Terry Southern and the
American Grotesque

Terry Southern and the American Grotesque

DAVID TULLY

Foreword by Nile Southern

McFarland & Company, Inc., Publishers
Jefferson, North Carolina, and London

Unpublished works are used by permission of the estate of Terry Southern and executor Nile Southern and the Henry W. and Albert A. Berg Collection of English and American Literature, The New York Public Library, Astor, Lenox and Tilden Foundations.

LIBRARY OF CONGRESS CATALOGUING-IN-PUBLICATION DATA

Tully, David, 1970–
    Terry Southern and the American grotesque / David Tully ; foreword by Nile Southern.
        p.   cm.
    Includes bibliographical references and index.

    ISBN 978-0-7864-4450-2
    softcover : 50# alkaline paper ∞

    1. Southern, Terry — Criticism and interpretation.
2. Grotesque in literature.   I. Title.
PS3569.O8Z88   2010
813'.54 — dc22
                                                                                2010009184

British Library cataloguing data are available

©2010 David Tully. All rights reserved

No part of this book may be reproduced or transmitted in any form or by any means, electronic or mechanical, including photocopying or recording, or by any information storage and retrieval system, without permission in writing from the publisher.

Front cover: Terry Southern (photograph by Pud Gadiot, courtesy Pud Gadiot and Nile Southern).

Manufactured in the United States of America

McFarland & Company, Inc., Publishers
  Box 611, Jefferson, North Carolina 28640
    www.mcfarlandpub.com

For my parents, for everything

Acknowledgments

I would like to thank Dr. Kenneth Silverman for his inspiration, expertise, and unflagging enthusiasm during the long arduous haul of this project. I am also indebted to Prof. Josephine Hendin and Prof. Robert Sklar for their support and astute advice.

This biography could not possibly have been written without the generosity and trust of Nile Southern and Carol Southern, in sharing the Terry Southern Archives (and their memories) with me. I am honored by the privilege they have granted me, and hope the results that follow do it justice.

I would also like to give a big thank you to Peter Matthiessen for the enlightening conversation, the extremely helpful insights, and the warm reception of the early version; to Lee Hill, for showing the way; and to George Plimpton for the kind and encouraging words about the first draft.

Heartfelt appreciation to one T. Michael Kelly, esteemed Curator of Rare Books at Amherst College, for his valued critical insights and awe-inspiring librarial skills. As a wise former child star once advised me: "Keep smiling!" And for her invaluable help with getting the manuscript in presentable shape early on, a big thank you to Melissa Moser.

And last but not least, endless gratitude to my wife Daniela, my family and my friends, for putting up with this for so long.

Table of Contents

Acknowledgments   vii
Foreword by Nile Southern   1
Preface   5

Part One: The "Quality Lit" Years

Introduction to Part One   9
  1. Texas Summers   19
  2. You're Too Hip, Baby   25
  3. Don't Get Hot   30
  4. Give Me Your Hump!   47
  5. The Mad Tradition   65
  6. Making It Hot   74
  7. Grooving in NY   82
  8. Hipster   96
  9. Beyond the Beat   107
Conclusion to Part One: Bedtime Stories   115

Part Two: The Movie Years

Introduction to Part Two   123
  10. The Great Stanley K.   128
  11. Riding the Black Humor Wave   136
  12. The Southern Cult   140
  13. The Hollywood Kid   149

14. Excessive Verbiage	155
15. The Epic Sensibility	160
16. Come and Get It	163
17. King Weirdo	167
18. Blue Movies	171
19. Lost Weekends	177
20. Grossing Out	183
21. Saturday Nights of Terror, Days of Weird	188
22. Limbo	194
Conclusion to Part Two: The Priest of Pagan Nature Laid to Rest	200
Source Notes	203
Bibliography	213
Index	219

Foreword by Nile Southern

After my father died in 1995, I inherited forty boxes of papers and his bewildering legacy. The fact that Terry's reputation had morphed at some point from disciplined writer to popular culture "pied-piper" hadn't helped him during his lifetime, and wasn't helping me keep him in bookstores, either. Through the publication of a new anthology *Now Dig This: The Unspeakable Writings of Terry Southern 1950–1995,* and the letters-driven *The Candy Men: The Rollicking Life and Times of the Notorious Novel Candy,* my efforts to draw attention to the wide range and serious nature of much of my father's work were critically well-received, but did not resolve the unstated underlying puzzle: "Who *was* Terry Southern?" Rather, they bolstered the accepted axiom that Terry was a man who could write just about anything, and had been everywhere that mattered. David Tully takes us beyond the awe-struck, which is where most Terry Southern observers, including myself, have been, and casts us into the hagiography of his soul — where Terry Southern's life and *oeuvre* meet in a place uniquely determined by his times.

As Tully brilliantly reveals, what my father left behind was an extraordinary body of work reflecting a seriousness, depth, and world-view whose lineage of high-level Decadence, Grotesquery, and Satire has historically been marginalized — precisely because it is, at its sharpest, culturally critical, and, as former *Harper's* editor Lewis Lapham observes, "A *tragic* view of human nature ... that simply *does not sell.*" As Terry's Executor, what mystified me most was not just the seemingly instant academic bias against the "pop-culture" successes of *Candy* and his film work — as if that somehow made him less of an artist than his novel-writing compatriots who didn't achieve such pop-art breakthroughs — but the fact that Terry didn't fit into any neat categories that institutions typically need to amplify or fill in their collections: novelist, essayist, screenwriter, journalist, humorist. Terry fulfilled each of these categories with confidence and a style all his own, but because of that, I suspect, he fell through the cracks — as he continues to do today. Rather than identify Terry Southern as a "keystone species" of American Studies and post-war American Lit — my father tends to be mentioned as an eccentric literary adjunct to the Beat Generation, the Gonzos, or the "literary outlaw" of the *Paris Review* set. To me, and to those who have long taken his work seriously, he's the bridge between the Beats and the Beatles; the link between Poe and Kubrick. It's a sad reflection on our times that such fluidity for a writer should be considered a detriment — as opposed to a model for the hybridized new media scribes of today.

David Tully contacted me in the late 1990s — hoping to gain access to Terry's archive and begin work on his Ph.D. dissertation on my father's work, work that he found extraordinary and underappreciated. At the time, Terry's archive, now safely housed at the New York Public Library's Berg Collection, was stuffed into a small locker at the Chelsea Mini-Storage facility in New York City. The archive contained over forty boxes of handwritten and typescript material, a good deal of it unpublished at the time. It took twenty minutes and great upper-back strength just to unload the archive from its roost at the beginning and end of each day. Countless hours were spent poring through material that spanned Terry's writing life from 1948 to 1995, items that included novels, short stories, plays, financial records, legal documents, journals, essays, contracts, fragments and ephemera. Tully created his own dense resource guide, compiling a massive amount of previously uncollected and in many cases unknown writings, along with Terry's well-known works. Tully's investigation remains one of the highlights for researchers of the Southern archive — for he donated his five volumes of bound materials to the Collection — a perfect starting point for any researcher setting out to navigate the deep waters of Terry Southern.

The idea of someone getting a *degree* in Terry Southern was certainly appealing — but besides his dissertation topic, what impressed me most about this young man and his enthusiastic, forthright nature was something Terry would have appreciated: a private inscrutability, tempered by conspiratorial gleam. "A veritable Feelix Treevly," I thought (one of Terry's great characters from his first novel, *Flash and Filigree*), and clearly someone who would uncover the deeper meaning to my father's life and work. Armed with notebook computer and portable scanner (a high-tech novelty even today), he was one of the few stable components in the posthumous world of Terry Southern.

Tully understood that Terry's great impulse to write came from his exposure at an early age to the elaborate prose of E.A. Poe. He reveals how

Poe became Terry's key technical strategist—for he had cracked the code between seemingly authentic reportage (where *credibility* is paramount), and the timeless terrain of the "far-out" tale. My father was smitten by Poe's ability "to render as real the most weird." How appropriate, then, that David Tully's thesis advisor was one of the foremost Poe scholars, the Pulitzer Prize-winning Kenneth Silverman.

Tully does not linger on Poe, nor on Hawthorne, another literary antecedent for the young writer, for as Terry develops, his influences encompass a broad range of styles and tones. Most compelling to me was Tully's previously unexplored assertion that Terry was influenced equally not only by Hawthorne, but by the "*chthonic*" (David Tully's aptly chosen word) Natural world and the "terrible beauty" he experienced in his rural boyhood in Texas, and later in the fields of Connecticut. The philosophical idea that Nature will always trump contrivance was, as Tully points out, a constant theme of Terry's, weaving throughout even his most unnatural settings, from *Flash and Filigree*'s sterile waiting rooms, to Guy Grand's ever-shifting metropolis. Another unexplored idea put forth by Tully places Terry as a practicing student of the Surrealists and Situationists. After David showed me some of Terry's early surrealist texts, such as *C'est Toi Alors*, his thesis was further confirmed by a recent discovery: a treasure trove of reel-to-reel audio tapes that my father recorded in his apartment in Greenwich Village in the early '50s.

The radio-show routines, some of which are in French, captured much of the vibe and intensity that still resonated from his life spent in Paris between 1949 and 1954. These recordings (soon to be released) are like an audio odyssey into what Tully calls "the quicksilver philosophy" of Terry's Existential world: a place where dreams and absurdist invention puncture the ubiquitously growing and ever-crass commercial culture. On one of the tracks, Terry's voice sounds a bit like William Burroughs from his own 1950s tape-recorded experiment, *Nothing Here Now but the Recordings*. Terry's voice, reading Tristan Tzara's 1918 *Dada Manifesto*, captures the pure state where hipster persona meets mad-cap Bunuelian intensifier. Embodying the surrealist impulse, the voice is dreamy, provocative and eerily defiant:

> *I am writing a proclamation, and I want nothing. Yet, I say certain things. And I am against proclamations, as a matter of principle, as I am also against principles. I write this proclamation to show that one may perform opposed actions together, in a single, fresh respiration. I am against action, for continual contradiction. For affirmation also. I am neither for, nor against. I do not explain, because I hate good sense—but there exists an art which does not reach the voracious mob.*

In some ways, Terry's haunting pronouncement came true. For as Tully reminds us, Terry's role as the musical genius side-man, blowing note-perfect riffs on now-classic film dialogue is often how he's remembered — at the expense of his written work. The best-selling *Candy* reached the "voracious mob," however, and many of Terry's most far-out ideas (space burial, media pranks, diving for dollars, A-list erotic films) are current cultural phenomena.

More importantly, Tully reminds us that in Terry's literary output his true brilliance and originality endures; a *capacity to astonish*, hard and precise as a diamond. For the first time, David Tully shines a bright and penetrating light on the profound aspects of Terry's *oeuvre*, showing us a writer who, though he threw in his lot with Film, had a bedrock existential praxis, combined with a magic ear for dialogue, and a fine, filigreed prose style that gives his written work a powerful, skeptical, scouring truth — unachievable in film. David Tully's book may finally lay to the rest the "party boy" image of Terry Southern — and confirm him as an accomplished artist of moral strength who found "beauty in every form," and never lost sight of the powerful impulse to *make it hot for them*.

Nile Southern, the son of Terry, is the author of *The Candy Men: The Rollicking Life and Times of the Notorious Novel Candy*, and the editor (along with Josh Alan Friedman) of the Terry Southern anthology *Now Dig This: The Unspeakable Writings of Terry Southern, 1950–1995*.

Preface

Terry Southern and the American Grotesque performs two functions: it is a biography of the American writer Terry Southern, and a critical analysis of his literary output (novels, short stories, screenplays, journalism, and essays), a significant portion of which has never been published.

Such an analysis is possible only because I was generously granted access by Southern's family to his private archives; at that time, they were contained in a forlorn warehouse on Manhattan's West Side. Happily, the Terry Southern Archives are today housed in the Berg Collection at the New York Public Library, and are readily available to scholars. They are an invaluable resource, housing a wealth of unpublished material. However, even though several stories and interviews have been officially released in the years since his death, much still remains unread and unknown outside the Archives.

The value of the unpublished material dates from a time when Southern was finding his voice, and therefore was not trapped by his own reputation as "outrageous satirist," which was the sad fate awaiting him down the line. Here, we find a serious young writer with something to say; not repeating his best bits, not mimicking himself, lost in the labyrinth of his own personal mythology ... this is the record of a consciousness open to the world, valuable and worth preserving, experimenting with a multitude of styles and media, moving between personal journal, fictional prose, poetry, essays and film. These writings open an entirely new window on Southern's imagination, immeasurably enhancing and transforming our perception of him.

Take, for instance, the folder bearing the simple title "Fifties Journal." Here, we have come right to the well, the source of the tales and essays. Written in the early '50s, the journals were neatly typed on numbered pages — but so carefully arranged and collated that it would seem the author intended to publish them as a whole. The Journal is a treasure trove of ideas and sketches (reminiscent in its collage structure of later works like "Love Is a

Many-Splendored"), as well as influences: the Journal ends with three pages of quotes from the *Iliad* and *Odyssey*—one of the quotes served as epigraph for the first draft of *Flash and Filigree*. Filled with aphorisms and observations, its style recalls the Nietszche of *Twilight of the Idols*—perhaps a latter-day Existentialist attempting to pay tribute to his illustrious predecessor. And this is but one example of what lies in the Archives—no portrait of Southern as artist is possible without this material.

This critical study, therefore, presents a more all-encompassing sense of Southern's canon than has yet been offered, or even attempted. The acknowledgement of Southern as a major satirist is fairly common; a sustained analysis of his body of work has been, until now, nonexistent.

Southern's writings are examined in the chronological order of their composition and publication, following his career from its beginnings in Texas, through study in Chicago, to wartime experiences in Europe, and postwar study in Paris on the GI Bill. Once in Paris, Southern's career as a writer begins in earnest, as he attends lectures by Sartre at the Sorbonne while helping Peter Matthiessen to start *The Paris Review*, where they are joined later by George Plimpton.

Part One then follows Southern as he moves from the expatriate scene in Paris, to the underground and literary elite of Manhattan, championed by the likes of William Faulkner and Henry Green. Southern's cult celebrity status earns the attention of Hollywood, and the story ends at the dawn of his career in films where, despite writing the screenplays for several landmark films, his talent soon self-destructs.

Part Two chronicles that breakdown as Southern pursued the film muse—yet also exposes the intermittent flashes of the old genius, glimpsed amongst the wreckage. Until now, nearly all of the work from this era has gone unseen by the outside world. The value of this later material lies in its record of an artist struggling to hold on to his voice and vision and then expand upon it, even as the vagaries of public taste and show business pulled him in too many directions, eventually pulling him apart.

Although he was reluctant to discuss his own writing, Southern did have one stated goal in his work: "to upset complacency." His tales are set in a strange twilight world akin to Hawthorne's, a disorienting realm where naturalism and myth, realism and surrealism blend. For all his grotesquerie, Southern is a serious writer. His grotesque is derived from Poe, Lovecraft, and a childhood immersion in the Pulps; but Southern's is a kaleidoscopic vision, presented in a dazzling array of media and styles.

Terry Southern and the American Grotesque explores the quicksilver philosophy sustained throughout the impressive and bewildering field of his writing, placing Southern in a context of surreal American humor stemming from the Southwest, and a canon of Decadent Romanticism that begins with the violent, horrific black humor of Sade.

It's likely that Southern's output has eluded critical commentary so far because it is so varied, hard to pin down, and disorienting. *Terry Southern and the American Grotesque* offers a comprehensive analysis that reveals a cohesive vision.

Part One: The "Quality Lit" Years

Introduction to Part One

I. "Now Dig This...."

> America's single and singular virtue is that its ground is invented, based not upon a myth of natural right or of ethnicity as ground, the kind of foundation that one finds in European history or in world history at large, but upon groundlessness as such.... The vivid common culture that all Americans possess is the yield of the decidedly artificial polity that America has always been even if it did not begin to know it before 1950.[1]
> — Perry Meisel, *The Cowboy and the Dandy*

It was about midnight every night that the cops started beating them. August of 1968, and the Democratic National Convention in Chicago was quickly degenerating into a free-for-all riot, the Pigs against the Peaceniks.

'Round midnight, more or less like clockwork, the police would don their gas masks and enter Lincoln Park, clubs a-swinging. And in the midst of the fray, running for cover with the rest of the Yippies and Hippies, was a small band of journalists-for-the-moment, sent by *Esquire* magazine to Bring Back the Story.

This was a group comprised of what was at the time waggishly referred to as the Alternative Establishment: Jean Genet, William S. Burroughs, and Allen Ginsberg — well, Ginsberg was not actually sent by *Esquire*, but he was on the scene nonetheless, in an attempt to control potential violence through various Buddhist chants. This was a noble aim, to be sure, but one that seemed to have little discernible effect on the Chicago police department.

These three counterculture superstars were teamed up and on the run with one more hero of the era — Terry Southern. Of these four intrepid reporters, Southern was in fact the sole member whose credentials did include a fair degree of work in legitimate journalism. If any of these four was at all inclined to relate what they were seeing in Chicago in a straightforward just-the-facts fashion, it was most likely to be him.

This did indeed turn out to be the case, when the *Esquire* edition about Chicago finally appeared in November of 1968. While Genet discusses his lust for various policemen and Hippies, and Burroughs extols the virtues of life in Red China before slipping into a reverie about a baboon running for president, Southern manages to give the reader a vivid feel for the chaos of those nights in Lincoln Park: "'They're coming,' screamed a girl in absolute terror as she passed. Running behind her was a boy of sixteen or so, blood covering one side of his face. Now at the rear of the crowd we could see the cops chasing and flailing."[2]

Hiding from the cops in the lobby of an apartment building near the park, the gang of four were soon discovered: "'You communist bastards,' one of them snarled. 'Get the hell outta here. Now move.' And he raised his club at the nearest person who, as it happened, was Genet — but the latter, saint that he is, simply looked at the man and shrugged, half lifting his arms in a Gallic gesture of helplessness. And the blow didn't come; another tribute to Genet's strange power over people. Instead, they pushed and prodded us out onto the street where they talked about taking us to the station; but they were soon distracted by activity farther down the block and they rushed away, because it wasn't really us they wanted to get it — it was the children."[3]

Southern's fabled penchant for embellishment and fantasy is held firmly in check here — what fiction could equal the insanity of that weekend in Chicago? American society was apparently spinning out of control, a morass of riots, assassinations, fragmentations; violence on both the home front and across the seas. In this new America of 1968, the apocalyptically comic sensibility of Southern — which had seemed so fantastic and shocking to the stable Eisenhower America of ten years before — was now positively tame.

Southern's Hipster sensibility is certainly in evidence in the piece, from the article's title ("Grooving in Chi") to his affectionate labels for his compatriots, ("Jean 'Jack' Genet," "Big Bill Burroughs," "That Loony Fruit Al Ginsberg") but these are stylistic flourishes, a gilding of his presentation. The substance of the piece is simply an astonished transcription of what he saw — events speak for themselves.

Southern finished the job; the convention, that downtown bloodbath, in the town that Carl Sandburg labeled "The Hog Butcher to the World," was over. He'd be called back soon after, to testify at the trial of the Chicago Seven, but for now the work was done. And so the outlaw, after a weekend spent being chased by cops, left the heartland — as he had a quarter of a century earlier — and headed east. His ultimate goal this time wasn't New York, though — nor was it London, or Paris. It was home: East Canaan, Connecticut.

Nestled snug in the heart of the Canaan Mountains in northwest Connecticut, the township of Canaan is comprised of two sections: North and East Canaan. It's the only blue collar town in affluent Litchfield County; its quarry, a stone's throw from Southern's house, provides the limestone for the small local factory producing magnesium. East Canaan, where Southern lived, is a land that time forgot: a charming, sleepy chunk of Norman Rockwell Americana, composed of a white clapboard New England church and a post office.

North Canaan, right down the road, offers one movie theater on the minuscule main street of the tiny town; it still proudly announces on its marquee that its latest offering is being presented in Technicolor.

What lured Terry Southern to such a remote spot as East Canaan, Connecticut? What kept the notorious literary outlaw, darling of the underground and avant-garde, in this wholesome setting from 1960 until his death in 1995? In the answer to that question lies the key to understanding his entire artistic vision.

When Southern first settled into the homestead in the early sixties with his wife Carol and their infant son, Nile, he had virtually no money: the family ate the deer and small game that Southern shot, as well as the tomatoes that Carol canned. Despite this mode of subsistence farming, they were still in debt by 1963, when *Candy* was finally published in America. And then, things changed.

Candy quickly climbed up the *New York Times* best-seller list. His first screenplay, for *Dr. Strangelove*, resulted in a smash-hit film right on its heels, in 1964. That same year, he would head out to Hollywood, where he would rent a beautiful Spanish Mission house in the Hollywood Hills and begin collaboration with Tony Richardson, on his film version of Evelyn Waugh's *The Loved One*. *Flash and Filigree* and *The Magic Christian*, though poor sellers, were praised by critics, and World Publishing had given him a hefty advance for his next novel, *Blue Movie*.

He was the toast of "the Quality Lit Crowd" (as he referred to it) both in the U.S. and abroad: a writer's writer, his work was admired by everyone from Irwin Shaw to Norman Mailer to Henry Green. He was a cult figure to the Beatniks and Hipsters, a pal to Burroughs and Ginsberg — the psychedelic jester whose comic apocalyptic vision helped to usher in the just burgeoning sixties sensibility, that would forever place to rest the complacent mask of fifties America.

In 1967, The Beatles would include him on the cover of their *Sergeant*

Pepper's album, standing right next to his beloved Edgar Allan Poe — one of a group of characters that the Beatles selected as the most influential individuals of the past hundred years. In 1968, he would revolutionize independent film-making by coauthoring *Easy Rider* with Peter Fonda and Dennis Hopper.

This was the situation of the man who settled in East Canaan in the early sixties; this was the pastoral setting that the bruised and battered Southern returned to after the trauma of Chicago in 1968. What lured this prominent rebel against American social complacency to a town that seemed the very model of All-American conservatism — especially since, for all intents and purposes, after 1968 he rarely ever left the town again (save for the odd foray into New York)? What appealed to him? What placed such a hold on his imagination that the boy from Texas designated this spot as home and refuge?

II. The Donkeyman at Twilight

In 1964, the novelist Nelson Algren, a good friend of Southern's, wrote an appreciative essay about the latter's work ("The Donkeyman by Twilight"), in which he observed that:

> Southern's true kingdom ... is neither contemporary criticism nor that hilarious mocking world of Guy Grand playing Donkeyman. The world he creates most hauntingly is that of the nocturnal dreamers with whom our literature began: he is closer to Nathanael Hawthorne than to Nathaniel West. This is a world rooted in American earth, yet lit by moon or twilight, a land never before seen. A place where wild dogs never bark but race, heads low, down a midnight road; but where a plague of green roaches slowly settles and descends upon rows of human faces strangely drowsing. Southern finds the settings for which Poe had to go to Ulalume in seasons that never were on the BMT, or at an excavation site in the Bronx.[4]

The evocation of Poe and Hawthorne is an apt one. After all, the dust jacket of the first American edition of Southern's first novel, *Flash and Filigree*, tells us that: "Between the ages of 11 and 15 (spent in his native Texas) he filled 67 thin blue notebooks with narrative-adventure based on the stories of Edgar Allan Poe, and from 16 to 18 he rewrote as exercise all of Hawthorne's stories and about half of Poe's."[5]

Again and again throughout his life, in his own writing and in interviews, Southern returned to Poe (and in particular, his one novel, *The Narrative of Arthur Gordon Pym of Nantucket*) as the source and inspiration for his own work. In an interview conducted only days before Southern collapsed on the stairs at Columbia University (before being rushed to the hospital where he died a few days later), he again returned to this primal well: "The way it began, I recall, was ... reading a story called *The Narrative of A. Gordon Pym*.... [Our teacher] got so upset reading us the story that she had literally shuddered with disgust. I thought that was so great, I rewrote the story using members of the class and her."[6]

He showed it to his friends, who were shocked: they circulated it in utter disbelief. "It was some sort of turn-on for me," he said, "that possibility for attention and communication."[7] In early interviews, Southern had cited H.P. Lovecraft and the whole *Weird Tales* pulp-fiction school of writing as primal influences on his developing imagination. But such writers were only descendants of a Grotesque style that Poe had already developed to perfection in *Pym*—and when Southern encountered it, his own voice was first activated.

In his biography of Poe, *Edgar A. Poe: Mournful and Never-ending Remembrance*, Kenneth Silverman tell us: "Poe created in *Pym* a classic adventure story, through which he gave body to the classic theme of illusion ... a dizzying verbal hall of mirrors that confuses ... fact and fiction. The narrative proper brings the reader into a treacherous world of disguises, forgeries, and impersonations, where appearances lie."[8]

Beyond the mere surface similarities between Poe's grotesque excesses in the novel and those in Southern's own work, there is this essential shared core of meaning: illusion, deceit, the notion that appearances lie. Ever reluctant to discuss his own writing, Southern did have one stated goal: "...to upset complacency."[9]

His tales are set in a strange twilight world akin to Hawthorne's, a disorienting realm where naturalism and myth, realism and surrealism blend. They are existential fables from an American Kafka, hinting at what Perry Meisel speaks of in the opening epigraph: America is built on fictions, and if you don't like the America that you're given, simply disorder the senses, change perceptions, and come up with a new one.

It is often difficult for people to take comedy seriously, but Southern, for all his grotesque comedy, is a deadly serious writer. The grotesquery comes from Poe, Lovecraft and a childhood immersion in the pulps, but Southern's is a kaleidoscopic vision, presented in a dizzying array of media and styles. It contains the Hemingway-like naturalism of "Red-Dirt Marijuana," the Henry Green-cum-Raymond Chandler impressionist noir of *Flash and Filigree*, the children's tale for adults (and *Great Gatsby* sequel) *The Magic Christian*, the *Blithedale Romance*–meets–*Deep Throat* farce of *Blue Movie* (his Tinseltown rewrite of Sade's *120 Days of Sodom*) ... and that's only scraping the surface.

Indeed, it's highly likely that Southern's output has eluded critical commentary so far precisely because it is so varied, so hard to pin down, so disorienting. At a memorial service held on December 16, 1995, at the Unitarian Church of All Souls in Manhattan, Southern's eulogy was given by Kurt Vonnegut. An old friend of Southern's, as well as a fellow veteran of the Black Humor Wave of the early sixties, Vonnegut told the crowd that: "Terry had two speeds: legal family man, fifty-five miles an hour, perfectly civilized; and the wildest sorts of maneuvers and outlawry at supersonic speeds."[10]

In other words, Southern has two modes: realism and surrealism; and two speeds: dreamy and gentle, and frenzied Keystone-Kops-style farce. But this two-sided coin had one unified purpose. Southern never said in any explicit manner what the intent of his writing was, but hints for solving the puzzle can be found in comments from other writers, preserved in an old journal from the early fifties that Southern kept when he was starting out on his own career as a writer in Paris. The first comes from his beloved Henry Green: "Prose is not to be read aloud but to oneself at night ... a gathering web of insinuations which go further than names however shared can ever go. Prose should be a long intimacy between strangers with no direct appeal to what both may have known."[11]

A "gathering web of insinuations," working at an almost unconscious level, in a region below appearances, below masks — this is an essential element for understanding the random events of his picaresque tales. The second comment, from Samuel Beckett, provides insight into the meaning of his humor: "The bitter laugh laughs at that which is not good; that is your ethical laugh — ha! The hollow laugh laughs at that which is not true; that is your intellectual laugh — ho! ... But the mirthless laugh is ... the laugh of laughs, the *risus purus* ... the saluting of the highest joke, in a word the laugh that laughs — silence please — at that which is unhappy. It is down the snout — just so: HAW!"[12]

That "HAW!" reappears again and again in Southern's prose, indicating the laugh that he desired for his humor: refusing to accept the unhappiness caused by a repressive culture, by false appearances and deceit, and undermining it through an appeal to the unconscious. Southern's laugh of nature explodes the lies of culture.

This is what Southern found and returned to, again and again, in his remote farmhouse in his Hawthorne woods and fields: it was the source and wellspring of his vision. In Algren's words, it is "a world rooted in American earth yet lit by moon or twilight"[13]; that is to say, it is nature, the earth, the twilight realm and, via Poe and Hawthorne, the language of what Greil

Marcus has termed "the Invisible Republic," America's folk culture subconscious (also termed by Marcus, "The Old, Weird America"[14]).

A quicksilver philosophy is sustained throughout the impressive and bewildering field of Southern's writing, placing him in a context of surrealist American humor (stemming from the Southwest, and becoming increasingly pervasive in American popular culture after 1950), and a canon of Decadent Romanticism that begins with the black humor of Sade. This is founded on Camille Paglia's notion of Decadence as a "skirmish between the Apollonian and Dionysian elements"[15]; that is, culture (Apollonian artifice) aware of the power of nature (Dionysian chaos). Southern's surrealism subverted appearances and played with masks, while his Decadent Romanticism made him a proponent of nature.

In conversation,[16] Peter Matthiessen was initially resistant to the notion of categorizing Southern's work in a convenient slot, with a label like Decadence, and its attendant, potentially confining, tradition or history; and Nile Southern[17] at first resisted a Decadent reading of the surrealist short piece "C'est Toi Alors!" though he later came to agree with the assessment.

Such reactions are understandable, as criticism and/or exegesis can rob art of its mystery and its power, while tradition may rob the individual talent of that quality that renders him or her unique. But the labels work.

Albert Goldman once described the tales of Southern as "a *Terry Toons* version of the Marquis De Sade"[18] — specifically, he was addressing *Candy*, most notorious of the tales, but one would be hard to top this as an apt and succinct appraisal of Southern's entire oeuvre. Yet to consider Southern as a Pop Sade is not to denigrate him, but rather to realize how he brought a fascinating new dimension to Decadence in the Jet Age of the American Century. As Southern told *Life* in 1964: "The important thing in writing is the capacity to astonish; not shock — shock is a worn-out word — but astonish. The world has no grounds whatever for any complacency. The *Titanic* couldn't sink but it did. Where you find smugness, you find something worth blasting. I want to blast it."[19]

A decorated demolitions expert in the Army during World War II, Southern continued this work after the war ended, carrying it over into the field of writing. Southern remembers that as a child he alienated one of his friends with one of his stories: "...my best friend — by using his sister in a really imaginative piece, perhaps the best of this period ... and this slowed me down for awhile in daring, but finally I learned not to care too much and would write wholly for an imaginary reader — whose tastes were similar to my own. And this is, of course, the only way to work well."[20]

Southern was saddled with a Decadent aesthetic sensibility in the seemingly barren Baptist Texas of the thirties; no wonder he found a soulmate in Poe, a Decadent Aesthete who felt he was artistically starving in what Poe perceived to be the culturally barren America of the 1840s. Southern's monster stories and Hipster bildungsroman sketches offer glimpses of hidden freedom and hidden limits. His freaks remind us of our ties to nature, as his vision evolves and moves ever more towards the Grotesque, away from realism towards surrealism; as he reinvigorates and reinvents the pulp form of the monster story to serve as cultural criticism.

Southern was a Southwestern humor variation on Poe and Hawthorne. In rewriting their tales as a teenager, recasting their images and events in more contemporary terms (as he began with his version of *Pym*, and continued to do until his death), he reintroduced us to an America that, in the words of Marcus, "No one has exactly inhabited before"[21]: a twilight, unconscious dream-world, halfway between our plastic, waking pop culture America that we all share via TV and the Internet — and death, the abyss, the other side, another world.

Southern's Pop Art is Decadent. It neither evades nor embraces morality, but simply perceives morality as part and parcel of a cultural artifice that seeks to evade or conquer nature. Decadence pits nature against culture and knows that, in the end, nature is always the winner.

Candy Christian, for instance, is the Christian impulse in the face of ravaging nature, a prophecy of the failure of the Hippies ten years later (charted also in *Easy Rider*). Southern's work still resonates because he tapped in, however intuitively, to the Dionysian energies of America's Invisible Republic, and showed how they could be both liberating and unforgiving.

And what is "the American Grotesque"? The American Grotesque is that element in American popular and pop culture that accentuates the freakish aspect of the carnival that is American culture: the freak show at the edge of town. It is a unique form of Decadence that accesses and utilizes the Invisible Republic, in highlighting and depicting the conflict between nature and culture. The Invisible Republic, like all of culture, turns on the conflict, the lack of harmony, between nature and consciousness; but it is closer to nature than high culture. It is earthier — it welcomes chaos.

Candy Christian is the sort of archetypal virginal blonde that Hawthorne loved to use in his allegories: the emblem of innocence and purity. In Southern's hands, she is defiled by a monster and loves it. Poe feared chaos more than Southern, which is what drove him to create the murder mystery, the detective story, the imposition of order on chaos. In the fifties, learning his trade, Southern half-heartedly composed a few detective stories (with a drug addict detective seemingly modeled on Coleridge, a Romantic forebear of Poe's), but it is obvious his heart wasn't in it. Unlike Poe, Southern welcomed chaos.

One suspects that for Poe, *Pym* was a nightmare — for Southern, it was a manual for living. And although, like Poe, he recognized nature as the ultimate limit that could not be evaded (see the dark, bleak conclusions of "The Road out of Axotle" and *Easy Rider*), he also welcomed the excess that freed you to find out for yourself, that liberated you from artificial limits. Southern speaks in his best work in the language of dreams, and with his pop art, connects our waking world with the Invisible Republic: he brings dreams and nightmares into the waking world to shock us out of waking dreams ("this flaw, this fissure in the fabric of reality is the basic theme of Terry Southern's work,"[22] is how William S. Burroughs put it).

His novels and tales are children's books and fun houses of horror; horror stories in which masks are manipulated, cast aside for freedom or welded on to the face for imprisonment forever. And beneath this play lies the blackness of the void, a hungry nature that consumes.

Southern envisions America itself as a carnival — complete with freaks, burlesque dancers, and acrobats — in his final short story, "Repentance." The original manuscript bears the even better title "The Refreshing Ambiguity of the Déjà Vu,"[23] signaling Southern's enthusiastic return to the sort of fullbore surrealist short stories he wrote in his youth — he's come back home again. The tale was written in the early nineties, and was his most oblique exercise in the surreal since the mid-fifties. After years adrift, he'd returned to his roots.

The portrait is bleak: the crude circus presents itself as the last chance for anyone in the midst of a world that has become a desert, and the "repentance" of the title seems to be Southern's own, for in some way contributing to the creation of the mad carnival that is American pop culture — two of the show's big stars, after all, are Candy Christian and her hunchbacked lover.

But there is still, in the careful delineation of the features of the carnival, a love betrayed for the freakish odd-ball nature of American culture. "Repentance" is not only a final statement of sorts — it is also one of Southern's most forthright declarations of how he views America; as forthright as a surrealist who speaks through insinuation can be.

The American Grotesque is a certain kind of American Decadence; exploring America's night world, its culture as side show and carnival — the "Pandemonium Shadow Show,"[24] to borrow a title from Ray Bradbury's *Something Wicked This Way Comes*. It is the freak show subconscious to popular culture consciousness, always undermining the dominant cultural narrative. The American Grotesque loosens up the rigid façade of American culture, exposing the abyss that lies beyond, working against all cultural forms that rigidify, repress, and deaden.

We find the American Grotesque all around us, from the literature of Flannery O'Connor, to the horror films of Tobe Hooper, to rock stars of the sort typified by Alice Cooper or Rob Zombie, for instance — a subconscious to mainstream culture's conscious face, a corrosive agent necessary to keep American culture from rigidifying. These are surreal visions that spring from the American unconscious, keeping liberating glimpses of nature always present.

Writing, for Southern, was both an attack and a game; and the reason for his put-ons, his trickster behavior, may be glimpsed in a comment on the Decadents by Camille Paglia: "In *Un Chien Andalou*, a tennis racket is hung like a crucifix on a wall, expressing the surrealist insight that social institutions and philosophical systems are a game."[25] The social institutions critiqued by Southern the Satirist may be gone, but his true, central preoccupations (the clash of nature and culture, the need for compassion, the drive for freedom) are still very much with us.

Grotesque Decadence is a kind of Romantic Decadence unique to America, spawned by the Invisible Republic, keeping our culture shaken up and vital. All of Southern's work, like that of other surrealists before him, is a game — one that is rewarding and enlightening, however shocking, to play. And why did Southern play it?

Southern found on his farm a connection with nature, and with the Invisible Republic of Hawthorne and Poe that liberated him as a youth in Texas, offering a way out of the deadening and violent culture that stifled him. Early trauma in the brutal milieu of Texas (the deaths of childhood friends, including one by his own hand) made Southern shrink from violence; early disappointment with his alcoholic father made him contemptuous of authority, turning him into an inadvertent but true American Gnostic.

Southern sought out alternate father figures in Romantic writers who liberated the imagination: role models like Poe and, later, Henry Green. He sought freedom in nature, a natural world of impulse and passion that trumps and transcends the limitations of reason and repressive culture. That liberation is what Southern looked for in the wilds of Connecticut, after the crackdown on the children in Chicago.

That liberation is what we can find in the surreal games of Southern's tales.

1

Texas Summers

Texas occupies a special place in the landscape of Southern's fictional universe: it is a locus of extreme violence and brutality. He was born there on May Day — May 1, 1924, in the small town of Alvarado, to Terry Southern I, a pharmacist, and his wife Helen, a sweet, pretty Irish woman who tended the house.

Like his son, Terry Southern Senior seems to have been a gentle, funny, but rather lost individual, and what discord there was in the house between the parents and their only child came as a result of the father's alcoholism. It was a regular part of Helen's routine to hide the car keys, as Terry Sr., when drunk, would always threaten to take out the car. Terry Jr. later recalled to Carol (his second wife) how he would take the keys from where Helen had them hidden, hurling them at his father and yelling, "Go ahead, kill yourself!"[1] The drinking, and the strife it caused in the home, eventually seem to have driven an irreparable wedge between Southern and his parents.

But Terry also cherished happier memories, such as when his father took him to the carnival that had come to town, called "The Big Onion." A black midget was on display in one of the tents, billed as "The Monkey Man, Mister Dan." Terry Senior waited for the proper moment, when he and Terry Junior (ten at the time) snatched up Mister Dan, whom Terry Senior referred to as "The Funny Little Old Monkey Man," and took him to a bar nearby, buying him a drink, then returning him to the tent afterwards.

The escapade so thrilled the young Terry that it later resurfaced in his final novel, *Texas Summer*, published in 1991.[2] In the novel, Mister Dan the Monkey Man is kidnapped by Harold (the protagonist based on Southern himself) and his best friend, Big Lawrence (based on Southern's childhood friend, Big Herb) — a substitution that indicates an avoidance of the pain still likely involved in any reminiscences about his father.

When Terry was in the seventh grade, the Southern family moved to

Dallas, and bought a small place in Montclair, a suburb not far from the schools he attended — Winnetka Elementary in Oak Cliff, where he is remembered by his childhood friends as an excellent baseball player on the Winnetka diamond; and then Sunset High, where he was in the ROTC and the Biology Club.

Although Texas is treated in Southern's fiction as a bleak locale, he also would later recall it as "ideal, from a Huck Finn point of view."[3] The contrasting cultures, black and white, that he was exposed to in Dallas did much to shape his evolving vision.

So, too, did the discovery of Edgar Allan Poe, whose tales he first heard courtesy of Elsa Dinsmore, his fourth grade elementary teacher, whom he remembered in his final interview, given to *Paper* in 1995, as "a big fat pain in the ass."[4] She read "The Gold Bug" to the assembled class, then assigned to each student a report on a chosen story by Poe. Southern went to the library and found a selection of Poe's complete works; upon leafing through it, he stumbled on the story that would change his life, shaping all of his subsequent work: Poe's only novel, *The Narrative of Arthur Gordon Pym of Nantucket*.

A sensational "history" of murder, shipwrecks, cannibalism, and bloodthirsty natives, *Pym* piled shock upon shock for over two hundred pages. So taken was Southern with the novel's "weirdness"[5] that he immediately set about rewriting it, now featuring his fellow classmates and Ms. Dinsmore as characters in the narrative. He showed the finished product to Big Herb, who offered the critical assessment: "Goddamn, you must be crazy."[6] Southern later recalled that Big Herb's horrified reaction to his grotesque first foray into novel-writing marked the moment "when we began to drift apart ... Texas and me."[7]

The other component of Southern's education, as vitally important to his development as the discovery of Poe, was that found in the section of Dallas known as "Central Tracks," located near Deep Elum. It was the heart of the African American community in Dallas, until the central expressway came through and the district was torn down, and was known in the Dallas of the thirties as "Nigger Town."

Southern was first exposed here to soul food, to Blues, and to other aspects of African American culture. With friends such as Big Herb, A.B. Ord, and Louis Gillmour, Southern would head into Central Tracks every Saturday night, after the football game at Sunset High, to the clubs on Greenville Avenue, such as Luann's, The Plantation, The Blue Room, and Papa's.

There, they would feast on the extremely hot barbecued ribs and chicken drenched in red pepper, and the extraordinary music of bands such as Joe Liggins and His Honey Drippers or Andy Kirk and His Clouds of Joy, their name derived from the fact that the bandstand, when they played, was constantly engulfed in marijuana smoke. Even when the bands weren't on the stand playing, the jukeboxes would offer what were then known as "race records," the African American music that couldn't be found outside of Central Tracks; records such as Bullmoose Jackson's "Big Ten-Inch": "My gal don't go for smoking, liquor just make her flinch / Seem she don't go for nothing, except for my big ten-inch."

Southern and his friends never encountered any hostility from the locals when exploring the wonders of Deep Elum: "It wasn't antisocial then," he later recalled; "I guess they needed the money and I think they liked the idea that we dug the music and food."[8] What Deep Elum offered to the young Southern was a culture of greater freedom, even of greater possibilities, as opposed to the white Southern Protestant culture in which he had been reared, which seemed to Southern to offer only limitations, only fear. This shared experience of "Southern Protestant"[9] culture would bind him in friendship with the novelist William Styron, who grew up in a similar social milieu, when they would later meet in Paris, in the early 1950s.

Central Tracks also provided Southern and his friends with pleasures beside music and food. Along the railroad tracks that ran through the center of Deep Elum were rows of whorehouses, where a fourteen- or fifteen-year-old boy could lose his virginity for $1.00 — or even $1.50, if he chose to be a big spender that evening. These establishments were run by imposing madams sporting names like "One-Armed Annie" (a one-armed prostitute) and "Big Red" (an enormous black woman in a giant red wig). One night, when wishing to sample the wares of One-Armed Annie, Southern was warned by Big Red: "Be careful with Annie, she's a settled woman," meaning that she was not up to any strenuous activity.

The violence that underlies all of Southern's fictional reminiscences of Texas may stem in part from an incident that took place during one of these Saturday night outings into Central Tracks. Southern and an unnamed friend, standing at a bar, got into an argument; Southern struck his friend, who fell against the bar's marble top. The friend died instantly. It was an accident, and no one, even at the time, blamed Southern for what happened, but the guilt hung over him for the rest of his life. Carol observed later: "Terry avoided conflict like the plague, and I think that [the accidental murder of his boyhood friend] is why."[10]

Soon after that event, violent death struck close to him again, when his friend A.B. Ord was also killed, only months before their graduation from

Sunset High. A.B. had gone hunting with Big Herb in a field just outside of Clarendon, a suburb of Dallas. As Big Herb was passing the gun to A.B. through a barbed wire fence, it accidentally went off. Southern was one of the pallbearers at his funeral, and later recalled the experience as "devastating ... I think it did have a sobering effect on me — for a while, anyway."[11]

One of the first chapters of *Texas Summer* that Southern composed was published separately in the late fifties, decades before the novel, as "A South Summer Idyll." In it, Southern paints a loving portrait of Harold's hunting expedition with Big Lawrence; no death to a human being results in that tale's outing, but it quietly revisits that devastating experience, attempting to make peace with it — an attempt more fully discussed in a later chapter.

The father in *Texas Summer* is distant and remote — as, it seems, Terry Sr. increasingly became, detached and drinking heavily. The father *figure* in the novel, however, the true guide to young Harold, is C.K., the black hired hand on Harold's farm. C.K. was a composite of many people that Southern met during his sojourns into Central Tracks, as well as a man who worked on his cousin's farm back in Alvarado. One particular inspiration for C.K. was a shoeshine at Tubner's, a barber shop that Southern passed every day on his way to Sunset High.

The man was "extraordinary ... a philosopher, very well read,"[12] and provided Southern not only with ideas but also a steady supply of marijuana. Southern had had his first joint at the age of ten, back in Alvarado, and he was afterwards rarely without, especially once he moved to Dallas. It became a regular event for Southern and Big Herb to make the rounds of Central Tracks, looking to score some weed, and so the shoeshine proved an invaluable source and influence.

Southern graduated from Sunset High in May of 1941, and in September 1941, he attended North Texas Agricultural College in Arlington, Texas (later the University of Texas at Arlington). He took courses in biology, chemistry, mathematics, algebra and trigonometry and, at the urging of his mother, who wanted him to become a doctor, planned to become a pre-med student, following in the footsteps of his father as a pharmacist. Southern was turned off by his pre-med classes, finding that it was not at all a "friendly doctor kind of thing," but very "abstract" and clinical.[13]

As a former member of ROTC, Southern tossed aside his pre-med deferment, voluntarily enlisting in the Army in March of 1943. In the Army, he became a demolitions technician; his job was to render enemy objects unusable "by means of explosives," which could have served in later years as an apt description for his mission as a writer as well. During the war, he received a Campaign Medal with two Bronze Stars, a Good Conduct Medal, a Victory ribbon, and three overseas service bars.

Carol was astonished, after his death, to find these medals in his attic; he never spoke of his war experiences to anyone. Southern's only recorded meditation on his time as a soldier was that "the main benefit of the war for me was the opportunity to travel. There were some tedious times, and some scary times, but all the negative stuff was outweighed by the emancipating experience of seeing the world."[14] Near the end of his life, he confided to an interviewer that he planned to write a memoir of his experiences during the war, but died before penning a word on the subject.

He was honorably discharged as a corporal in November of 1945, at Fort Sam Houston in Texas. Returning to Dallas for his discharge, Southern reunited with Big Herb, who was now a member of the Dallas police force; there, they had one final, disturbing foray into Central Tracks. The brutality of Big Herb and his fellow policemen towards the inhabitants of Deep Elum horrified Southern, who watched from the squad car; he left Dallas soon after, not returning again for another fifty years.

During this final visit to Dallas, while briefly attending Southern Methodist University, Southern was also exposed for the first time to the music and culture that would have probably the greatest influence in shaping his artistic sensibility: jazz. Jazz is a more complicated outgrowth of the Blues and R&B that thrilled Southern in high school; no doubt Southern made an emotional connection with the jazz world because it was likewise populated by people who were, perhaps not fleeing the culture that had spawned them — but at least trying to create a different one.

After leaving Texas, Southern seems to have had very little contact with his parents; Carol remembers that to her, it was as though he "sprang fully formed from Zeus's head."[15] As Emerson remarked, "all true Americans are orphans," and the Hipster who began to emerge in Chicago, who fully developed in Paris and Greenwich Village, kept up that tradition. Birthday and Christmas cards from Helen tell of warmth and affection between the two, but also a certain sense of distance: "It was so nice to talk with you on the telephone. I wish that we were closer so that we could do it often.... I get lonesome to hear from you both but I am so negligent about writing to anyone myself that I cannot very well say anything."[16]

Helen had endured and suffered Terry Sr.'s drinking, staying with him until the end; when she died in 1955, Terry Senior seems to have come completely unglued. A series of heartrending letters from him to his son, scrawled on stationery bearing the addresses of various hotels from Texas to Florida, chart the disintegration of a man utterly lost, quickly drinking himself into his grave: "Dear son ... have had the toughest time in my hectic life, auto wreck, broken ribs, heart attack, jail, hospital, etc."[17]

On January 17, 1957, Southern checked into the Royalton Hotel in Miami, where he was found dying two days later; it was unclear whether the excessive drinking was a deliberate suicide or simply that the problem had gotten out of his control. He was sent to Jackson Memorial Hospital, where he died of an "overwhelming infection of the left upper extremities complicated by acute and chronic alcoholism. Infection arose in an injury of the left hand"[18] — an injury sustained when he'd been beaten up and robbed by a hitchhiker he'd given a ride to only a few days before. By this time, Terry and Carol were living in Geneva, and Terry was unable to return home for the funeral.

Carol remembers that Terry Junior always spoke warmly of his mother, but rarely of his father. All of the letters from his father were carefully saved and filed, however, and the death seems to have haunted him — in some ways, Southern's final years would come to seem a sad echo of his father's end.

The death of Southern's parents did not come until the mid-fifties, but would prove the final physical break of any ties that Southern still had with Texas, the last link in a chain that had begun to sever when he went off to war. Carol thinks of Terry as "a real Texan but ... I think he really hated Texas,"[19] while his son Nile doesn't see Terry's relationship as quite so cut and dried, but rather "odd."[20] He remembers that his mother had told him that the Southern family was related to Sam Houston, but also mentions that Terry never spoke to him about that. He is, however, as firm as Carol in maintaining that when Southern left Dallas in fact, he left it completely behind in mind, as well.

In a certain sense, however, Southern never did leave Texas, at least not subconsciously. No matter where his tales are set, be it Paris, Manhattan, Hollywood, or India, they are products of a Texas temperament, a subtly Southwestern humorist. Read in this light, Guy Grand stands revealed as a Sut Luvingood for the Jet Age, and Paris as just a more glamorous Central Tracks. Until his dying day, all the songs that Southern blew on his horn — be they raucous or mournful — were Texas Blues.

2

You're Too Hip, Baby

Southern briefly attended Southern Methodist University because of its convenient location in Dallas; having outgrown Texas, however, he soon transferred to the University of Chicago. His brief sojourn at Southern Methodist did manage to expose him to a French professor named Lon Tinkel, a highly literate individual who first interested Southern in all things Parisian; in 1960, Tinkel would review *The Magic Christian* for *The Dallas Morning News*, giving his former pupil's work a rave. Tinkel's digressions in class on all aspects of French culture began opening Southern's mind to European high culture, much as Central Tracks had first opened his eyes to African American culture.

He transferred to the University of Chicago after hearing of the Dean Robert Maynard Hutchins and his celebrated "Great Books" program. However, on arriving in Chicago, he happened one day to visit the campus at Northwestern and, on seeing these "beautiful, blue-eyed blondes in their yellow convertibles who were taking the sun by the lake.... [He] transferred to that school pronto."[1]

What Tinkel had begun at Southern Methodist was continued at Northwestern by an English professor named Bergan Evans, and a philosophy teacher named Arthur Schlipp, both of whom inspired Southern to extensive study in those areas (Southern, in fact, majored in philosophy at Northwestern). He roomed with an Indian man, Nandan Kagal, who introduced him to yoga and spicy Indian cuisine, which proved no challenge to someone weaned on Tex-Mex cooking.

Northwestern University conferred on Terry Marion Southern II the degree of Bachelor of Science on August 31, 1948, and having been prepped and inspired by Tinkel, Evans and Schlipp, Southern set off for Paris.

He studied at the Sorbonne under the G.I. Bill, from 1948 on into the early fifties. Class attendance at the Sorbonne was not participatory — as students simply enrolled for the doctorate and chose a thesis (in Southern's case,

"The Influence of Mallarmé on the English Novel Since 1940")[2] and researched it for defense at some point in the indefinite future. There were no exams given, simply the opportunity to attend lectures by the likes of Sartre, Camus, and Cocteau (one lecture that had a particular impact on Southern was given by Marcel Raymond, author of *From Baudelaire to Surrealism*).

The golden age of foreign film-making was beginning in the late 1940s and early 1950s, and Southern often attended the Cinemathèque, viewing such classics as *L'Age d'Or*. At night he would visit the jazz clubs, where he would witness Miles Davis, Thelonious Monk, Charlie Parker, and Dizzy Gillespie in action. The glory days of the twenties were still being replayed by the young expatriates of the fifties, and Southern attended the bullfights in Spain, going to San Sebastian in late April, then on to Pamplona to run with the bulls. Each of the bullfight festivals would last about a week, and Southern would so arrange his schedule that all spring, or about six weeks, would be spent going from bullfight to bullfight. These trips to Barcelona inspired an early story written in the Hemingway mode (like the later "The Butcher"), a story that went unpublished until Southern chose to include it, fifteen years later, in his anthology *Red-Dirt Marijuana and Other Tastes* (an inclusion which shows a certain amount of pride in it).

"The Face of the Arena" is set in the familiar Hemingway territory of the Barcelona bullfights, and pits the lone fighter against the hostile crowd. However, where Southern diverges from the Hemingway path is in the character of his warrior. Rafael Marulanda is no noble gladiator — he's a coward: "They say, or did say, that Marulanda was a typical failure through ineptitude and cowardice ... it was strange, in fact, that he should have been a bullfighter at all ... and he must have wanted it very badly ... all later memory turned around his father's proud sacrifices and the make believe arena."[3]

Southern finds the dreaming child within the bullfighter, the sensitive soul coming up against the brutal reality of his failure, in a landscape not unlike that of the later tale, "The Sun and the Still-Born Stars": "Now, it may have been the heat, for certain August afternoons in Barcelona blazed with a strange and terrible light. [But] the filled arena rose up and around like the inside of a great cauldron, the living walls a huge, tortured mosaic that wavered in the black lined heat as though the whole thing were slowly corning to a boil."[4]

The epiphany in this tale, however, is not a moment of courage, but an absolute failure of it. A child runs into the arena; Marulanda grabs the boy and tries to take him outside of the arena space. However: "At a point, perhaps ten feet from the barrier, when he knew the bull was upon him, he turned to face it or avoid it, still holding the child before him, almost, it appeared now, as a shield."[5]

Marulanda tries to flee the arena after sacrificing the child to the bull, but the crowd will not let him: "The face of the arena, a livid white, all the small faces fused by the heat into a single screaming mask ... [Marulanda] began to cry, quietly, not with pain or remorse, but like a child or puppy, incredulous, whimpering a weird gratitude."[6]

Southern's concern here is the innocent child in a hostile world; Marulanda knows that he too will be a sacrifice, like the child he has offered to the bull. And he is grateful to leave this world that has risen up against him, this hostile nature, white and unified (reminiscent of the white figure rising from the milky depths at the conclusion of *Pym*).

The European approach to literature fascinated Southern as well — not as a means to become rich or famous, but as an end in itself. He recalled that "in Europe, writers tend to approach it in a kind of mythological way, dealing with themes ... such as war and peace and patricide."[7] "Patricide" is an odd thing to cite in this context, a concept not generally viewed as being so universal and central a theme as "war" and "peace" in literature. It would, however, become a major driving force in Southern's own work: an attempt to come to terms with the father who so frustrated and disappointed him.

The jazz music and existential philosophy that held sway over Paris's intellectual culture in this era did much to stimulate Southern's evolving perspective; so, too, did the expatriate American crowd that he soon began socializing with. Making the rounds of the Paris society, Southern fell in with the likes of George Plimpton, a young Harvard graduate looking to start a literary journal in Paris; Peter Matthiessen (whom Southern referred to as "Bush Master Math"), a young fiction-writer who, between forays into Africa, would spend time honing his craft in Paris, working as an editor on various literary journals and newspapers there; William Styron, a young novelist selling stories to the journals; Aram "Al" Avakian, a young fledging film-maker and editor; Mason Hoffenberg, a New York poet and trust-fund child; Alex Trocchi, a young Scottish novelist; Richard Seaver, an editor at *Merlin*, one of the literary journals; and more established writers, such as Samuel Beckett, even Jean Cocteau himself. Also passing through on occasion were such notables as Truman Capote, Tennessee Williams, and Norman Mailer and, in the later fifties, emerging Beat luminaries such as Allen Ginsberg, William S. Burroughs, and Gregory Corso.

Replay of the twenties it may have been, or even the thirties of Henry Miller and Anaïs Nin; still, in the early 1950s, for a young writer, Paris was the place to be. Newspapers like *The Paris News-Post*, published by Harold

"Doc" Humes, and journals like *Merlin*, *Zero*, *New-Story*, and *Paris Review* would give a platform, if not much revenue, to a young writer attempting self-expression. In fact, it was largely because of an early Southern story, "The Accident," that *The Paris Review* came into existence at all (this will be discussed, like all works here, when we arrive at the story's publication date).

But when Southern credited "Doc" Humes with publishing his first story in *The Paris News Post*,[8] he was mistaken in his recollection. In fact, his first published story was "The Automatic Gate," published in *New-Story* in June of 1951. In it we see the emergence, the first appearance, of Southern's subtly recurring theme of patricide.

The tale is, in essence, a retelling of Kafka's short story "In the Penal Colony." Where Kafka's tale was concerned with a government official who has created an elaborate torture device, a contraption that eventually claims the official himself, Southern's story focuses on an older keeper of the Paris Metro gate, who has devised a foolproof trapping mechanism to stop anyone who tries to enter without paying his or her fare.

In both Kafka's tale and Southern's, the official who has created the torture device has become so obsessed with his notions of law and order that he has become alienated from any context in which his notions made sense, and in the end, is himself ensnared by his own elaborate machination. In Kafka's case, it was the actual official who winds up in the machine; in Southern's, the gatekeeper loses his prey, but claims an innocent bystander instead. An innocent pays for the follies of authority.

Monsieur Pommard is trying to stop a young man who torments him nightly, by sneaking through the automatic gate without paying the fare. In speaking to his fellow gatekeeper, Pommard vents his disgust at this young man, who constantly flouts the conventions of the Paris Metro:

> "He's an anarchist," said the old man gravely. "Anarchist?," echoed the other, really surprised. "Certainly. What did you expect? He has no respect. No respect for the regulations."[9]

The other (unnamed) gatekeeper, younger than Pommard, silently resents him but says nothing, while the non-paying metro traveler acts on the very desires that this impotent younger man feels inside. In discussing the gate and the people who break it, the young man says to Pommard, "'the people are crazy.' Just as one day, he thought, they will break these city gates again. 'And as for the fat pigs then....'"[10]

In the end, the metro traveler again escapes Pommard; but caught in the automatic gate is an innocent young woman: "On the young lady's face was a look of astonishment, child at a magic show, blotted over now by the rush of blood from her nose and mouth."[11] As will so often happen in later Southern fiction, to protagonists like young Candy Christian, a young innocent is caught and harmed due to the machinations of the old and power-mad.

The next Southern story to appear in print was "The Butcher," also published in *New-Story*, this time in November of 1951. In early stories like "The Automatic Gate" and "The Butcher," Southern has not yet discovered his true voice, but they remain interesting genre exercises, fine examples of a young craftsman learning his trade. There is no freak-show element to this story, no hint of the carnivalesque; Southern is still working here in the Hemingway mold. But again, we find a preoccupation with the dilemma of the old destroying the young.

"Patricide" was perhaps what Southern wished to effect with his literary explosions of old patriarchal conventions, but what he displayed in his work more often was how the old prey on the young, whether intentionally or unintentionally. It is an accident that the young girl is caught and crushed in "The Automatic Gate," and the father in "The Butcher," Monsieur Beauvais, wants to be a supportive father for his son returning from the war; the son's mind and sensibility are blasted by what he has seen. But M. Beauvais is deaf to what his son has told him in relaying the horrors of war: "'Of course,' he said to himself, 'the boy is getting it off his chest.'"[12] The father and his generation have created this world awash in blood that has, perhaps unwittingly — but no less surely for that — destroyed his child. The story climaxes with a portrait of Beauvais at work:

> He cut the throat as smooth and quick as a surgeon would lance a tiny boil, laying the whole of it open with such speed and grace. Then the blade was sliding like a razor in cream cheese through the white throat of the next.
> By the time Beauvais reached the end of the rack, his feet were sloshing above the ankles in blood.... "I haven't noticed Louis around," he said carefully, leaning back, "and the boys from the disposal. They seem late in getting around with the brooms this morning."[13]

Unthinking butchery has destroyed the younger generation; the world is awash in blood spilled by the fathers. And no one is cleaning up the mess.

Southern's first two published stories were set in his newly adopted home of Paris; but they carried undertones from Texas, brooding on the unresolved relationship with his father. Freud tells us that all our future relationships begin in the family romance; and though Southern may have convinced himself that he was looking at the new world around him, on an unconscious level, he was still coping with the world he had left back home.

3

Don't Get Hot

His next story, "The Sun and the Still-Born Stars," was published in *The Paris News-Post* in February of 1952. This is the piece that "Doc" Humes published, and that Southern in later years remembered as his first published story. Here, Southern returns consciously and vividly to the landscape of his youth, to Texas — and he moves forward as well, into the realm of the surreal and grotesque, inching closer to his true voice. "The Sun and the Still-Born Stars" marks a major stride forward for Southern, from the quasi-realism of "The Automatic Gate" and the stark realism of "The Butcher" — towards the unique variety of Grotesque that would come to characterize his best-known writing.

Set on the barren Gulf coast of Texas, the tale reads like a fusion of Flannery O'Connor and H.P. Lovecraft, and can be viewed as Southern's nightmare vision of what his own life might have been, had he chosen to stay in Texas; this is the life he might have lived without what he gained from his heightened sensibility, his taste for literature, and his exposure to African American culture:

> Sid Peckham and his wife were coast farmers, and Sid was a veteran of World War II. They were eking out the narrowest sort of existence on a little plot of ground just east of Corpus Christi.... Sid and Sarah were of a line of unimaginative one-acre farmers who very often had not owned the land they worked, and whose life-spring was less connected to the proverbial love of the land than twisted somehow around a vague acceptance of work, God's will and the hopeless, unsurprising emptiness of life. The only book in their house was the Bible, which they never read.[1]

These are people who question nothing, who accept surfaces — and, consequently, live in a flat version of reality, relieved only by their weekly visits to the movies:

> Sid had come to use the word "realist" to describe certain films, but instead of realist, it sounded as though he was saying "reel-less." ... But somewhere behind this, the mask of each expressed life, deep under the dead wood and simplicity of their ever separate, unspoken awareness, little things were crawling alive, breathing and taking on great secret shape.[2]

This, here, is the very core of Southern's vision. Behind the flat dead surfaces of our culture, nature is teeming with life — and no matter how we try to repress, choke, strangle, or ignore it, it will still burst through. In the case of "The Sun and the Still-Born Stars," nature bursts through in a fashion more strange and fantastic than Sid and his wife Sarah could ever possibly imagine, bursts through like a figure from Jung's Collective Unconscious — in the form of a monster that roars up out of the Gulf and onto their farm, coming from the sea to raid their melon patch. "'I reckon it's a hog,'" is Sid's deadpan reaction.[3] He then unemotionally, but dutifully, engages the monster in a duel, transforming the pair into a rural Texas version of Saint George and the Dragon.

The struggle between man and monster continues for a time, until Sarah, who has been refraining from doing anything but watching due to her pregnancy, behaves in an unexpected fashion. She abruptly runs into the midst of them, grabbing Sid's spear, and seemingly kills them both:

> Great cloud head image on the silver screen ... growing, swelling, swelling ... "*Stop!*"
> Lilt. And the surf around them feathered out all white-edged rose. Their motion faded to an end as gradual and even as the close of slow music.[4]

Having destroyed both monster and husband in a fantastic film of her own creation, she then slips back into her usual semi-catatonic state. She trudges to the movie theater, buys a ticket, then turns "back to the man in the glass box, her face a serious frown. 'Going to be reel-less?'"[5]

In a land that is a "flat, burning waste,"[6] all that endure are the pregnant woman and the melons, images of fertility. And her last, questioning "reel-less?" seems a mocking of any reductive visions of nature. Nature is far stranger than "realism," a literary and film convention, could ever hope to convey.

What unites these three seemingly disparate published tales, and what unites all of Southern's work, is a recurring theme of distrust of authority figures, who are usually male and older (patriarchal), and a refusal of the repressive culture that they represent, or that in turn represents them. Simultaneously, there is an embrace of nature as a strange, freakish, unpredictable, grotesque, invigorating, life-giving alternative, represented alternately or simultaneously by female figures and by African American culture.

Southern's next published work was "The Accident," which later served as Chapter Three of his first novel, *Flash and Filigree*, published in 1958. It appeared as a standalone story in the first issue of *The Paris Review*, in September of 1952. Peter Matthiessen credited Southern and this tale with the very founding of *The Paris Review* itself: "Harold Humes (who owned *The*

Paris News-Post) had hired me to be the paper's literary editor, to find short stories to publish in the newspaper. The first story I found was Terry's 'The Accident,' and Humes and I agreed it was too good to appear in this newspaper, and that's really why we decided to form our own magazine to publish short stories.... So Terry was really the catalyst."[7]

"The Accident" makes more sense when seen in the context of *Flash and Filigree*, but even this fragment continued the theme of a preoccupation with complacent authority figures getting their comeuppance. The story opens with cool, confident Dr. Frederick Eichner leaving his Beverly Hills office; with exquisite care, Southern paints a portrait of a man in complete control of his environment:

> "Morning, Doc," the attendant said. "Swell car you got there." It was a Delahaye, 235. Dr. Eichner came down the steps slowly. "This is interesting," he said, "my experience has given me to believe that the majority didn't care for foreign cars ... at the far bottom of the hill below was a crossroads with a traffic signal, and at a quarter way on the descent, a white stone marker showed the distance from there to the intersection of one-eighth mile. It was Dr. Eichner's habit to time his descent on leaving the crest so as not to pass the stone marker until the warning amber had shown on the traffic light below, and then to race down the hill at full throttle and beat the red. The duration of the amber was five seconds, so that to clear the intersection ahead of the red light, he must do the eighth mile at an average of ninety."[8]

But Eichner is caught up in the middle of an attempted mob hit, one truck driving another car off the road at this intersection, and is himself involved in the accident. This is followed by Eichner's interrogation by two incredulous policemen, Officers Stockton and Eddy. The tale climaxes with the collected Eichner completely losing his cool and exploding at the two cops, which causes Officer Eddy to try to calm Eichner with the admonition: "Take it easy, fella, don't get your shit hot."[9]

George Plimpton later remembered that his earliest experience with Southern was encountering Southern's wrath; Matthiessen had asked Plimpton to help him edit *The Paris Review*, and Plimpton was caught in the line of fire when the magazine attempted to censor the potentially offending line: "In those times (the early fifties), the U.S. Customs was even more rigid and conservative than the U.S. Mail.... After much discussion, the offending word was changed to 'crap,' and at last the line became the feeble and rather unlikely 'Don't get hot.'"[10]

Southern wrote a three-page letter demanding reinstatement of his original line, demonstrating his outrage at any form of censorship. *The Paris Review* dutifully published an erratum, though not the line or letter — and Southern was slow to forgive Matthiessen.

Southern's humor was evident in "The Accident," in the contrast between the down-to-earth policemen and the insufferably pompous Eichner, while a sense of righteous outrage is evident in the letter to *The Paris Review*; he had arrived as an angry young man with a keen wit. He was living at 53 Rue de la Harpe, making the rounds of the Montparnasse scene; his student I.D. photo from the Sorbonne shows a hawk-faced young man with his eyes on the main chance, a man already becoming legendary among the young expatriate crowd in Montparnasse for his wit, his intelligence and his unflappable Hipster cool.

Matthiessen remembers that when he first met him to discuss publishing the story, Southern was "on the nod from grass or something stronger like heroin, leaning against the wall, nodding off, responding to questions an hour after they had been asked"[11] (Carol Southern maintains that Southern never took heroin, and that it was probably hashish).

William Styron recalls Southern as "really rather shy and unboastful. I was amazed by the quality of the prose, which was intricately mannered, though evocative and unfailingly alive.... What I read ... was fresh and exciting. I sensed the need for real encouragement when he said, 'I trust, then, Bill, that you think this will put me in the Quality Lit game?'"[12]

What Southern showed Styron at this point was "The Accident," part of his novel-in-progress. Meanwhile, Southern was carefully cultivating the persona of the Hipster, while also diligently honing his craft. John Phillips, who stopped over in Paris in the early '50s en route to Africa, and stayed on to help Matthiessen launch and run *The Paris Review*, remembers Southern as being:

> ... among my first mentors on the scene.... Terry's was a silent, inscrutable presence on the Boulevard Saint Germain. Night after night he sat with one or more equally inscrutable friends like Aram "Al" Avakian [later the director of *The End of the Road*, for which Southern wrote the screenplay] in the Old Navy and stared at our table of earnest Ivy-Leaguers ... Terry Southern and Al Avakian hobnobbed with bizarre companions talking a strange—"hey, man," "ho, man," "haw, man," "man!"—patois.
>
> If, after many evenings of being solemnly scrutinized by Terry in those cramped premises, one tried to acknowledge his presence with an overture of any form—an innocent wave or friendly nod, a wink or mere "Hi there"—which could be construed as collegiate and uncalled for, it was mercilessly ignored. There was no penetrating that Texas cool."[13]

Phillips, as an advisory editor, was out searching the cafés for young poets of promise and had, in fact, lost a manuscript from one of them, somewhere on the floor of a café. While he was bending over looking for it, Southern came and stood above him. "It's not worth looking for," Terry said.

> But we were going to publish Terry Southern, strange as he was. Those who knew him best were careful not to tell us that when he first came to Paris under the G.I. bill, slender and silent as the owl he kept for a pet in his rented room, Terry had been about as callow as the rest of us. His persona had not yet developed into the aloof enigma one met in the Old Navy. It was further still from the jocular cosmopolitan [he became in his old age].[14]

Phillips remembered Southern's letter to the *Review* regarding "The Accident" as "a ringing blow for creative freedom."[15] The erratum that appeared in issue number two was composed by Matthiessen, and read: "Terry Southern is most anxious that *The Paris Review* point out the absence of two words from his story 'The Accident.' The sentence, 'Don't get hot' should have read, 'Don't get your *crap* hot,' an omission for which we apologize to all those concerned."[16]

Art Buchwald, who at that time was writing a column for *The Paris Herald-Tribune*, thought it was the funniest erratum notice he had ever come across (Southern disagreed, remembers Matthiessen, and would scarcely talk to him for months). Buchwald wanted to write about it in his column, but he knew his editor would never allow that word ("crap") to appear. "It was a problem that bedeviled everyone then,"[17] Plimpton recalled.

Southern's next published piece was a reprint of "The Sun and the Still-Born Stars" in *The Paris Review* in February 1953. But after the splash that "The Accident" made, it's odd that his next new story to appear was not until December of 1954, when *London Mystery Magazine* published "His Second Most Interesting Case" in their issue No. XXVI, with authorship credited to one "Terrave Burnerm." Southern had been collaborating on a series of detective stories with David Burnett, the son of Martha Foley and Whit Burnett, of *The Best American Short Stories* fame. Their original shared pseudonym had been the swanky "Maxwell Kenton," a name that would finally see the light of day covering his next published collaboration (with Mason Hoffenberg), on the novel *Candy*.

The hero of "His Second Most Interesting Case" is Professor Hartmann, described as "an unpleasant man,"[18] but whom his students regard with "reverence." Hartmann teaches his students how to commit perfect murders and is, therefore, needed by the police to help with their investigations — but they do not like him. They regard him as "unpleasant" because he knows how the criminal thinks — a hero who explores and understands the dark corners of the mind.

The story is a fairly straightforward, mundane detective tale. The one curious twist on the genre that it offers is that we are given, in Professor Hartmann, a detective modeled on the likes of Samuel Coleridge and Thomas

De Quincey. Hartmann tells his student, Lewis Weber, that "Perhaps you've heard me lecture. Some say I'm the greatest speaker since Coleridge. It may be that I am greater than Coleridge. There are resources I have not yet drawn upon."[19] Here we have De Quincey's English Opium-Eater as master detective, the Romantic drug addict as cultural hero. Perhaps this is not too great a leap from Sherlock Holmes's own cocaine addiction, but it is certainly more pronounced; and in this case, drugs are an aid, rather than a hindrance to deduction.

Professor Hartman made a return (of sorts) in an unpublished radio skit written during this period, "The Mad Monk," dating from about 1954. While not as rich as the later sketch "C'est Toi Alors," it mines the same vein of Poe-influenced surrealism, while also moving towards the realm of Second City sketch comedy. And this time around, Hartmann had even more in common with Guy Grand than he did previously, as he pulls a Treevly-like con on the hapless Dr. Ames, devolving from learned medical expert to used car salesman in mid-interview.

The address for "Terrave Burnerm's" original manuscript for "His Second Most Interesting Case" reads 269 West 11th Street, NYC 14 — a long way from Southern's Paris address of 53 Rue de La Harpe. All throughout the early fifties, Southern made several trips back and forth between Paris and New York, living in Greenwich Village — first alone, then with his first wife, the model Pud Gadiot, and finally with his second wife, Carol. John Phillips paints a vivid portrait of Southern's home life in New York in this period:

> Tex [Southern's nickname from *The Paris Review* crowd] was living in a walk-up on West 11th Street with his then-wife, a stunning fashion model whose name was Pud. They owned ... an illuminated tropical fish tank which contained Siamese fighting fish ... bred to extreme viciousness. The males must be separated in the aquarium by a pane of glass lest they devour one another in sexual jealousy ... the dominant light in the living room came from the tank, in which the fish, lurking in green and purplish shadows had, even in those pre-psychedelic times, a psychedelic effect upon the visitor, no matter what he was smoking.[20]

There, constantly reminded by his pets of vicious, beautiful nature, Southern and Phillips would watch T.V. with the sound off, listening to Miles Davis, "two Americans in search of the Grail.... It brought us right back to the Old Navy when we sat like owls in the chilly dark."[21]

In New York, Southern not only wrote a series of detective stories with Burnett (of which only "His Second Most Interesting Case" survives), but also two short films — his first forays into filmmaking, an area that fascinated him perhaps even more than prose, even then. The shorts are "Candy Kisses," a macabre tale of a man poisoning children at a playground, and "Children at Play," which is the light to "Candy Kisses'" darkness. In "Children at

Play," the children at a playground overcome their hatred and disgust of each other to celebrate love, as they band together to repair a snowman who has melted in the sunlight. In this very early attempt at screenwriting, for a (very) short film, we don't find a confrontation between Apollonian and Dionysian — merely a celebration of "peace and harmonious relationships" in inevitable triumph over the forces of hatred, warming the winter landscape.

Also from this period is a brief, unproduced screenplay entitled "Night Light"— the portrait of a poor boy in a tenement (Arnold) struggling to be a jazz musician, to create art and beauty in a squalid New York City landscape.

What all three films share is a characteristic concern with innocence: innocence destroyed by an evil adult, destroyed or imperiled by the unfeeling harshness of Manhattan, or innocence triumphing over nature's indifference. These films offer some of the earliest glimpses in Southern's work of "the Smallest and Dear"— the heroes of his only children's book, *The Donkey and the Darling*, written just a few years later.

Southern's last story published during this early fifties Paris era was another reprint of "The Sun and the Still-Born Stars," this time in *Harper's Bazaar* in July 1955. But during the crossings back and forth between Paris and the Village, his attention grew increasingly focused on the New York literary scene.

The most memorable (perhaps *only*) job that Southern held in this period was as the captain of a barge that hauled rocks on the Hudson River, between Poughkeepsie and Far Rockaway:

> Alex Trocchi got me the post. There was a period when these positions came into favor with persons creative who needed a robot type job. There were few or no duties. George Plimpton can explain barge life to you since he used to take young girls out on Trocchi's barge and try, as he said, to "get them." ... [I]t got to be a social must, going up river on the barge. Nelson Algren came a couple of times, David Solomon and Seymour Krim, Christopher Logue and Jimmy Baldwin. And, of course, Mason would come along quite often.... So life on the barge was not without interest.[22]

Soon after his first marriage dissolved, Southern met his second wife, an aspiring painter named Carol Kauffman. Carol's memories of her first meetings with Southern dovetail quite nicely with John Phillips' memoir, providing a complementary portrait of the jazz hipster underground of the Village in the fifties, balancing Phillips,' Plimpton's, and Matthiessen's memories of the Paris underground of the same period:

> Greenwich Village was a Mecca then for writers, artists and dancers. I was very drawn to "the scene," specifically the "hipster scene." These people had a certain

style, cool, detached, skeptical, ironic. The overriding idea seemed to be that everything had a double meaning, and God forbid you should express any emotion.

I was crossing Washington Square Park and I bumped into Mason Hoffenberg sitting on the edge of the circle with someone who was looking away. He introduced me to Terry, but I couldn't imagine Terry even saw me since he was being ultra cool and not making any contact, much less eye contact. Judging from his profile, he looked very bored.

[Later, at a date at the White Horse] he was so appealing and interesting looking. When we were leaving he said, "[a]re you going to take me home with you, or do I have to introduce you as my cousin from Nebraska?" Who could resist that?[23]

All through this period, Southern was writing steadily: everything from short stories to poems to screenplays to plays — and a novel in progress, one that he was continually working on from the early 1950s until its final publication in 1992 (in drastically truncated form) as *Texas Summer*. It was a bildungsroman ("full-on JEAN-CHRISTOPHE, you know, introspective"[24]), one that began life under the title *The Hipsters*, continued on as *Youngblood*, and eventually ended up as *Texas Summer*. The novel was to take the protagonist, obviously modeled on Southern himself, from Texas to Paris to New York. Southern eventually lost interest in the project, no doubt because, as always, he was reluctant to discuss himself — when asked about the novel in the late sixties, Southern seemed dismissive of it: "...I don't know whether I'll ever get back to that. The idea was to take the development of a man — I mean beginning in childhood ... very conventional, very simple. It doesn't really interest me much anymore."

However, he did ultimately return to the early chapters set in Texas — probably when he realized that the focus was clearly more C.K., the father figure, than it was Harold, the youth modeled on Southern.

If *Texas Summer/Youngblood* comprises Volume One of his bildungsroman, *The Hipsters* is then Volume Two. Like the essay "The Bird Is Gone" (see below), this long-gestating, ultimately abandoned first novel is, at its heart, self-portrait. And like that essay, this novel was never completed by Southern — the mirror was apparently not his favorite source of inspiration as a writer. However, it is rewarding to read *Texas Summer* as prologue to what follows, and "Put-Down" (collected in *Red-Dirt Marijuana and Other Tastes*) as its coda — bringing this ensemble from the badlands of Texas, to Chicago, New York and the transatlantic crossing, and ultimately to the abyss they face in the heart of Europe ... and themselves.

The novel is not only self-portrait, but also a portrait of the environment that most vitally formed him as a writer — and if the philosophic discussions described in painstaking detail here might strike readers as puerile, they are also invaluable as a first-person account of how this generation of expatriates thought and behaved.

It also contains — within its kaleidoscopic ensemble of students, Situationists, musicians and philosophers — the only attempts Southern made at depicting homosexuals as fully formed characters, rather than campy comedy devices. A close friend of such noted gay writers as Frank O'Hara and William S. Burroughs, Southern obviously never had any personal problem with homosexuality, but must have found, after this effort, that such a voice and milieu was beyond his reach to capture authentically. Too bad, as Peter has potential as a character, and Southern's later tales could have used more such variety.

As it moves from ship to train to hotel to taxi to café to salon to jazz club to school, the manuscript has the feel of an eyewitness report, a reporter taking dictation while occasionally flying into rhapsodic reverie — and perhaps it was because Southern left the scene that the novel faltered and broke off. More's the pity, as what remains is some of his most engaging — and potentially crowd-pleasing — work. There are no chapter numbers or titles — only page breaks between episodes.

The manuscript begins with one couple, Priscilla and Aaron, as they lie in a ship "in the port at Cherbourg." Attention is first focused on Priscilla, lying in a bunk in her cabin, as she prepares herself to see Paris for the first time:

> She had to turn on the bunk almost crying aloud, closing her eyes against her mother, fighting to doubt the betrayed image behind them, but could only doubt the betrayer. And yet could she still save herself now by falling back on their final scene alone, drawing on the anger and resentment she had spent there, had respent a hundred times since....
>
> Above at rail on the unloading side and watching it was Aaron Vrobel, another young American, and not unlike Priscilla, a past breaker, except that, unlike Priscilla, he had broken once long ago and since had held no past but a series of unrealized futures.[25]

These are people who have broken with mothers, with the past, with "the debt and the trap." With a cinematic eye, Southern leaves this couple and moves on to others, from couple to individual to couple, examining the lives of the Hipsters of Paris. These include Harold, the protagonist of his Texas tales, now grown up and left Texas, working as a jazz musician in a Paris night club. The sequence set at a party gives only brief snippets of dialogue, always coming back to one topic ("'And what was that, sir?' 'The death.'"[26]). No past, no future, death the only inescapable fact — these are people skating over the abyss.

Like all of Southern's novels, *The Hipsters* was not a tightly constructed, large-scale story, but rather a series of sketches. Though the majority of these sketches never saw the light of day, a few were eventually published as isolated short stories ("Put-Down" and "You're Too Hip Baby"), just as fragments of the earlier Texas-boyhood section were also published as isolated stories ("Red-Dirt Marijuana," "Razor Fight," and "A South Summer Idyll"). These will be discussed in the order of their publication.

While working on his bildungsroman, his Great American Novel, Southern continued to publish. His next short story to appear was "The Panthers," later reprinted in his anthology *Red-Dirt Marijuana and Other Tastes* as "You Gotta Leave Your Mark." Published in *Harper's Bazaar* in 1955, it is of a piece thematically with the short films Southern had made with David Burnett. Unlike the surreal monster that erupts into the flat world of Sid and Sarah in "The Sun and the Still-Born Stars," or even the muted endorsement of the psychedelic mind-set presented by Professor Hartmann in "His Second Most Interesting Case," "The Panthers" returns to the austere, gritty realism of "The Butcher" and "The Face of the Arena."

"The Panthers" (or, "You Gotta Leave Your Mark") opens on the same terrain, populated by the same characters, as the three short films:

> It was one of those huge jagged emptinesses left wherever a building is improperly torn down in the tenement section of a city, actually it was New York. But seen out of context — say in a cropped photograph — one might have said it was someplace in Europe destroyed by war ... except there was nothing recent or mysterious about this rubble. It had settled in impossibly uneven, hard-packed mounds all molding and covered with soot. The children in the neighborhood called it "the lot" ... there was a certain bleak wildness about the broken terrain and the lighting was always bad, unreal, like that on the print of underdeveloped film.[27]

This is the urban equivalent of the forbidding wasteland that is the Texas Gulf coast of "The Sun and the Still-Born Stars." The sun in that Texas was harsh and unforgiving, the stars still-born, dead, incapable of supporting romance or dreams; here, "the lighting is always bad"— false, electric, equally unyielding, ungiving. After the murder and shattered lives are played out in this tale, we are left with a detective and a tiny boy looking at each other:

> They were standing like that, in that strange embrace, the detective looking down with a certain sadness in his eyes when the little girl with the cloth doll appeared down the sidewalk near the lot, slowly approaching, carrying her cloth doll on one arm, she raised her eyes and saw them, gave them a serious look, and turned away in a wide arc to pass, cradling the doll in both arms now, shielding it from their sight.[28]

Like Sarah in "The Sun and the Still-Born Stars," this child represents the more benevolent face of nature: maternal, giving, a face which shuns the male, violent culture that has created the urban wasteland all around her. Compare this with the end of the short film "Children at Play," in which the children have fought, the snowman has melted:

> CAMERA BACK to reveal one of the three's (tiny child! little Carolyn Windham White! *Smallest and dear*!) who has replaced the snow and continues now (with touching maladroitness) in her effort to patch up and sustain the snowman ... other children drift back towards the snowman and are seen, in the growing distance, to be working on it once more, together. FREEZE ON child's smile.
> FIN.[29]

Innocence and nurturing love are the antidote in Southern's universe to the violence, aggression, and hostility found in such vistas as the flat Texas landscape (the harsh side of nature) or the urban hell that The Panthers find themselves in. For innocence is the nurturing, benevolent side of nature, and the only solution to a crushing, repressive culture, which is what Southern perceived American culture of the 1950s to be — the culture that had created a situation like the Manhattan of this tale must take the blame for it.

"The Sun and the Still-Born Stars" and "The Panthers" together form a complementary paired portrait of country and city, in which one can be as harsh and unyielding as the other. Southern greatly prefers nature to culture, and though nature has two faces, harsh and benevolent, it is only that benevolent side of nature that can transform harsh, unforgiving culture.

Portraits of an urban nightmare can also be found in unpublished sketches from this time, like the uncompleted short story "The Pusher":

> Being a pusher had taken him outside normal society ... indeed, he was the most loathed and put-down person in an area which extended from Greenwich Village to Harlem.... He camouflaged and distorted any show of emotion so severely that you couldn't really tell what was happening with him. But from his general behavior, you would assume that the one thing he did want was to be considered loathsome.[30]

For all of Southern's relentless pursuit of the Hipster persona in himself, he was also capable of seeing the dark limits to which it could be taken, pushing a person so far out that there was no way back in to human contact, to love. The poetry he was writing in this period also reflects his ongoing concern with children's outlooks on a hostile world, and their survival; it also again demonstrates his preoccupation with the drug user who exists on the fringes of society, be that drug user a professor, as in "His Second Most Interesting Case," a loathsome, grotesque freak, as in "The Pusher" — or, as in the poem "Song of the Old Hemp-Smoking Woman by the Fireside," even an old woman:

> How pretty is the fire, how pretty tonight/...
> the wood burns red is close in dead.[31]

Working again in the medium of poetry, he also crafts a song of innocence, his "Funny Little Children's Song":

> Is ever no matter the same?/
> As pearl to wine or world to time, as day and night or wrong to right,/
> and black as white./
> Is ever no matter the same?[32]

Southern was no accomplished poet, certainly, yet these ballads do posses a certain primitive charm. In these singsong bits of verse, we find distillations of recurring themes: the old woman is a benevolent earth goddess figure who achieves a psychedelic vision, and the young children are confused by a world in which nothing is clear-cut, a world in which perception has to be adapted to constantly changing situations, and the innocent are always in peril. It's also notable that there are two versions of the "games" in the manuscript contained in the Terry Southern Archives — and that the slight variations revolve around the word "white." Once again, the white goddess of Poe's *Pym* casts her spell over Southern's vision; the "whiteness of the whale" still haunts the American poet.

In another poem from this period, "Play a Game of Diplomats," another favorite theme of Southern's is explored, that of politicians who play with people's lives as if they were toys or card games:

> Two players sit and watch the deal as children follow a spinning wheel/
> and the time is shadow, white and raw/
> so what will it be, stud or draw/
> It is the last, look at the clock, feel for the shadow under the rock.[33]

Southern's conception of politicians and the military as overgrown malevolent children (those who "feel for the shadow"; that is, those who pursue darkness) — as opposed to the sweet innocence of the children in the short films, in "Panthers," and in "Funny Little Children's Song"—first surfaces here. Later, it is given fuller imagining with the politicians and generals of *Dr. Strangelove* (most clearly seen in the excised pie-fighting sequence that originally concluded the film), as well as the generals who open their weapons like children under a Christmas tree, in the final scene of the unproduced screenplay *Grossing Out*.

In 1963, in an article for *Esquire* entitled "Looking for Hemingway," Gay Talese wrote a memoir of the *Paris Review* crowd during the early fifties period, at that time a decade gone: "They are obsessed, so many of them, by the wish to know how the other half lived. And so they befriend the more interesting of the odd, avoid the dullards on Wall Street and dip into the world of the junkie, pederast, the prize fighter and the adventurer in pursuit of kicks and literature, being influenced perhaps by that glorious generation of ambulance drivers that preceded to Paris at the age of twenty-six."³⁴

Certainly, a dominant concern of the *Paris Review* crowd in this era in Paris, or the Beat crowd that was simultaneously congregating in New York, was the lives of those on the fringes of what was then considered conventional society—the lives of junkies, of the jazz underground, etc.

Southern wrote the Paris sequences of *The Hipsters* before he began working on the Texas boyhood sequences, and tales like "The Pusher" show his attempts as a writer to convey portraits of the "seamier" side of life in Paris and New York. Such sketches appear in his fiction and lyric poetry, and in unpublished non-fiction pieces such as "Jazz Scene" and "The Bird is Gone," a memorial tribute to Charlie Parker:

> There shall always be artists and wise men like Shaw and Gide and Bertrand Russell, who somewhere check their pace and, waxing sage, age to mellowness and respectability, while the world grows somewhat better for it. But then there is another breed, a race apart, who pulls out all the stops and throws them away, has not time to consult physicians or priests, and creates and recreates himself to the point of speeding over icy mountain roads, getting syphilis on a South Sea island, or dropping dead from too much absinthe or heroin. These are not the self-styled stereotypes of romantic agony, but the few, the Nathanael Wests ... with their mercilessly schizoid, uncompromising integrity who cause the blood of an art to *move*.... They give by exchanging their own.³⁵

In a restrained tone, Southern, in this essay, attempts to create his own version of Mailer's "The White Negro," his echo of Ginsberg's *Howl*—while also foreshadowing the title and subject of his later tale "The Blood of a Wig," published in 1964. Of course, his efforts in the field of the serious, studied essay hardly compare to Mailer's, nor do his forays into poetry demonstrate evidence of the heir apparent to Baudelaire, or a rival to Ginsberg's evocation of the urban fringe dwellers' existence in *Howl*.

Still, the essay is fascinating. Of all the unpublished pieces in the Archives from this period, the essay was one of the most difficult to reconstruct—the original manuscript is a confusing tangle of typescript, handwritten text, hastily scribbled marginalia, crossed-out sections and arrows indicating restructuring. Such relentless revisions indicate the importance to Southern of the subject, and of getting his thoughts on the matter down in just the right way; it was, unfortunately, never quite finished to his satisfaction, surviving only in chaotic manuscript, this last draft never fully abandoned.

Judging by the amount of revision and fine-tuning, it was obviously quite important to him, and one might conclude that he felt ultimately frustrated in expressing himself as clearly as he wished. Perhaps that is because the subject is less Charlie Parker than jazz itself—and given the kinship between jazz and Southern's own writing, the influence that the music had on his work, one can only wonder if Southern was here trying to describe, to get at, the "blood" of his own art—and that because he could not achieve a certain level of detachment in self-portraiture, the subject got away.

This may be due to the fact that sustained long-form essays, like sustained long prose works (i.e., novels), were not Southern's metier; his strength lay in the moment, the riff, the joke. In a few years, Southern would find an outlet for his serious meditative side in the short essay pieces he published in *The Nation*. But his greatest vehicle for creativity still remained not film, not poetry, not the essay—it was always the short story, the pulp tale.

His next published piece appeared in *Harper's Bazaar* in February of 1956, and worked out themes already developed in "The Bird Is Gone" (the academy versus the underground) in a far more entertaining (and therefore convincing) fashion. "The Night the Bird Blew for Doctor Warner" tells of an erudite, accomplished musicologist who attempts to immerse himself in, and thereby understand, the jazz underground:

> "I'll have to be a *hipster*," Doctor Warner said, "if not, indeed, something *more*...."
> "Something more?" said Professor Thomas, stressing his mock surprise with a sickly smile. He loathed strange jargon. "Don't tell me there's anything more, Ralph, than being a hipster!"
> "Yes," he said evenly, "you might say that a *junky* is something more than a hipster."[36]

Warner hopes to classify, to understand the fringe dwellers, those who dwell in the void. And so he goes downtown in search of heroin, hoping that the procuring and sampling of this drug will immerse him in the mindset of the jazz musician. There, in an alley, he meets up with a boy he suspects to be a pusher:

> Dr. Warner nodded with grave knowing. "Crazy," he said and then, with a slow wink of confidence as he departed, "Later, man."
> The boy blinked with disinterest and sank carefully back against the wall.... [Warner] had just succeeded in freezing *riff* in italics when the word and the phrase exploded in a flash of blinding white, as an arm swung out from the darkness and laid a short segment of lead pipe across the back of the Doctor's head. As he staggered between two mountains of refuse, he was hit again, and the white light was shot through with coils and bolts of purple and gray and flooded out on a heavy wave of blood blackness.[37]

The Professor comes up against the junky, and doesn't survive the encounter—the fringe will not be categorized or understood. This tale is not exactly complex, but it is a memorable pulp evocation of the clash between high culture and low, between culture and brute savage nature, and of culture's absolute vulnerability and inefficacy in the face of it.

An unpublished tale from this period plays out the same confrontation from a different angle. In "Paul's Problem," a bright young graduate student ("a physics student at Columbia"[38]) must deal with the brutal treatment of a prostitute, in a room upstairs in the hotel in which he is working as a night clerk. Again, we see not only how an eruption of sex and violence can fracture the frail philosophies of culture, but also the abuse of power — the corrupt authority of Johnson and its cruel treatment of "the smallest and dear," as represented by The Girl, in a variation on the same triangle found in "The Automatic Gate." But this time, the young idealist is ultimately willing to go along with those abuses, in order to get along — making this tale all the more tragic.

The story begins with a detailed portrait of a night clerk's menial tasks. When Paul is finally left alone at the desk, he begins musing on his academic work and, more particularly, on:

> ... a small discussion group meeting once a month, made up mostly of people from the physics department. [Its] purpose had been to present and clarify, mathematically, new unproved theories in physics ... [but] gradually the discussions had assumed another dimension, philosophy ... Paul enjoyed these new discussions.... He supposed there would be a quoting of ... Sartre and Camus ... emphasis on the necessity of the individual's awareness of responsibility for his acts ... he was hoping to formulate some contributions of his own.[39]

He is called away from his musings by a disturbance upstairs: a prostitute is being beaten by her client. In the face of this violence, he is paralyzed with fear, unable to act as anything but mute witness. Through meeting the prostitute and being offered a glimpse into her mode of being — by seeing his own helplessness and moral cowardice, his refusal to act on her behalf — he comes to view his group and their activities with sudden distaste:

> He knew too that he wouldn't go to his group meetings anymore either. Moral responsibility. The irony would be a little too final, and at that thought, he felt a moment of sorrow for himself that he had never before felt in his life, and having lost that as well, such a simple pleasure, harmless ... what the hell difference did it make, it was probably nothing but talk anyway.[40]

Southern never did finish his thesis on Mallarme, and this tale offers an insight into why he lost interest in his graduate studies; it is yet another ineffective cultural bulwark against chaos, incapable of equipping us to deal with violence (truth to tell, though, his interest in academia was probably never terribly keen to begin with — the G.I. bill was more than likely just an excuse to sample life in Europe). Paul, the hapless night clerk, is not unlike Kafka's clerk Joseph K. in *The Trial*, or Todd Hackett in Nathanael West's *The Day of the Locust*, even West's *Miss Lonely-Hearts*: a soul adrift, ravaged by forces beyond his control, coming up against the brutality of the world and finding his perspective insufficient as a means of coping.

There is another story written in this same period that offers a slightly subtle shift in the role of the "hapless" protagonist, hinting at the more prominent work to come. The story was unpublished in Southern's lifetime, and survived in a manuscript offering the same address that "Paul's Problem" did (269 West 11th Street). Though it was not to see print for over half a century, in retrospect the story offers a significant milestone on Southern's road to finding his true voice and subject.

"A Run of Dimes" seems to give the reader yet another harmless clerk in the person of Fred Merkle, a small cog in the giant machine of the U.S. Treasury Department. But the tale focuses on Merkle's sudden questioning of the details of his neat, ordered existence, and, more importantly, shows actual consequences resulting from that questioning:

> Merkle, who had been with the Treasury Department for twenty-four years, [is] one of that legion of conscientious, apolitical employees who managed to survive the ravaging spoils of administrative and policy change by dint of sheer unambitious hard work, and by the concomitant fact that their positions are usually of a category below general or rather particular notice. However, through 24 years of conscience work in any conceivable organization, one does obtain, by degree, to positions of quasi-and/or momentary authority. And so it was with Merkle. Today, for example, he was in charge of a run of dimes.[41]

Merkle, however, has of late been increasingly nervous and has taken to "reading the morning paper very closely.... 'Lay off things like that for a while,' the doctor had said grandly, 'you're worrying too much. Sit in the park with a good book, *fiction*.'"[42] The doctor's prescription of fiction as safe and escapist, helping Merkle to cease questioning the status quo, demonstrates Southern's contempt for any fiction that does not seek to question or to challenge; that does not, in short, act as an explosive device.

Merkle refuses to escape or take comfort in fiction, and instead "had subscribed to the paper, and it was there every morning on his desk." Merkle becomes obsessed with a speech the president has made in which he "asks faith for the nation." He calls the president, finally reaching him after going through many channels, and confronts him about the notion of faith, even as a run of C-3 dimes is waiting to go: "...I read your speech, the speech you made yesterday about faith, and I've been reading the newspapers about the ... investigations and so on...."

Merkle is troubled because the current dime (Lady Liberty), with a woman's head on it, bears a prominent demonstration of faith:

> "It has the woman's head," Merkle continued, "and liberty around it, you know, in big letters. Then at the bottom, 'In God We Trust,' in small block, sort of bal-

anced by the date of issue.... [W]ell, from your speech and the way things are going in the paper, it didn't seem right to me somehow, having the emphasis...."

The president is shaken by what Merkle is slyly insinuating:

"I can only say we are doing the best we can...."
"No," said the president, and Merkle had to strain to hear, "we don't want it like the penny."
"All right, Mr. President, we are going ahead with the regular run then."
"Yes, yes, of course."[43]

Over the span of their conversation, the president goes from "tolerant good humor" to being shaken by what Merkle is implying, through his request to change the run of the dimes. The point of the tale is that even the tiniest cog in the machine ("the smallest and dear") can, when he or she starts to question the way things are, shake up the highest powers-that-be. Merkle is an ancestor of Guy Grand, the Magic Christian — and the first example, in one of Southern's tales, of somebody "making it hot for them"[44] — as Southern himself was about to do.

4

Give Me Your Hump!

Throughout this period (the early- to mid-fifties), Southern's voice was developing, his central themes and preoccupations emerging, as his style moved from character sketches of New York and Paris, and the portraits of the Underground thriving in both cities, to a concern with questioning — and even attacking — the "Aboveground." And in focusing his vision, he had found a role model.

In 1955, soon after they met, he went for a date with Carol at the Riviera Bar on Seventh Avenue in the Village. As Carol recalled, "I had met Terry and bumped into him at a party, and he asked me for a date. And I had arrived at the date, which was at a bar, and the first thing he said was 'Do you know the work of Henry Green?' And I had never heard of him, but it was so uppermost in his mind. So he described his work and he felt that it was the freshest writing being done and that he was really expanding the form of the novel in a very interesting way."[1]

Green was the British author of the novels *Loving*, *Living*, and *Party-Going*, among others; his work is highly reminiscent of Southern in style, if not necessarily in substance — though Southern, in his early years (grounded in realism), as well as in his final work, *Texas Summer*, is closer in terms of subject matter as well (though his concern is, of course, American culture, as opposed to British culture).

Green's work is highly cinematic, mostly comprised of dialogue, quickly sketched surfaces, and appearances hinting at unplumbed depths; all elements highly akin to Southern. When Terry and Carol moved back to Europe, an initially epistolary relationship with Green would soon blossom into a close friendship. Meanwhile, as Carol remembered: "When I first met him, I was living on the Lower East Side. He didn't like taking the F train to East Broadway, he wanted to be in the Village. So he got us a room on Charles Street. His life was so exciting ... he seemed plugged into everything interesting that was going on. He always had plans. One thing I adored about

Terry, he certainly was a man with a plan.... He very much lived out his fantasies."[2]

Carol and Terry were married on Saturday, July 14, 1956, in Tupper Lake, New York. They lived on the barge, towing rocks between Poughkeepsie and Far Rockaway for the summer; he was beginning to earn a reputation at home, after "The Sun and the Still-Born Stars" and "The Panthers" had made their splash in *Harper's Bazaar*; nevertheless, they took a freighter back to Paris. Terry spent the voyage reading *The Scarlet Letter* aloud to Carol.

They stayed briefly in Paris, with Mason Hoffenberg and his girlfriend Coquette, before heading off to Geneva, where Carol had a job as a nursery school teacher at the Ecole Enfantine des Nations Unies.

Before leaving New York, Southern had another story, "A South Summer Idyll," published in *The Paris Review* of October 1, 1956. It was the first appearance in print of Harold, the boy protagonist of *Texas Summer* who would, as an adult, move to Paris and find success as a writer in *The Hipsters*. Moving the focus from Harold's adult life in Paris in *The Hipsters* back to his boyhood in Texas, allowed Southern to explore (as did his work back in New York) the matter of children and violence, the confrontation between innocence and evil. No longer is his foregrounded concern simply the delineation of an alternative lifestyle, an urban underground (that territory was being trademarked and copyrighted anyway, by Ginsberg, Kerouac, and their fellow Beats).

"Idyll" is the rural version of "Panthers," evoking not the urban milieu in which Southern had been living, but rather the bleak, forbidding landscape of Texas, of "The Sun and the Still-Born Stars," the land that had reared him. At this point Harold's name was Howard (his name would not be changed to Harold until the publication of "Red-Dirt Marijuana" in *The Evergreen Review*, four years later), and the story opens, appropriately enough, with Howard cleaning a gun:

> A summer Saturday in Dallas and the boy Howard sat out on the back steps, knees up, propping in between, an old, single load, twelve-gauge shotgun.[3]

Howard goes to his friend Big Lawrence's house and, with a third friend, Crazy Ralph, they sit in the room, talking and reading comic books, while Big Lawrence leans out the window with his own gun, aiming at a cat, pretending to fire — and eventually doing so:

> The cat seemed to have hardly moved.... But in the screen now, next to a hole made in opening in the screen from the outside, was another, perfectly round, flanged out instead of in, worn suddenly, by the passing of the bullet, all bright silver at the edge.[4]

Howard and Big Lawrence, indifferent to this violence and death, then go hunting. Southern evokes the landscape of Texas with loving detail, but it is a land governed by brutality:

> Heat came out of this dry stone, sharp as acid, wavering up in black lines. Then at a bend before them was the water hole, small now and stagnant....
>   The sound came as one, but within one spurting circle of explosion, the two explosions were distinct....
>   "Goddam!" said Lawrence, frowning. One side of the rabbit, from the stomach down, looked as though it had been pushed through a meat grinder.[5]

The rabbit is skinned, birds shot, hornets crushed in Big Lawrence's hand and eventually, as evening comes on, they go home, there to encounter the aftermath of their morning activities:

> ... a little girl was holding onto the dress with both hands, pressing her face into the apron, swinging herself slowly back and forth so ... she stroked the child's head with one hand, and in the other she was holding the dead cat.[6]

Like "The Panthers," the tale concludes with the innocence of a young girl blighted by a harsh violent terrain, now not sheltering a baby doll, but mourning her dead cat. Southern achieves his effect not through direct commentary, but juxtaposition of images. In the case of "A South Summer Idyll," no adult world, patriarchal figure, authority, status quo, or convention is called to blame. Here, it is simply that the harsh side of nature wins out over its more benevolent face. In the Texas of Southern's imagination, the two polarities of nature, harsh and benevolent, come in daily conflict with each other. In the Texas of this "Idyll," brutal always wins — however, in his next Texas tale, "Red-Dirt Marijuana," a possible solution to this stark dualism will be found.

Life in Geneva, and marriage to Carol, gave Southern an order and discipline that his life seems to have lacked before, and would lack again thereafter. However, Southern told Carol that he felt cut off from his "material" in Europe, and so they returned to New York, buoyed by the critical success of *The Magic Christian*. It is there that his alcohol and drug consumption would begin to get the better of his health and his talent.

Though his work in the early- and mid-fifties was concerned with the drug culture, and though Peter Matthiessen remembers him as being stoned when they first met in the early fifties, Carol Southern remembers that for "most of our marriage, we had no money. We could not afford more than a couple of glasses of wine a night, liquor was not a problem. But then when he started making money, he started drinking a lot and taking a lot of drugs."[7] In Geneva, however, far from Manhattan and Paris, he found quiet and focus.

Southern did some of his best writing in Geneva. In this period he was developing his style, moving beyond prose, into varied experiments in script writing. These include an "Untitled Narcotics Sequence" set in Manhattan, in which people from all walks of life are busted by cops for drug use. Even more interesting is a short surrealist skit named "C'est Toi Alors, A Scenario for Existing Props and French Cat," in which a young student in Paris is driven mad by a cat, and *The Year of the Weasel*, a lengthy play that developed out of his experience observing the children in the United Nations School, and an experiment that he conducted with the children, involving one of his signature themes — masks:

> My wife was teaching in the kindergarten of the United Nations School in Geneva, and we lived in rooms above the school, not unlike a situation in a Kafka novel. My desk was by a window overlooking the courtyard and I would watch the children play. They were all children of diplomats, so there was a spectrum of nationalities. It was unsettling to observe their behavior was so absolutely stereotypical. The American children were willful and bullying, and so were the Germans. The English were snobbish. The French were effete, clever and silly. The Orientals were very bright and ultra polite. I got so fascinated watching the children that I stopped working on anything else. I took notes on their behavior just like a child psychologist. At one point I went to a local costume shop and bought a bunch of animal masks — lion, fox, donkey, etc.; then I persuaded my wife to hang them in the children's cloakroom, so I could see what child would choose which mask. Interesting stuff. The head mistress, however, was a rather strict Meg Thatcher type, and she put an end to my experiments before they ever really got started.[8]

Southern's preoccupation with children was still strong, as the above shows. He was more inclined to use women as nurturing figures and men as repressive authority figures; the "Meg Thatcher type" from the actual school has been transformed in the play into "The Director," described as "a dynamic fellow of fairly eccentric manner." Other characters include Miss Smart, described as a "nice looking young woman, rather prim," a precursor of Babs Mintner in *Flash and Filigree*; Mr. Dexter, a "pleasant young man, well mannered," bland father of Johnny, one of the children in the school; and Smeller and Teller, "two bomb shelter salesmen, sharp dressers, vaudeville team manner,"[9] a duo who (if they had appeared) might have been reminiscent of Officers Stockton and Eddy from *Flash and Filigree*.

Although the manuscript's title page indicates otherwise, there never was a second act even in rough manuscript, and the first act, which exists in polished final draft, is self-contained and self-sufficient; even if there were plans for a second act, what we have here works quite well on its own. The only indication of more to come is the listing of comedy team "Smeller and Teller" in the cast listing, but the act's end seems fairly final.

Weasel represents a major advance in script writing after the short film sketches like "Children at Play" and "C'est Toi Alors." And unlike *The Big Touch* (or, for that matter, most of Southern's film work, discussed below), *Weasel* is not work-for-hire ... it's all Southern, the Surrealist emerging in a longer-form work, beyond the Naturalistic reporter of *The Hipsters*. The inspiration came from watching the schoolchildren that his wife was teaching in Geneva, but Southern took it in a direction all his own, down an avenue of Absurdist Theater via the drawing room comedies of Noel Coward — creating a pure product of Bomb Culture. And in put-ons of The Director, despite his malevolence, we can even detect early signs of Guy Grand himself.

The play opens on Miss Smart reading to the children from "the government booklet on fallout protection." The children are then led in a sing-along by Miss Smart for the delight of The Director, singing lyrics such as "HEE-ROW-SHE-MA, HERE I COME! / RIGHT BACK WHERE I STARTED FROM! / MUTILATION! RADIATION! / YOU'RE A FUNNY SIGHT! / ... AND THE FREAK SHOW'S ONLY JUST BEGUN."[10]

Southern is beginning to make a freak show of his fictional universe — just as education, he implies, is doing with the world, and with the young. As the sing-along comes to an end, The Director begins to distribute the masks:

> THE DIRECTOR BEGINS PRANCING ABOUT IN HIGH-STEPPING MARCH TEMPO, DISTRIBUTING GROTESQUE PLASTIC MASKS. WHEN EACH CHILD HAS RECEIVED ONE, THEY FALL IN SINGLE-FILE BEHIND DIRECTOR AND TROOP AROUND THE ROOM AFTER HIM. WITH THE LINE, "YOU'RE A FUNNY SIGHT" EACH CHILD RAISES MASK OF MUTILATION TO HIS FACE AND TURNS POINTING TO THE CHILD NEXT TO HIM.[11]

Moving into the territory of surrealism, and the Theater of the Absurd of Ionesco, the play is an interesting experiment (as were the masks), but a rather heavy-handed indictment of the teaching of fallout safety in schools, and the preparation for nuclear war. Ultimately, Dexter and his son, wearing masks given to them by The Director, sink into a "tomb" — the fallout shelter that Mr. Dexter has dug in the school's backyard, since he has "no room at home."

> THEY STAND MOMENTARILY, MASK OF WEASEL AND MASK OF MUTILATION, FACING AUDIENCE ... THEY SINK DOWN INTO THE SHELTER AS LIGHTS DIM. AS THESE LIGHTS DIM, FIVE SMALL SOFT SPOT LIGHTS GRADUALLY COME UP, EACH FOCUSED ON A CHILD'S GROTESQUELY MASKED FACE, LYING ON THE PALLETS, FACING THE AUDIENCE.
> THE SCHOOL-DIRECTOR, UNMASKED, LIES ON HIS BACK LIKE A MAN IN A TRANCE.
> THE SMALL LIGHTS DIE WITH THE SLOW CURTAIN.[12]

And so the play ends. In moving from the realism of "Panthers" and "A South Summer Idyll" into the Theater of the Absurd, Southern offers a more nightmarish vision of what he feels a violent, death-driven culture does to children ("the small lights die"). The children are transformed before our eyes into monsters, sunk into tombs, while the repressive authority figure lies in a trance, his victory complete and his mind, like the culture he has created and fostered, dead.

While he was writing *The Year of the Weasel*, Southern was also working on his first and only children's book, *The Donkey and the Darling*, which remained unpublished until the late 1970s (when it was released in a limited edition by the Whitney Museum, illustrated by the pop artist Larry Rivers, a close friend of Southern's). In the fantasy world of *The Donkey and the Darling*, Southern's concerns remain the same that they were in the stark landscape of "The Panthers" or the Absurdist theater of *The Year of the Weasel*. Again, there is the conflict between innocents and monsters (the Ass and the Angel, Body and Soul, an early version of the hunchback and Candy Christian); between those who are open to the world and those who seek to control perceptions, twisting innocence into grotesquery: "There are in the wide world around a group of things apart, and these are called *Tiny Splendid Things*. Of such, for example, are *Cricket ... Kitten ... Baby Fox ...* and THE DARLING."[13]

So Southern opens his fairytale, introducing us to the "Tiny Splendid Things," creatures akin to the "smallest and dear" of his short film, "Children at Play." And soon after that, we are introduced to their opponents:

> In Sillicreechie, where the Darling lives, all the books are owned by Bad Witch ... it is true that Bad Witch has several false editions of the *Book of the Darling*, but such false editions are unsatisfactory and cannot be used *against* the Darling, whose own books are kept fresh by proper dusting each day.... Donkey has one book, *The Donkey Book*. It is filled with various likenesses of Donkey ... each night after Thin Wisdom leaves, Pig Man and Bad Baker are employed to come in and stir the books up with long poles.[14]

In these opening moments, Southern establishes the theme of his tale: how perceptions can be controlled. There are those who delude others, like Bad Witch, Pig Man and Bad Baker (controlling and confusing the books, which can change perception), and there are those who delude themselves, like Donkey — interested in nothing but himself. And then there are the Tiny Splendid Things, simply open to experience: the innocents. The book is a collection of adventures, not one sustained narrative — not unlike A.A. Milne's *Winnie the Pooh*, and like *Pooh*, it has the flavor of an Oriental fairytale, not only in its style, but in its substance. Ultimately, its message, like Milne's *Pooh*, is essentially that of the *Tao Te Ching*: namely, the virtue of the small.

The book concludes with an outing of "the Smallest and Dear" (as "the tiny splendid things" have been properly named by book's end), at which Donkey insists on preparing a broth for all the Smallest and Dear to eat. They are apprehensive, "for it was well known that Donkey broth was a tasteless guk."[15] But the Darling believes in him, and through her belief and affection, she transforms the broth:

> And then did the Darling see the Donkey and marvel at his manner, how he pranced about the cooking pot adding spices with a flourish.
> "That Donkey is *true cooker!*" she cried, "see him add his spices with a flourish!"
> And due to the magic of the Darling words, the broth became excellent indeed and a delightful aroma filled Meadow Green. Then the Darling began to fall asleep under the Big Tree with her Donkey-broth, and her words became all sleepy and distorted. "That ... Donkey ... is ... *true* ... *cooker!*" she meant to say, but said instead, "That ... Donkey ... is true coo-coo." And so the Donkey-broth at once became a tasteless guk — but no harm was done because the Darling and the Smallest and Dear were already full of good broth.[16]

Donkey, continually bumbling, deludes himself, not even taking pride in his own creation ("Pah, I've no time for this broth!"[17]). Bad Witch tries to control all the books and, therefore, all thoughts (essentially, she censors, as *The Paris Review* had done to Southern). But Darling simply loves, and in doing so, she transforms the world.

Both *The Donkey and the Darling* and *The Year of the Weasel* are concerned with innocence and experience, with perception and delusion. Education, it is implied again and again in Southern's work, is no guarantee of true vision. More often than not, true vision is only attained by the innocent; this warning against the dangers of organized education connects these two works with earlier tales like "The Night the Bird Blew for Doctor Warner."

Another work written in Geneva offers a surreal variation on the theme explored in the earlier "Paul's Problem," that of an overly educated student coming up against something he cannot comprehend. The sketch, "C'est Toi Alors," is not only a development of "Paul's Problem," but an ode to Poe's tale "The Black Cat" as well. The action opens on:

> ... a small apartment in late evening, [as] a sensitive-looking young man sits at his desk scrutinizing the pages of a telephone directory. The soundtrack is military marches, he gets up from the desk, crosses the room and dons a U.S. Army helmet which he carefully adjusts. He takes up a machete or bolo knife which stands in the corner of the room, and a pistol from under the rug. He faces the direction of the door, holding the bolo knife in his right hand and making a narrow menacing arc with it, while slowly taking aim with the pistol.[18]

In the small apartment, with the "sensitive" young man, we are again in the world of the over-educated young student visited in previous Southern tales. But this is someone desperate to present an air of authority, to cleave to the harsh masculine world of the military — a world he is carefully recreating and preserving in his personal cocoon, a world of order represented by the telephone directory. This small universe is soon invaded, however, by "a cat entering the room at a trot, as on the way to food, but it sits down near the desk to wait."[19] The short sketch is an escalating encounter between the young man and the cat, as the cat drives him to distraction and to madness:

> ... he leaps at the cat, holding the bolo like a dagger. The cat jumps aside and the young man grovels on the floor, kicking his feet like a child and plunging the bayonet repeatedly against the floor, his face buried in the rug...
> (shrieking insanely)
> *C'est toi alors! C'est toi alors! C'est toi alors!*
> CAMERA PULLS UP to show the cat sitting in the helmet which is slowly spinning on the desk.
> FADE TO BLACK.
> FIN.[20]

Strange as this skit seems at first glance, it is a fairly straightforward variation on Poe's "The Black Cat," centered not on an alcoholic, but rather a sensitive (i.e., more feminine than manly) man trying desperately to assume a hard Apollonian aura, a masculine persona. But nature — with all its Dionysian mystery — in the form of the cat, erupts into his closed world, destroying the rigid order he sought his military regalia and his telephone book. The cat's impassive feminine resistance to his imposed order drives him to madness. And in presenting the confrontation of repressive, masculine Apollonianism with mysterious, feminine, Dionysian nature, "C'est Toi Alors" develops and expands upon the themes that Southern has been developing, while paying discreet homage to his spiritual forefather, Poe.

But while — in his unpublished dramas and children's books — Southern had been moving away from the realism of his published short stories, towards the surrealism that would mark his celebrated novels, he was still writing in a more realist style in the prose tales. And though also concerned with the confrontation between nature and culture, innocence and experience, these tales were also offering a new angle, a new form, for that confrontation: the collision of two cultures. In the unpublished tales "Janus," "Brandy for Heroes," "The Strangest Breed," and "Color-Blind," opposing cultural sides transcend their differences and come to a warmer understanding of each other — or at least, they attempt to.

"Janus" focuses on David and Vivian West, a young couple driving from France to Italy; they are not all that dissimilar, it can be surmised, from Terry and Carol Southern as they explored Europe (Carol and Terry often drove from Switzerland into France, for instance, to sample the better restaurants found over the border). David is cynical and jaded, while Vivian is happy and open to new experience — exactly as Southern may have pictured himself and his wife. David represents experience with a touch of bitterness; Vivian, innocence — together, their outlooks comprise Janus, the two-headed god, and the question at hand is whose outlook will prevail:

> "Aren't the *colors* marvelous," said Vivian happily. She was looking out the window on her side of the car.... "They're so much *stronger* than in France ... the difference is just amazing."
> David grunted while reaching for a cigarette, an assent meant as marked dissent.... "All right, Viv," he said, rubbing his hands together, "now let's get with it. Don't be so afraid of showing a little emotion once in a while. Christ, that's what makes this business of living the wonderful, big business it is. The biggest darn business on earth, to my way of thinking."[21]

Their opposing viewpoints play off each other throughout the story. When their car gets a flat tire in a remote section of the countryside, an old man comes to help them, fixes their tire, and asks for nothing in return. Afterwards, they drive in silence for a while:

> "What a wonderful thing," said Vivian finally, in a sort of full-throated way, turning to David, expectant, dry, soft and big.
> David started to say something, but cleared his throat instead.
> "Well, it takes all kinds, my dear," he said then, in a senator's voice, patting the inside of her leg, "it takes all kinds. A grand old maxim...."
> She snuggled against him. "Yes," she said, smiling.[22]

This charming slice-of-life self-portrait of the Southerns during the Geneva period is perhaps culled from an actual incident. Even more so, it's a loving Valentine to Terry's wife Carol, his own "smallest and dear," and the necessary counterpoint to his own jaded Hipster worldview, which receives a bit of a reproof here. Also notable is his (or, rather, David's) use of the term "color-blind" to denote sensitivity — a clue to the meaning of that tale as well: receptivity to other modes of seeing. There is also the atypically rhapsodic prose as the Wests watch the surf in Italy — the priest of nature is singing a hymn, and it even gets David to shut up ... for a moment.

"Janus" offers a touching glimpse into the serene existence that Terry and Carol led in Geneva; it's a bit of autobiography demonstrating how the power of kindness can transform even the cynical cool of Southern himself. The work he did in Geneva, unlike his earlier stories or his later films, nearly always ends on an upbeat note; Southern did not only some of his best, but some of his most joyful, work in this period.

"Brandy for Heroes" is again concerned with the meeting of two different cultures, and is an odder tale than "Janus." Though also concerned with a slice of mundane life — the filling of a cavity, as opposed to the changing of a tire — this tale's subject and characters begin to veer into the surreal mad-scientist/Dr. Eichner territory that will increasingly preoccupy Southern. Doctors, like the clergy, the military, and politicians, will come to occupy a prominent role in Southern's vision, as absurd yet dangerous paternal authority figures. Yet here, the approach is still more genial than fearful ... though the potential for pain is very real.

Working in similar territory as "The Face of the Arena," this is a more light-hearted send-up of the Hemingway brand of heroism. Members of Southern's generation had a choice between two literary lions of the previous generation to choose as patron saint: Hemingway or Faulkner. Here, once again, Southern comes down firmly on the side of "The Fab Faulk." Like "Janus," this is about different cultures, different views of reality, finding connection. Unassuming, unpretentious and gently funny in its absurdity, this unpublished treasure is probably my favorite Southern tale.

In a remote village in Spain, the unnamed protagonist, an American, finds an unusual dentist: Hernandez works in a dim, dark building, with an apparatus out of Kafka's penal colony (echoes of "The Automatic Gate") in a building reminiscent of Kafka's Castle:

> Hernandez was a man of good appearance ... looking more like those photographs of William Faulkner. Anyway, he had a good gray look, a quiet, kindly and wise look, yet, too, a certain pride and twinkle with all.[23]

Hernandez, it soon becomes clear, is no malevolent Eichner, but a healing figure, an artist:

> It was a tall structure resembling a massive wooden painting easel, and it occurred to me that perhaps Pablo had subconsciously drawn his image ("it is an art," he had said) from this association. Suspended from one of the upright arms was the terrible drill.[24]

In order to prepare the narrator for the painful operation, Hernandez gets him drunk on brandy. In fact, they share several glasses of brandy together before Hernandez begins the operation. Afterwards, the American visits his friend Pablo, who had recommended the dentist:

> "Do you a drink now?" he asked, glancing towards where the waiter was standing.
> "No, I believe not. As a matter of fact, I had quite a lot to drink there with Hernandez. Brandy."
> "Ah, yes," he said quickly, nodding, "*ah, yes*— the brandy" when he looked up again, the smile was a real one, even shy, seeming to hold its own modesty at being surreal. It was a smile of shared experience. He cleared his throat.
> "Well," he said, "what is the English saying — 'claret for women, port for men ... and brandy for heroes.'"
> And he raised his glass then in a little gesture which seemed, for that moment at least, like his smile, very real, warm and all — embracing.[25]

The American and the Spaniard bond over the shared experience of pain at the hands of the dentist. As much as this tale resembles "Janus" (foreign cultures find common ground, understanding and friendship), it is also, like the early story "The Face of the Arena," a send-up of Hemingway. The characters do not bond over war, but rather, a cavity filling. And it is not insignificant that the benevolent paternal figure, the dentist, resembles William Faulkner.

As Southern recalled in an interview: "Since college days and before, I had regarded Faulkner as the most influential American writer of our time and always came down vociferously on his side whenever one was obliged to choose between him and Hemingway."[26] It is Faulkner, then, who benevolently presides over this sly send-up of Hemingway's brand of heroism.

Another unpublished tale from this period, "Color-Blind," explores the dark side of two cultures meeting (or colliding), of two differing modes of perception attempting to find common ground — and failing. This short story, like "Janus," draws on Southern's own life for initial inspiration — merely in the situation of the American student and his foreign room-mate, though in Southern's case, his roommate at Northwestern was from India rather than the Philippines. From there, one can assume that reality and fiction diverge, as it's hard to imagine Southern being so self-involved and emotionally, culturally deaf (or "color-blind") as the narrator. And here, as in "Paul's Problem," we see the contempt for academic philosophy — perhaps, at root, a guilty reaction brought on by Southern's own unsuccessful struggle to finish his thesis?

A young American philosophy student (again, like "Paul") is living with a Filipino student, living in America on a sports scholarship. The young narrator is working on his doctoral thesis:

> I was lying on my bed, morose, and trying to choose ... some isolated precept of existentialism for the subject of my thesis.... [I] wanted it to have a real value or practical application, so to speak. And Yonda came in.... I sighed aloud to express my annoyance, then deciding I was too tired to get up and dress, I simply closed my eyes as though he weren't there, and went on tending my own dark thoughts.[27]

Yonda wishes to engage the narrator in conversation; he had been upset by an incident at a picnic earlier that day, when his hostess and fellow guests went swimming in cold water. Yonda asks the narrator why they would do such a thing, and whether he should go along with such an odd custom. The narrator attempts to respond:

> Of course, I tried to tell him that, in America, certain circumstances ... carry with them the almost moral necessity to "go in" ... but I checked myself with a cough and instead, suddenly recalling the childhood cry, "Last one in is a rotten egg ..." excused myself and plunged into what should be a really crackerjack thesis.[28]

Abruptly, Southern's narrator abandons the conversation, turning away from communication and focusing intensely on his thesis — the tale culminates in a final paragraph that is completely underlined for emphasis, save for the final two words (and thereby emphasizing them all the more):

> The ultimate effect of such a thesis is far from certain. What I'm hoping will happen ... is that one Sunday in July I'll just step out of the penny arcade and there it will be ... like a gigantic Kodachrome slide blazing in majestic desolation and really monstrous silence ... Coney Island.[29]

Yonda cannot understand why Americans do the absurd things they do; the narrator cannot explain American behavior to him, and so simply cuts himself off, refusing to interact with Yonda, drawing back inside himself like a turtle, as alone as he was before their brief interaction. Like Paul in "Paul's Problem," and the tortured young man in "C'est Toi Alors," the narrator of "Color-Blind" has tried to protect himself from what he cannot understand, to lull himself into an imaginary realm, what Henry Miller had called — in a phrase co-opted by Lawrence Ferlinghetti for a celebrated poem, published just before the composition of "Color-Blind" — "a Coney Island of the Mind."

Unlike David and Vivian in "Janus," or the narrator of "Brandy for Heroes," the narrator of "Color-Blind" refuses to reach out, choosing instead to retreat within himself. His doctoral thesis, his work in philosophy, offers no insight, only an amusement park of the mind to get lost in, isolated from others — the blindness that the title speaks of is blindness to other people, other cultures ... and other colors.

Incidentally, the manuscript for "Color-Blind," which gives Carol and Terry's address ("1146 rue Schaub, Geneva, Switzerland"), is signed by one Maxwell Kenton, like "His Second Most Interesting Case" before and *Candy* soon after. Normally, Maxwell Kenton was used only for Southern's collaborations. "Color-Blind," which is not a collaboration, is credited to Kenton as well, for reasons known only to Southern himself.

The unpublished tales of this period also include Southern's second return to Texas, after "A South Idyll" and before "Red-Dirt Marijuana." Originally titled "A Stranger Breed," Southern crossed that title out in the manuscript and penciled in "The Strangest Breed" — emphasizing even more firmly the unique quality of his loner protagonist.

It's an odd, brief sketch, an encounter between a cowboy coming to a ranch looking for work, and the foreman who cannot hire him, not needing any workers. Though a realist sketch of Texas life, the story does mark the second appearance in Southern's prose of a freakish monster — though one more subdued, certainly, than the monster of "The Sun and the Still-Born Stars." Nevertheless, the horse that the cowboy tries to ride is described as:

... a fantastic horse, a tall, freakish animal with a head too small and legs too thin for its body, but in the neck and the diamond-coated shoulders was the mark of a strange pure breed. The wild eyes rolled and glittered, and the teeth bared repeatedly.... The cowboy was looking into the chute, "Don't think I've ever seen a horse like that," he said. The foreman laughed and spat, "Not you or nobody else," he said. "One of old crazy Morley's horses, Justice Morley. He's dead now too, passed on a month ago.... Wasn't exactly right in the head, I guess. Shame."[30]

The cowboy tries to ride the horse, and is quickly thrown. Afterward, when telling the foreman that he, along with his wife and children, should be "pushing on," the foreman remembers another ranch nearby that "might be shorthanded," but the cowboy refuses him. "'Well, thanks,' said the cowboy, looking back across the square, and beyond, up at the two o'clock sun, 'I reckon we'll just push on.'"[31]

The cowboy is as much a freak and a loner as the horse he tried to ride, and the two will always remain isolated. The story is Southern's tribute to the cowboy, the western hero, the loner who never fits in and will never be tamed. Turned out or driven mad by society (by Justice Morley, or by the ranches that won't hire) the loner keeps "pushing on"; heading, like Huck Finn, out for the territories.

"The Strangest Breed" makes an interesting companion piece with "The Sun and the Still-Born Stars," in that both are early portraits of Texas and center on a confrontation between man and "monster." However, in this case, that brush with the savage face of nature does not destroy the man, but instead liberates him. Like the horse, he will never again let anyone ride him.

Still, this celebration of a cowboy going it alone is an odd message for a story written amid a group of tales about the need for contact, for communication and understanding; but it's a tribute to Texas and the code of the loner. And like the other tales of Texas that Southern began to write in this period, it indicates that even with the happiness he found in Geneva, there was still a sense of homesickness for America, and for the Texas he claimed to have hated.

One of Southern's closest friends at this time (though their relationship had been kept active almost entirely through correspondence) was Mason Hoffenberg, the American poet living in Paris. Hoffenberg had little success in his vocation as poet, but did enjoy a regular income from the Olympia Press, where, under the pseudonym "Faustino Perez," he had written several erotic novels for Olympia's "Traveller's Companion" series, with titles like *Until She Screams* and *Sin for Breakfast*.

Southern would occasionally go up to Paris to visit Mason Hoffenberg or Alex Trocchi (who like Southern, had gotten the barge job on the Hudson). One of Trocchi's close friends in this period had been the French surrealist painter and film maker Jean Cocteau; Southern and Trocchi would often go over to Cocteau's apartment to smoke opium, while listening to Stravinsky and Berlioz. In his essay "Flashing on Gid" (published in *Grand Street* in 1992, and intended to serve as Chapter Three of *Making It Hot*, his unfinished memoir), Southern recalled: "It was during the Cocteau opium period that I wrote a short story called 'Candy Christian,' about a ... darling who's compassion incarnate ... so filled with universal love, that she gave herself fully and joyfully to ... a demented hunchback. Of course, that was merely the surface, the flimsy trappings, as it were; the meat and potatoes of the piece lay elsewhere."[32]

According to Southern, it was Alex Trocchi who alerted Maurice Girodias, the head of the Olympia Press, to the existence of "Candy Christian." Girodias later approached Southern with the idea of turning the tale into a full-fledged novel of erotica. However, it should be noted that John de St. Jorre, in his *Venus Bound: A History of the Olympia Press*, credits Hoffenberg with going to Girodias and telling him about *Candy*.

The genesis and publishing history of *Candy* is messy, a series of squabbles between the Southern-Hoffenberg team and Girodias over who owned the copyright. *Candy* was published by the Olympia Press in 1958, but outlawed in both France and the United States. When it was finally published in the U.S. in 1964, it spent over thirty weeks on the *New York Times* bestseller list, but Southern and Hoffenberg received money for royalties for a mere few weeks due to the complicated copyright technicalities, since it was in the public domain. Their contract with Putnam stated that royalties would cease if the book was pirated,[33] which it promptly was.

Candy would stand as the first instance of Southern foolishly ensuring that he would receive no profit from his work, a career course that would continue in Hollywood, with particularly unpleasant results in the case of *Easy Rider*. De St. Jorre chronicles in detail the legal squabbles over *Candy* (see also Nile Southern's *The Candymen*); the correspondence between Southern and Hoffenberg during this period, as they sent chapters back and forth, is filled with references to Girodias and the money: "Thanks for your recent, though I do hope Gid is not beating us for crack ... decency vies with cunning; in your restatement of terms, Mas, my understanding was that we were going fifty-fifty on the overall figure, and it seems to me rather cruel bait to suggest otherwise."[34]

The letters show evidence that Hoffenberg (probably incapacitated by his heroin addiction) actually contributed relatively little to the composition of *Candy*, but that Southern, ever generous, was determined to share the profits with him fifty-fifty, though Hoffenberg did not begin to work on the novel until Southern had already conceived the idea and written several chapters.

Hoffenberg, it seems, was far too innocent, far too good a friend, to abuse Southern's trust — and Girodias, by withholding any sort of sizable payment (added to the public domain status of *Candy*) ensured that there wasn't much money for Hoffenberg and Southern ever to fight over anyway.

But as Carol Southern remembers, Terry "was so hopeless with agents. He would make his own deals and not tell the agent.... Sterling Lord [his literary agent in the fifties and early sixties and again in the nineties] just sort of gave up on him."[35]

Southern was, from the outset of his literary career, hapless with money. But it appears that Mason Hoffenberg was even worse in this regard. In a letter to Hoffenberg dated "May, 1957," and sent from Geneva, Southern teases: "As for your attitude towards money, however, I must say it is not the greatest ... I see in this blind spot of yours, Hoff, and I can tell you now, with all due respect, how it happened. Let's say it first began when you realized as a small child, and you told me this once yourself, that certain of your friends liked you more for your money than for your true self. So this gave you an odd feeling about it, money."[36]

Southern urges generosity at all times as the mark of a decent human being. This explains why a man who amassed so much money in a brief time in Hollywood in the late sixties died virtually penniless. Like his heroine Candy Christian, he was almost childlike in his naïve openness and generosity, a trait that would not serve him well in the ruthless world of Hollywood, and one that was already being taken advantage of by Maurice Girodias in 1958.

The central event of the novel *Candy* occurs in Chapter Ten, which is also the original standalone story "Candy Christian," the seed from which the rest of the novel sprang. In this bizarre little tale, Southern's true strength fully emerges for the first time: his representation of the American Grotesque. And what are the "meat and potatoes" that Southern spoke of? What is being played out in the confrontation between the young girl and the hunchback? The story begins with their meeting:

> There was only one tree on Grove Street. This was the sort of thing Candy was quick to notice and to love.... And that was where she met the hunchback. It was late one airless summer day when the sky over Greenwich Village was the color of lead.[37]

Already, with the girl and the landscape, there is the familiar confrontation between joy, openness, and optimism, and the deadness of hostile nature, a "sky the color of lead." Candy tries to speak to the hunchback as he gazes into the window of a men's underwear shop, but he is capable of saying only one phrase:

> "Rubatubdub!" he said.
> Candy laughed. She heard a wisdom and complex symbology in the hunchback's simple phrases. It was as though she were behind the scenes of something, the Dadaist movement, even creatively a part of it. "This is the way things happen," she thought.... And here she was, a part of it.[38]

Candy brings the hunchback to her apartment for tea; through a series of misperceptions (the hunchback wants to rob her, while she simply wants to make him happy, to be Christian), the two of them finally wind up in bed together, in what is perhaps the ugliest sex scene the Olympia Press ever published in its *Traveler's Companion* series:

> ... as he began to strike her across the back of her legs she sobbed "...yes, hurt me as they have hurt you." ... as it continued she slowly opened her eyes, that all the world might see the tears there — but instead she herself saw, through the rise and fall of the wire lash — the hunchback's white gleaming hump! The hump, the white, unsunned forever, radish root white of hump.... With a wild impulsive cry she shrieked "GIVE ME YOUR HUMP!"... And she teetered on the blazing peak of pure madness for an instant.[39]

This chapter, the standout segment of the novel, is a magnificent, disturbing and hilarious example of the American Grotesque: Southern's true voice in full flower. Plimpton remembers that "its famous line, 'Give me your Hump!,' was a greeting one heard around the cafés when it was first published."[40] And it is small wonder that a literary vignette so outrageously freakish could elicit an immediate reaction. The entire encounter between Candy and the hunchback is an admirable example of the two traits that George Plimpton had pinpointed as dominant characteristics of Southern's work: "Misunderstandings, ambiguities, odd juxtapositions and the comic aspects that result ... all that is very much a staple of Southern's work. So are monsters."[41]

This particular misunderstanding arises from two different perceptions of how the world works, coming in contact with each other; or, rather, coming up *against* each other, and not achieving any sort of contact through speech, only in the madness of their sexual union.

What are those two sensibilities? A benevolent view of nature as represented by Candy Christian, a view of mercy inherent in nature that has sustained the Judeo-Christian tradition; and a harsher view of nature, a perception of what Camille Paglia calls "the chthonian"[42] — the "bowels"[43] of nature, its blank hostile face. The white hump is akin to Melville's white whale, and (again) to Poe's white figure rising out of the milky ocean of *Pym*'s finale.

The monsters of Southern's work are the freaks rising out of chthonic nature, out of its harsh, less giving side. What is at stake in this story is which side of nature carries more weight, and the victor is clearly the hunchback. For the first and only time in the novel, through all the countless givings of herself to men, Candy achieves an orgasm; her only release, her surrender of self-control, is through the hunchback. And he, monster though he is, becomes the one true "love" whose image sustains her through the rest of the novel.

Though *Candy* has often been likened to Voltaire's *Candide*, that "Quality Lit" reference seems more an afterthought than a motivating factor — the only real similarities being a pessimism about human benevolence, and the episodic misadventures of the innocent protagonist spanning the globe. A surer source can be found in the "Tijuana Bibles," the pornographic comic books that Southern read in his youth back in Texas: "When I was young they had what was called 'little fuck books' which featured characters from the comics. Most of them were absurd and grotesque."[44]

It can be argued that the rest of the novel is a letdown from this chapter, because none of the other chapters achieve its heights of visionary grotesquery. But the surrounding chapters do, in fact, offer a context that heightens and underlines what is going on in the confrontation between Candy and the hunchback. All the other men who take advantage of Candy's open, generous nature are figures of cultural authority: doctors, psychiatrists, professors, religious gurus — even, in the apocalyptic final sequence, the Buddha himself. None satisfy Candy; she simply gives away, and is given nothing in return. They are monsters of a sort, true, but monsters of cultural repression; monsters who take life and give nothing in return.

The hunchback, like the sea hog that enters the melon patch in "The Sun and the Still-Born Stars," is a monster of a different variety, a monster who gives. Candy achieves orgasm with the hunchback because she and the hunchback are two sides of the same coin. They are nature itself: giving, beautiful, benevolent, nurturing, while also harsh, seething, and monstrous.

In Southern's Decadent vision, nature must be embraced in its totality. To be only kind, benevolent, giving, willing to suffer for others, is a cultural lie, an embrace of only one-half of nature's complete face. Candy herself has been lying (or, at any rate, mistaken). In coming face-to-face with her other half, in moving beyond the lie or misrepresentation, she is transformed and fulfilled in an orgasmic explosion in which the cultural mask falls away ... and she is none the worse for it. The hunchback does not harm her, and her cute "Darn it!" at the end of the chapter (on finding the hunchback gone) shows that she is still happily, completely, herself.

Chapter Ten of *Candy*, the tale "Candy Christian," is not merely a scandalous freak show, but a recipe for embrace of the full self. And within the context of the novel, in which Candy comes up against the seemingly endless string of manipulative, deceitful representatives of cultural authority, it becomes also an image of life's beautiful, horrifying truth, undercutting all the pretenses and lies we tell ourselves to create a culture and get on with living.

Chapter Ten was the initial impulse, the "meat and potatoes," as Southern called it. And perhaps having Candy come up against one or two cultural figures would have been fine. But the fact is, the novel is a one-joke idea that goes on too long, as Southern himself knew. Carol remembers that "he got bored with actually executing it. He set himself a goal of two typed pages a day. I was typing as he wrote in longhand. He would pass over the pages and keep asking: 'Are you at the bottom of page two yet?'"[45]

Girodias, who in his memoirs describes Southern and Hoffenberg as a pair of "artful rogues," recalls Southern talking about *Candy* a bit differently. Having invited Southern out to lunch in Paris, Girodias remembers that Southern described Candy to him, with "captivating gestures, tracing her haunches, molding the fullness of her breasts." Southern joked to Girodias that when writing he got "an enormous erection ... he did not know what to do. He seriously wondered if his wife was going to leave him if he had to dedicate an entire book to this Candy."[46]

The conversation that Girodias recalls was obviously delivered to entertain, and to coax more money out of his publisher. But it seems likely that Southern was, in fact, bored with a novel that was hopelessly locked into the rigid Olympia Press formula: a sex scene every two or three pages. And those "other things" that Carol Southern recalls Southern working on, which occupied his attention more fully, were, first and foremost, the novel *The Magic Christian*, which he had just begun.

But before that came what proved to be his first published novel: *Flash and Filigree*, published in 1957 (although it was completed in 1954).

5

The Mad Tradition

It should be noted at this point that the term "novel," in regards to Southern's version of the creature, is used only in its most familiar sense, as a long work of prose on a subject that is admittedly or purportedly fictional. However, Southern's episodic, less-than-tightly-constructed "novels" fall more truly in the tradition of Menippean satire — or what Northrop Frye, in his *Anatomy of Criticism*, has labeled an "anatomy," the long-form prose evolution of Menippean satire.

Southern's four published novels from his Quality Lit era can be seen as, respectively, anatomies of the misuses of the medical profession (*Flash and Filigree*), of the misuses of money (*The Magic Christian*), of the misuses of sex (*Candy*) and of the misuses of film in trying to truthfully capture human feeling and experience (*Blue Movie*). Still, "novel" is a far more familiar term for contemporary readers than "anatomy" is, so "novels" we will call them.

The novel *Candy* grew out of the short story "Candy Christian"; likewise, *Flash and Filigree* evolved from the short story "The Accident," which had been published in the first issue of *The Paris Review*, back in 1952. It gradually metamorphosed through two unproduced teleplays that Southern wrote in the early 1950s, *The Accident* and *A Fairly Stubborn Case*. The character "Babs" (a nurse in the novel) first appears in the teleplay *The Accident* as the daughter of Dr. Eichner, and the plot of the script offers an intriguing variant on what takes place in the finished novel.

In *The Accident*, Eichner hires the detective Frost to find discrediting material about a young man named Ralph, so that he can prevent the engagement of Ralph to his daughter Babs. The accident and grand jury trial prove not to be a red herring in the true plot (as in the novel), but the catalyst of Eichner's involvement with gangsters.

In the concluding section, Act Three of the outline, Eichner sends Frost out to find material on Ralph, and then brings in the gangsters who caused the accident in which Eichner had been involved in the first scene. Eichner asks one of the gangsters to kill Ralph; the mobster indignantly refuses. Ultimately, the two rival mobsters, who had each been trying to rub the other out in the previous accident, shoot and kill each other; their dead bodies lay strewn across the floor of Eichner's office:

> Camera is on Eichner sitting alone at his desk, a dead man on either side of him, and shot lengthens gradually up and away — as he slowly turns to his miniature car collection and dreamily begins to move them about, childlike, over the toy terrain.
> Fade to Black.[1]

Religion was anathema to Southern, but if, as Harold Bloom claims, Americans "inhabit a gnostic cosmos,"[2] then Eichner and the other cultural authority figures/father figures in Southern's cosmos are repressive Jehovahs, trying to claim the void and control people as their playthings. Other people are as much toys to Eichner as his miniature cars, and the mobsters pay dearly for destroying one of his toys at the outset. In *The Accident*, Eichner remains triumphant, lord over his domain. And the "Fade to Black" here is an ominous dying of the day, unlike the peaceful fade to black and reemergence into light that comes at the close of "Candy Christian."

The next teleplay on the road to the novel is *A Fairly Stubborn Case*, which follows the events of one strand of narrative in the novel (the Eichner-Treevly thread) quite closely, introducing the pivotal character of Frederick Treevly for the first time. In this case, however, Ralph and Babs are dispensed with. And, probably to accord with the strict demands of staid 1950s television, the teleplay pulls a cop-out at the end, having the entire absurd adventure turn out to be a bad dream. *A Fairly Stubborn Case* ends with Treevly and Eichner happily discussing Treevly's medical problems in Eichner's office as the "scene waivers into lengthening distance, distortion and *black*"[3] — the underlining of the black implying that, perhaps, all is *not* well.

The novel (published in London by Andre Deutsch in 1958) achieves an artful fusion of the two strands of narrative developed in the teleplays that grew out of the original short story, paralleling the flight and pursuit of Eichner and Treevly with that of (the now Nurse) Babs and Ralph — the two strands never intersect, but comment upon each other.

An epigraph for the original manuscript of *Flash and Filigree*, cut from the published edition, offers a key enabling the reader to enter the bizarre world of the novel:

> And as in a dream, a man availeth not to pursue one that fleeth before him — the one availeth not to flee, nor the other to pursue — even so, Achilles availed not to overtake Hector his fleetness, neither Hector to escape [*Iliad*, XXII, 200–204].[4]

As is so often the case with life in Los Angeles (the city in which the novel is set), *Flash and Filigree* is about momentum, pursuit, chase without capture, quest without goal. Ultimately, that proves true only with one pursuit, that of Treevly by Eichner. And though Eichner does succeed finally in killing Treevly, it brings him no peace of mind.

However, in the case of Ralph's pursuit of Babs Mintner (herself a variant on Candy Christian), the hunt *does* result in capture, in a seduction sequence every bit as outrageous as Chapter Ten of *Candy*. As was the case with Candy's orgasm courtesy of the hunchback, sexual fulfillment here brings joy and transformation. The young, callow playboy Ralph is vastly altered by the time we reach the last moments of the novel, as his final exchange with Babs reveals:

> "Do you ... do you love me?" he asked with a soft finality, as though these might somehow be his very last words....
>
> It was almost midnight and, everywhere now, small night birds were beginning to flutter and, finally, to sing.
>
> "The way ... I love you," said the boy.
>
> And the birds sang softly, and in a way too, that did seem to promise they would sing right on through forever, dawn after dawn.[5]

Their narrative consists of his pursuit of her, his determination to seduce her, and — it is implied — his intention to move on after the conquest. But this quest culminates with Ralph's complete transformation, through a seduction that results in him falling in love with her; a vacuous male is offered meaning and fullness by a compassionate female. The joy and peace they find in a world full of "dawn into dawn(s)" offer sharp contrast to the paired narrative of Treevly and Eichner.

Treevly is Southern's first trickster figure, his first master of the put-on — an evolution of Fred Merkle. As Babs is a variant on Candy Christian, so Felix Treevly is a forerunner of Guy Grand, while Eichner is still every bit the manipulator and irritatingly complacent authority figure that he has been in previous incarnations, such as *The Accident* and *A Fairly Stubborn Case*. As Southern commented, "Eichner is like that Swiss machine: smug, highly specialized, everything is supposed to go very smoothly, then along comes this nut."[6]

Their relationship, translated into the Freudian romance, is that of rebellious son and stern father. The novel can be seen quite beyond the confines of any sort of social satire as a revisiting of Southern's relationship with his own father (who died soon after Southern finished writing the novel), the father who so disappointed him.

It can be argued that *Candy*, *Flash and Filigree* and *The Magic Christian* together comprise a trilogy, sharing and developing the common theme of assault on a father figure. This makes his next trickster figure, his next rebellious son, all the more fascinating. Guy Grand wears the guise of cultural authority and patrician father figure, and the novel that he dominates, *The Magic Christian*, is dedicated "To Henry and Dig" — that is, to the surrogate (and ideal) father figure that Southern had subsequently found in Henry Green ("Dig" was Green's wife), a relationship that will be discussed below.

The serene, pastoral conclusion of Ralph and Babs's chase is starkly contrasted to Eichner's fitful, unhappy, and restless resolution:

> Eichner lay in his own big bed in the total darkness of his room fully awake ... [he] snapped on the lamp first, then the Dictaphone. He picked up the mouthpiece ... lying flat on his back in absolute darkness, began to speak. "A letter, Miss Smart, to:
>
>> Editor
>> *Tiny Car*
>> 17 Rue Danton
>> Berne, Switzerland
>
>> Dear Sir:
>
> In your issue of 17 January you feature the article, by Jock Phillips, 'Should Miniature Cars Run?'
> First, let me say that I have *read* this article, that is to say, I have read ... let us consider the veritable host ... the veritable *host* ... underscore 'host,' Miss Smart ... veritable host ... do not repeat it, however ... the veritable *host* of implications posed here which might best be treated categorically, that is to say, in the strict sense of ... *category*.
> Underscore, Period. Now, by way of preface, let us take ... let us take ... do not repeat it ... let us *take*...."[7]

The grasping old man is cracking up; we leave Dr. Eichner alone in the darkness, descending into madness, his complacency forever shattered, his world of strict order and rigid categories left in disarray. Compare this to the conclusion of *The Year of the Weasel*, in which the sinister (and similar) Director ends the play in a serene trance, presiding over the dead world he has created — or the final shot of *The Accident*, in which Eichner is still contentedly playing with his tiny cars, still master of his universe.

Though Eichner has succeeded in killing Treevly, Treevly is victorious, his spirit living on in the gardener planning to blackmail Eichner. This is made more explicit in a treatment for a film adaptation of *Flash and Filigree* written by Southern in 1990, entitled *Nut Case*:

> Eichner watches the distant figure, noting his strange, uneven movement, like a wounded animal, odd and hauntingly familiar. And as he watched, inside his head, somewhere just behind the eyes, his brain began a slow and torturous arabesque ... as he realized it wasn't Garcia after all he was watching, but his nemesis and tormentor, none other than Felix Treevly himself.

CAMERA MOVES IN GRADUALLY TO CU, his distinguished features, which have suddenly gone grim and ash, FREEZE, and CREDITS RISE.[8]

The spirit of the put-on, and of the freak who disrupts the complacent surface of status quo culture, lives on triumphantly, though Eichner physically lives and Treevly does not. The juxtaposed resolutions of the doubled narratives — Ralph and Babs's dawning universe of youth, health, sexuality, and joy; Eichner's dark, midnight universe of authority, complacency, and death — make it clear which one, in Southern's view, will triumph in the end.

Though certainly this novel can also be read as a series of sketches, it is far less episodic and far more cohesive in structure than either *Candy* or *The Magic Christian*, which are both clearly collections of episodes rather than narratives with a structured beginning, middle and end. In setting the novel in Los Angeles (which at this point he had only briefly visited as a runaway during his teenaged years), Southern is invading the territory of Raymond Chandler and Nathanael West, creating a new genre for his generation that (along with Thomas Pynchon's *The Crying of Lot 49*) Malcolm Bradbury labeled as "surreal-absurdist California fiction."[9] And it is in that context that the novel starts to make a bit more sense.

As in a Raymond Chandler novel like *The Big Sleep*, it is never quite clear what the big picture is here, the large story behind the isolated vignettes. For example, take the mobsters involved in the accident that destroys Eichner's beloved car, a further shattering of his complacency after his initial encounter with Treevly, are never seen in this novel: they are only referred to offhandedly by the police, who clear Eichner of any involvement in the case in which he has become enmeshed. Babs is not Eichner's daughter in this novel, but only a nurse working in the hospital. Events are random, disjointed (not unlike Robert Altman's *Short Cuts*, a Los Angeles take on Raymond Carver's universe); characters are occasionally colliding into each other, but never quite cohering into any grand cosmic plan.

Eichner's position as a dermatologist indicates that he sees only skin deep, only surfaces, and not what goes on beneath. The healthy sexuality of Ralph and Babs offer a connection with the nature that teems beneath, the filigree underneath the flash of sliding plastic surfaces that is Los Angeles. Though not the case in the novels of West, sexuality does offer a solution here to the absurdity of life in this Southern California; darkness only results from isolation.

Again, a reading of the novel influenced by Freud's idea of the family romance offers the underlying key that connects its vignettes. Treevly is Southern, the rebellious son; Eichner is his father. In the encounters between

Treevly and Eichner, there is again a sudden flowering of Southern's true voice, paralleling his encounter between Candy and the hunchback, offering another facet of his unique vision. In Treevly, we have a master of the put-on, and of the American Grotesque:

> Mr. Treevly shifted in his chair as though about to stand.... "I should like to give you some *particulars* ... which may facilitate, or rather have some bearing-on ... the diagnosis."
> "Yes," said Dr. Eichner after a pause, "yes, of course." ... and as he spoke, standing very close, he brought the padded weight down sharply across the back of the young man's skull.[10]

Outraged by Treevly's grotesque and clearly untrue account of his lesion, and its implied mockery of the doctor, Eichner loses his "smugness" for the first time in the novel. This begins the long series of pursuits through Los Angeles — Eichner after Treevly, Ralph after Babs — culminating in Treevly's final put-on back at the doctor's office, the morning after the massive hash party/orgy that Frost had arranged, and Treevly had invaded, at Eichner's home.

Disguised as an enormously fat woman, "Mrs. Gross," Treevly details his suffocation of a small dog. And as the doctor listens to the tale of Mrs. Gross, the ugly truth begins to dawn on him: The full horror smothered the doctor, as in a valley filling from above with a mountain of snakes, that what was confronting him, laughing with sly insanity, was no less than Felix Treevly.[11]

The "valley filling from above with a mountain of snakes" compares nicely with the "gigantic landslide of black eels, billions of them surging past, one of which held the answer"[12] that fills the head of the hunchback as he makes love to Candy. These are seething images of chthonic nature straight out of Baudelaire, and convey exactly what both Treevly and the hunchback represent in Southern's cosmos: the face of chaotic nature, a nature that terrifies a bastion of repressive culture like Eichner. The healthy, innocent sexuality of Ralph and Babs represents the benevolent side of nature; Treevly, its more malevolent side. Together, they represent the full face of nature, the only truth in Southern's universe — and the only solution to smashing the smug complacency of a false, lying force like Eichner.

What is at stake again here is what is at the core of all of Southern's best work, pinpointed by himself in interviews, and reaffirmed by Carol Southern and Peter Matthiessen as well: the smashing of "smug complacency."[13] And though, as has been noted above, there are echoes of Nathanael West and Raymond Chandler, and of Edgar Allan Poe as well, in the horrific climax of the final encounter between Treevly and Eichner — still, the conscious stylistic model for this attack on paternal authority was Southern's chosen surrogate father figure, Henry Green.

As Carol noted, when she met Southern in 1955, he was already an ardent admirer of Green's work, but the close friendship between Southern and Green only began when he and Carol moved to Geneva, and even that was initially as a correspondence (Green's real name was Henry Yorke; he was a man so intensely private that he was never even photographed, save once from the back).

Southern claims that he wrote the novel *Flash and Filigree* in tribute to Henry Green, and that the title itself is, in his words, "an apt description of (Green's) style"[14]: the flash of surfaces, the filigree in the depths. The style *is* evocative of Green, though the subject matter is far more reminiscent of previously mentioned American influences such as West, Chandler and Poe — and the fast-emerging, unique voice of Southern himself, in his own surreal American Grotesque.

Back in the early fifties, a *New Yorker* article about Green had described his prose as belonging to a certain "mad tradition in English literature — Sterne, Carroll, Firbank, and Mrs. Woolf are predecessors"[15]; but Green's subject matter is far more rooted in realism than Southern's would increasingly become — or, by the point of *Flash and Filigree*, indeed already was.

Green's most famous novel, *Loving*, is set in an Irish castle during World War II, in which the gentry is Irish, the servants British — certainly an unusual twist on the standard situation in a British novel of manners, but still a far cry from the monsters and car chases in Southern's work.

Nevertheless, the two writers composed an ardent mutual admiration society, and if one goes past the apparently different surfaces of their work, past questions of realism or surrealism, one finds shared preoccupations with perception, with communication and miscommunication, with seemingly calm surfaces belying turbulent depths.

The "mad tradition" that *The New Yorker* vaguely spoke of is the Decadent tradition, the only one that could encompass writers as seemingly diverse as Lewis Carroll, Virginia Woolf, Henry Green, and Terry Southern: all these writers deal with glittering cultural surfaces that dance over roiling natural depths. And if *Flash and Filigree* is more frantic than *Loving* or *Party-Going*, it is only because it is more American — the concerns are the same. Playing with perceptions, showing up appearance as illusion, is the very essence of the put-on, and the inability to perceive correctly causes much of the pain experienced by the reserved British characters in Green's work as well.

Miscommunication and warped perception created an amusing incident during the interview that Southern conducted with Green for *The Paris Review* in 1958, after their friendship had fully gotten underway, and recalled by George Plimpton years later: "During the interview the two got into a mix-up over the word 'subtle' which Southern had used in a question and which Green, who doesn't hear very well, had mistaken for the word 'suttee'—the suicide of a Hindu wife on her husband's burning bier. 'How dull,' Green remarks when they finally get it straightened out."[16]

John Updike, introducing this interview in the posthumous Green collection *Surviving*, testily remarks that Southern is "more deeply deaf"[17] than his interview subject, a comment perhaps spurred by Updike's jealousy over Southern's close friendship with Green (Updike was a fervent admirer, even disciple, of Green, but never met the man)—as well as the negative, dismissive reviews that Southern gave to Updike's novels in the pages of *The Nation*.

The relationship between Southern and Green began when Southern sent an adulatory letter to Green, praising his work. Green responded warmly, and a correspondence was struck. Southern invited Green to come stay in Geneva, never expecting to be taken up on the offer, but Carol remembers that abruptly one day, out of the blue, they received notification that Green was coming. He wound up spending several weeks with the Southerns, and some months later, Dig came to visit as well.

When Southern completed his stylistic homage (*Flash and Filigree*), he sent it to Green and received the following note:

> Dear Southern,
>
> It is amazingly good. Frightening, extremely funny, wonderful dialogue. A *perfect* gift. And what is more, it sets one slap down in the U.S., as so few American books do. I really do congratulate you. I am proud you sent it to me. I want to read it again. I think it's too short, also scrappy, rather. If I may, I'll send you one or two suggestions.
>
> Yours in admiration, Henry Green.
>
> P.S. You must both come over here now.[18]

Carol and Terry did go several times to stay with them; Carol remembers "a wonderful Christmas"[19] they spent together. It was during one of these trips that Southern conducted the interview with Green that later appeared in *The Paris Review*.

Plimpton, in a letter to Terry about the interview after he received the manuscript, recalls meeting Green in London ("He talked at length of a stay with you in Switzerland and the drive to the south of France") but the problem at hand was a passage from *Loving* that Green and Southern had discussed, in which the word "cunty" was used. The word (much like the offending "shit" a few years earlier, when "The Accident" appeared) raised a furor among the staff of the *Review*, which Plimpton amusingly related to Southern: "Well, of course I called a crash meeting to discuss the four letter derivative spelled out in your last letter.... Consternation was immediate. Jean Stein didn't know what the word meant.... And as for Peter Matthiessen, who as you know, has been an anal man from way back, he suggested 'crap*y' or even (and he gulped) 'shi**y.'"[20]

The matter was eventually settled and the interview was published, offending word and all. Southern had set the tone for free expression in the very first issue of the *Review*— now, just a few years later, censorship was no longer a formidable matter, but a joke to be quickly tossed aside.

Carol Southern recalled Terry telling her that when he finished *Flash and Filigree*, "he got innumerable rejects on it. Nobody wanted to publish it. I think he got 26 rejection letters and then Henry Green helped him find an English publisher."[21] Green lavishly praised *Flash and Filigree* in a review in *The London Observer* when it was published in 1957 (it was published in New York by Coward-McCann, in 1958).

Green also appeared on a BBC book review radio program in 1957, in which *Flash and Filigree* was discussed, alongside Jack Kerouac's recently published *On the Road*. The panel of reviewers unanimously panned *On the Road*, but found themselves oddly interested in *Flash and Filigree* (though put off by the seduction sequence and a few other moments). Green, heaping accolades on the novel again, while admitting (as he had done in his letter to Southern) that it had a few flaws, also agreed with the other panelists in assessing the book as "essentially English" under its American clothes— which contradicts his comment to Southern in the letter that the book "puts one in the U.S. as so few American books do."

The reaction in London to *Flash and Filigree* was generally muted admiration, while in America it sank with nary a trace. However, Southern's first novel had been published. It would be followed the next year by the Olympia Press publication of *Candy*, which would bring down all the fury of the DeGaulle Administration, who immediately banned it in Paris (it was republished a few months later under the new title *Lollipop*, with not a word changed, and sold quite well under that name).

And in 1959, Random House would present, in New York, Southern's true American debut (as *Flash and Filigree* had first come into public notice in London, and *Candy* in Paris)—with the publication of his greatest novel, *The Magic Christian*.

6

Making It Hot

Throughout the period when Southern was writing *Candy* in Geneva, he was simultaneously working on *The Magic Christian*, developing it (like *Candy*) out of one central idea or joke: a millionaire who uses his money to foist outrageous pranks upon the public. In a letter to Mason Hoffenberg (addressed "Dear Mr. Sloth"), Southern responds to a comment Hoffenberg had made work about his work ethic:

> First, I think you're wise to suggest a policy of take it easy for getting this work out ... mostly just lolling about I should think. In fact, it reminds me of a scene in the novel I'm working on (*The Magic Christian*) about a billionaire who stages immense practical jokes, one of which is the swank one-class passenger ship, *The Magic Christian*.[1]

His letter goes on to discuss their progress with *Candy*; clearly, the two were being composed at the same time. The finished novels resemble each other quite a bit structurally, being a series of sketches, episodic and lacking the forward momentum of *Flash and Filigree*'s narrative. Though his letters to Hoffenberg belie an easygoing approach to the work, Carol Southern remembers: "The thing that was constant about Terry was getting up in the morning and going to work.... I remember when he was writing *The Magic Christian*, and he couldn't stop at one point ... he was so into it, and I would hear this laughter coming from the study."[2]

It is clear that he had a sustained level of inspiration with *The Magic Christian* and his adventures that he didn't find for Candy Christian and hers. The reason? Although Candy Christian was the benevolent face of nature and a send-up of naïve Christian charity, Guy Grand is Southern's clearest alter ego in his fiction, even more so than Harold in *Texas Summer*. Guy Grand is the prankster, the trickster, the master of the put-on; he embodies with his projects everything that Southern wished to achieve with his own writing. Grand's art is Southern's:

> What his associates managed to see in Grand was a reflection of their own dullness: a club member, a dinner guest, a possibility, a threat — a man whose hold-

ings represented a prospect and a danger. But this was to do injustice to Grand's private life, because his private life was atypical. For one thing, he was the last of the big spenders; and for another, he had a very unusual attitude towards *people*— he spent about ten million a year in, as he expressed it himself, "making it hot for them."[3]

Like the children who don masks in *The Year of the Weasel* (and the children wearing the masks that Southern provided at the United Nations School), Guy Grand also wears a mask. He creates an illusion in order to free himself, so he can play with illusions. His mask is the mask of Dr. Eichner, while his spirit, his "private life," is that of Felix Treevly. He is the two fused into one, Treevly using Eichner to perpetrate his deeds: the face of staid, complacent culture hiding the soul of roiling, chaotic nature. This is made evident in the very first scene, in which Grand perpetrates his first practical joke in the course of the novel, at the expense (and gain) of a hotdog vendor:

> Grand reached into his own coat pocket and took out a colorful plastic animal mask—today it was that of *pig*—which he quickly donned before beginning to gorge the hotdog through the mouth of the mask, at the same time reaching out frantically for the bill, yet managing somehow to keep it just beyond his fingers' grasp....
> When Grand finally drew himself back from the window and doffed his pig mask, it was to face a middle-aged woman across the aisle who was twisted halfway around in her seat, observing Grand....
> "Just having a laugh with that hot frank vender," he explained. "...[N]o real harm done, surely."[4]

Wearing the animal mask, he is revealing himself more fully than with his normal mask of patrician tycoon. Like Candy, Guy Grand lives out the Christian ideal of giving selflessly; in this case, he is the rich man who gives all his worldly possessions away. But unlike Candy, Guy does not give with charity naïvely; therefore, he is not used and abused by authority figures, nor is he ever surprised by animal nature.

Grand, embodying the spirit of Existential Hipsterism, transcends all these poses, all these cons, all these masks, and uses and manipulates each of them. The purpose of his con is to expose all other cons, to expose all beloved cultural poses and institutions as arbitrary illusions easily manipulated; to expose—in the true Decadent tradition, the "mad tradition"—that all culture is artifice, and the only truth is hungry, ravaging, abundant nature.

Everyone, Grand ultimately tells us, has an angle, a price—so don't get suckered, cheated, manipulated or abused. Grand's pranks demolish a culture of limitations, revealing a culture of possibilities and of freedom. In perpetrating these acts, Grand becomes a quasi–Situationist. No doubt Southern's close friendship with Alex Trocchi, himself a member of the Situationists, had some influence on Southern in developing the character of Guy Grand.

One piece of evidence that counters a perception of Southern as mere satirist of dated social situations is the comparison of the published version of *The Magic Christian* with the original manuscript. The two episodes in *The Magic Christian* which most clearly commented on actual cultural events of the era were excised from the final novel, granting it a more timeless feel.

In the first excised chapter, Chapter Twelve of the manuscript, Grand sends up celebrity media by replacing Grace Kelly and Prince Rainier's new child with a baby kangaroo, to the astonishment of the press below:

> A certain *monsieur,* who had been outfitted and made up to look just like the king ... carrying a bundle of swaddling, he went to the balcony and presented himself to the cheering throng below. His face was bursting with insane pride, as in a sweeping flourish, he opened the swaddling and proclaimed in a shout:
> "*It's ... thing!*"
> And in so saying, he brandished from the swaddling for all to see a wiggly, squirming, grease-covered baby kangaroo.
> Before this faulty impression could be corrected, the news and sensational photos were howling across the wires of AP, UP and INS:
> "HEIR APPARENT?"
> "AND HOW!"
> "WOW!"
> You can bet it set the public fairly hopping ... the joke was deemed by many to have been in doubtful taste.[5]

The second excised chapter, Chapter Thirteen, was, in the original manuscript, the climactic sequence of the novel, later replaced by the episode of the *Magic Christian* luxury liner. Perhaps inspired by the steamboat in Herman Melville's *The Confidence-Man,* the luxury liner sequence was the first episode written for the novel, originally conceived as a stand-alone and unpublished story like "Candy Christian." While being the original short story from which the other adventures sprang, it was originally placed much earlier in the novel. As published, the novel works better than the original manuscript, with the S.S. *Magic Christian* providing a suitably apocalyptic finale.

It is interesting to note, though, how Chapter Thirteen's send-up of the McCarthy hearings (which John Phillips had remembered watching with Southern in the West 11th Street apartment) gave a somber, even pessimistic, conclusion to Grand's adventures:

> Grand received the greatest setback of his career in 1953, when he was undone through a combination of madness and treachery by a key employee in his big project of that year. It all began about the time some Broadway wag put forward the slogan—*Nobody Ever Went Broke Underestimating The Intelligence Of The American Public*; a slogan which enjoyed a certain watchword vogue among the

cognoscenti of midtown commerce. Well, it rubbed Grand the wrong way, got his dander up.[6]

In an effort to disprove this maxim (which ultimately is proved true), Grand decides to back "a Midwestern senator who had based his election campaign upon the threat of American communism ... he was nutty as a fruitcake, of course, and Grand's first anxiety was that he would be put away before a bit of 'capital fun,' as he expressed it, could be had."[7] Grand's joke spins out of his control, however, when the senator brings on board a "young man" (obviously modeled on Roy Cohn) who skillfully maneuvers the whole thing into a rousing success. Grand realizes he was mistaken in ever believing that the senator would be put in "the looney bin":

> The men with the jacket never came and, in fact, no one raised a finger — a finger to topple the rotten egg from the wall; *no one*. Grand closed the affair with impatience and dispatch by having the senator poisoned. That afternoon though, he stopped around at the wag's office to see if he still had the banner up. It was there all right. Grand asked a few questions about it, how much it cost and so on, a little sadly it seemed — funny man.[8]

It's a bitter note to end the book on, as well as pointed social satire. Southern takes these two moments out, replacing them with more general antics (send-ups of the advertising business, of boxing, and of hunting), and concludes the book on a more optimistic note, when Grand whips shoppers into a frenzy by opening, all over the city, markets that offer incredible bargains. Just when he's bought the shoppers' devotion, these early versions of Wal-mart abruptly disappear, maddening the customers, who keep hunting the elusive goal:

> The people who had experienced the phenomenon began to spend a good deal of their time each evening looking for the new location. And occasionally now, two such people meet.
> And some say it does, in fact, still go on — they say it accounts for the strange searching haste which can be seen in the faces, and especially the eyes of people in the cities every evening, just about the time now it starts really getting dark.[9]

Again, as in many of his screenplays and short stories, we end with a fade to black. But in this case, Grand dances on into the twilight, not beaten or broken by jokes that spiral out of his control, but still firmly in command of his project, making it hot for the slumbering consumers.

Grand was occasionally to pop up in Southern's work after this novel appeared. In an unpublished 1973 piece ("The Day the Carlton Began to Slip"), Grand buys a luxurious hotel in Cannes in time for the film festival, carefully digging out all the earth underneath the hotel, so that when it's filled with festival-goers, it slowly sinks into the ground: a bitter commentary on the film industry that had by that point spurned Southern. In an unfinished piece composed in the early eighties, Grand goes to the Middle East, to perpetrate his pranks on Arab oil emirates; the sketch was never finished, so it's unclear exactly what Southern intended for Grand to do with these oil tycoons. Finally, in the late eighties, Southern developed a proposal for a weekly Guy Grand television series, a project that never got off the ground.

But in the late fifties, in this moment of inspiration, Grand was the clearest vehicle for Southern's vision, his greatest tool for "making it hot for them." *Flash and Filigree* was influenced in style and structure by the novels of Henry Green; the clearest model for both *Candy* and *The Magic Christian* seems the purely American pop-art form of the comic strip and comic book. *Candy* echoes, however unconsciously, the Tijuana Bibles that Southern and his friends read in their youth in Texas, while *The Magic Christian* seems a precursor of *Mad* magazine, and the more evolved psychedelic freakouts of *Mad*'s inheritor R. Crumb.

The Magic Christian became a cult sensation when it appeared; though it did not make the impact on popular consciousness that Candy and Dr. Strangelove later did, its influence was felt among the hipster cognoscenti. Mike Golden, interviewing Southern many years later, recalled that he had known many drug dealers over the years who kept it secreted away in their private stash — a fact which Southern noted as "the ultimate compliment." Hunter S. Thompson, a writer so influenced by Southern as to merit the title of Southern's heir apparent, later recalled his own first exposure to it: "I started reading it and I thought I was going to go insane ... it was an incredible influence on me. That last scene with the gorilla running around on the bridge of the ship, my God, it was so great."[10]

With the publication of this novel, Southern's reputation began to be cemented back home in America — a reputation that would steadily grow over the next five years, culminating in the simultaneous appearance of *Candy* and *Dr. Strangelove* in 1964. Southern had somehow stumbled upon the form that would be his greatest medium for his expression: the comic sketch. Not the sustained narrative of a novel, not the Pulp pastiche of his early tales (such as the *Weird Tales*/Lovecraft flavor of "The Sun and the Still-Born Stars," for instance), but a prose version of the comic book, one expressed in the back-to-back triumphs of *Candy* and *The Magic Christian*, and also in his later *Realist* pieces, all of which would shape the sensibility of late 1960s underground comix, *National Lampoon*, and *Saturday Night Live* (which Southern would come to write for, briefly, in the early 1980s), as well as latter-day descendants like *The Simpsons* and *Family Guy*.

Once Southern began submitting regularly to *The Realist* in the early sixties, he proposed to publisher Paul Krassner a comic strip detailing the adventures of a character he had created in the late fifties, around the same time as Guy Grand, and with a similar outlook:

> Now, what would you say to a comic strip, plot by me and drawn by Larry Rivers, called *The Adventures of the Vomiting Priest?*... You have this guy, dig, the priest, naïve, sympathetic sort of Karl Malden type. Wants to be a regular fellow ... except that he's constantly vomiting ... a source of alienation, it proves to be. People avoid him as a drag and a hangup ... he becomes embittered. The story gradually takes on a melodramatic quality, the vomiting priest strikes back, et cetera, then philosophic.[11]

In 1958, he published a piece in *Olympia* (the literary journal published by the Olympia Press) under the heading "The Spy's Corner"—a mock-newspaper article reportedly culled "from the *Canadian Sentinel*, Montreal," under the headline "New Art Museum in Hamburg Blown Up." The article, detailing the efforts of "the Neo-Dada School," focuses on an interview with "Thirty-two-year-old Ernst Badhoff, one of the leading exponents of the new school."[12] The Neo-Dada painters had recently blown up a museum in Hamburg, after having filled the museum with paintings composed of quickly dissolving acid—such is their exhibit. When asked what the point of their art is, "Herr Badhoff" answers:

> HERR BADHOFF: The point? What point?
> Q: Well, the whole thing.
> HERR BADHOFF: Ah, yes, that was the point, the whole thing. Yes, that was the point precisely.
> Q: To destroy the painting?
> HERR BADHOFF: No, no, the paintings do not exist.
> Q: To destroy the museum then?
> HERR BADHOFF: Well, that was another matter, quite peripheral, actually.[13]

All of these figures are Situationists of a sort, and, like Warhol with his soup cans a few years later, Pop Artists. Whether the protagonist is the Vomiting Priest (a figure who, ideally, represses nature, but is cursed by having horrific nature uncontrollably, continually welling up from inside him)—or the Neo-Dada painters, people who blow up museums, create paintings out of acid, and call it their art—or Guy Grand, whose art is simply to perpetrate practical jokes—they are given life by Southern in the pop form of the comic.

Whether these comics had actual illustrations or not is irrelevant—the spirit is there. This facet of his talent, for the comic sketch, is the one that would make the greatest cultural impact of any of his work. But simultaneously, Southern was also still nurturing the other side of his vision, the more serious, subtle, understated aspect. Carol remembers: "In Geneva he wanted to write about himself autobiographically, starting with these stories, but it was to go up through adulthood, and I don't think he ever knew enough about what was happening to him to be able to base a character on his own life.... I don't think he had the distance or the perspective.... I suggested to him that he end it ... with young adulthood, so that he doesn't have to cope with anything more; a coming-of-age novel."[14]

While writing the autobiographical novel that he had been working on since the early fifties (originally as *The Hipsters*, later as *Youngblood*, and finally published as *Texas Summer*), Southern came to focus more on the childhood aspect of it, turning from Paris to Texas.

However, another piece of *The Hipsters*, of Southern's life-in-Paris vignettes, was first to see the light of day: "Put-Down," a story that marks Southern's first appearance in *The Evergreen Review* (Volume 3, No.9), in the summer of 1959 (the same season in which Random House published *The Magic Christian*). Not being shown the name, it would be difficult to guess that the short story and the novel were published by the same author. "Put-Down" relates the experiences of two young couples who discover hashish for the first time:

> They stopped and half turned, standing uncertainly now, to appear surely as four Americans wholly, typically, lost in the rich summer afternoon of Paris.
> "Want to turn on?" Boris asked, absent and polite ... "Hashish!" Priscilla was delighted. She almost clapped her hands. "Baudelaire used to have it in his *confiture!*" she cried.[15]

Descendants of the protagonists of Hawthorne's *The Marble Faun*, or the novels of Henry James, the two couples are innocents in Paris, would-be Hipsters. Back in their hotel room, they smoke the hash and begin playing with a piece of mercury, which rolls into a crack in the floor:

> Just where it disappeared into the gray, there was a sudden treacherous movement, as of the angry living thing inside. And Priscilla screamed at the top of her voice....
> "You shouldn't let it bug you," said Boris from the floor....
> "I know, I know," said Priscilla, whimpering her gratitude — for she probably thought he was talking to her.[16]

Sustaining the spirit and influence of Green, the flash of the surface of this tale betrays the filigree of turbulent depths. As the flashing mercury is lost in the dark depths of the crack in the floor, so Priscilla is lost in the darkness inside herself, or at least glimpses that darkness when peering into the fissure, when the hashish cracks the bright surface of her psyche.

These American innocents, the tale tells us, are playing with fire when they experiment with the European experience (represented by the hashish), and they come very close to being a bright piece of mercury lost in the dark fissure themselves. Priscilla glimpses this, knows this intuitively, when gazing into the abyss that the crack in the floor has become.

The eminent Sterling Lord was Southern's agent. Random House had accepted *The Magic Christian* for publication, and the prestigious underground American literary journal *The Evergreen Review* was publishing "Put-Down," which probably meant far more to Southern than the glitzy *Harper's Bazaar's* acceptance of his stories a few years before. And so, coupling this success with Southern's fear, as Carol related it, that he was "losing touch with his materials"[17] (i.e., America), the Southerns packed up and left Geneva, and Europe; they headed home, even though Carol was very reluctant to go ("I was heartbroken."[18])

Time would prove that her reluctance was well founded, for Southern never again experienced the sustained creative growth and productivity that he found in Geneva. Whatever the reason for that growth (marriage, isolation, the friendship with Green, perhaps a combination of these and other factors), Southern's greatest period of artistic development and growth, and his three greatest novels, were behind him.

His great seven-year cycle was inaugurated with the publication of *Flash and Filigree* in 1957, and would conclude with the American publication of *Candy*, and the release of *Dr. Strangelove*, in 1964. Ahead in America lay fame, Hollywood, his greatest short stories, the creation of New Journalism in his work for *Esquire*, and a breakthrough in the form of pop satire in his work for *The Realist*.

But these were refinements of a vision developed in Geneva; once the refinements were fully evolved, the work was over. The triumphant return to America gave Southern the infusion of energy necessary to fine-tune and perfect the creative breakthroughs he had begun in Geneva. The first half of his great phase was finished: Geneva and Paris lay behind him, New York and America dead ahead.

7

Grooving in NY

With *Flash and Filigree* published in London and *The Magic Christian* about to be published in New York, Southern began to receive steady work as a book reviewer, in such prestigious publications as the *New York Times* and the *New York Observer* (the Olympia Press publication of *Candy* did little to help him in this regard). With this entree into the world of journalism, he also began publishing short essays of direct social commentary in *The Nation*: these serve as a sort of segue between his fiction and book reviewing, and his later breakthroughs in satire and New Journalism for *The Realist* and *Esquire*.

The Southerns arrived in New York in late spring of 1959, and stayed for a time with George Plimpton, in Plimpton's townhouse on East 72nd Street. There, he was interviewed by Maggie Paley for *The Paris Review*, to coincide with the release of *The Magic Christian*. Typically, Southern avoided speaking of himself, in this case turning the full attention of the interview onto Plimpton's maid, whom he referred to as "Catherine the Char." Asked by Paley what he would do if he were "given enough money so that you didn't have to work or make any commitments, and could do whatever you wanted," Southern replied that he would like to "give (Catherine) several hundred thousand dollars all in pennies. 'Mr. Plimpton asked me to give you this, Catherine; each coin represents the dark seed of his desire for you.'"[1]

Jean Stein, one of Plimpton's fellow editors at *The Paris Review*, had returned to New York; there, she was starting her own literary journal, *Grand Street*. It had been through Stein that Southern met one of his great heroes, William Faulkner. Carol remembers that Jean Stein "was a great fan of Terry's, and in those days she had salons, and Faulkner would be there, or Tennessee Williams, Dylan Thomas, or whoever was in town."[2] Stein recalled that Faulkner had been very encouraging to Southern after reading the story "The Sun and the Still-Born Stars," and Southern vividly described their first meeting in his unfinished memoirs.

Nervous at the prospect of meeting his idol, Southern had allowed Anatole Broyard to get him drunk and stoned at the San Remo bar, before he headed up to Stein's apartment. Once there, he was left alone with Faulkner in the kitchen, and nervously blurted out a joke that made fun of the racism of the South. Silence, for a moment. Then, Faulkner nodding unsmilingly, noting that "so long as the Negra maintains that sense of detachment, and that sense of humor ... he will endure."[3] A mortified Southern could only nod his assent.

Faulkner's "Letter to the North" (published in *Life*, March 5, 1956)[4] aroused the ire of northern liberals, in that it "advised against the readmission of the Negro student and author, Ann Lucy, to the University of Alabama." Southern immediately rose to Faulkner's defense with an impassioned essay for *The Nation* (unpublished) entitled "The Case of William Faulkner and the Cross-Bearing Liberals."

Southern, as a fellow southerner, lashes out against the blind political correctness that cannot foresee the violence and danger to Lucy that might erupt when immediately putting her in the midst of an all-white school: "Because of his stature as an artist and as an internationally honored American, we can hardly do less than make an effort to understand what he is saying.... After assessing Mr. Faulkner's position on this, 'the welfare of the southern Negro,' to the whole of his literature why, after all, suspect his motivations?"[5]

When Faulkner released his novel *The Reivers*, Southern again responded with a defense in the face of widespread criticism, with a review in *The Nation* entitled "Tom Swift in the Brothel" (probably he meant Tom *Sawyer*, far more applicable to the matter at hand than the boy inventor of the science-fiction series)— it was up to the author of *The Donkey and the Darling* to point out that *The Reivers* is, and should be identified as, a children's book:

> What will certainly mislead us readers into thinking the great man has fallen into some kind of complete inane senility, is that there is absolutely no indication of this fact [that it is for children] on the jacket of the book.... In short, *The Reivers* is a book which will prove both instructive and entertaining to the readership for which it was intended (children) ... trying to fob it off as a "regular Faulkner novel," or indeed as adult fair generally, is a very shabby business, and in serious disservice to one of the world's most respected authors.[6]

For the most part, Southern's book reviews are lazily written, consisting mainly of plot summary, followed by a brief paragraph in which he comes forward to say whether he liked or disliked the subject at hand. But they do give an indication of Southern's preferences among the literary offerings in this period (late fifties, early sixties). For instance, the article "After the Bomb,

Dad Came Up with Ice," a rave review of the early Kurt Vonnegut novel *Cat's Cradle*, helped cement a lifelong friendship with Vonnegut (Southern wrote an uproarious "Trib to Von," his tribute to Vonnegut, in the '80s, and Vonnegut was one of the speakers at the memorial service for Southern in December of 1995). And his most important book review, "When Film Gets Good...," published in the November 17, 1962, issue of *The Nation*, gives clear indication that Southern was bidding farewell to the world of Quality Lit, and getting ready to make his mark in the film world.

But in the late fifties, upon his return to New York, he was not content to just write book reviews and hang out with literary greats on the heels of his success with *The Magic Christian*. As the *Nation* article would soon give notice of, he was turning already at this point, more and more, to the form of the screenplay and the teleplay.

This was a natural development out of the cinematic prose he had learned from Henry Green, and refined into a style all his own. Green had even supposedly managed to get Southern his first paid work as a scriptwriter in 1957 (that was actually the doing of Ted Kotcheff, according to Carol Southern): he adapted Eugene O'Neill's *The Emperor Jones* for a live production on the BBC. Southern's version hews very closely to O'Neill's, only slightly altering and adjusting Jones's Southern dialect — a much-needed improvement by a true man of the South on the New England author's original dialogue.

He had written his full-length play *The Year of the Weasel* in Geneva, as well as the teleplays *The Accident* and *A Fairly Stubborn Case*, from which *Flash and Filigree* had developed. Upon returning to New York, he wrote a teleplay entitled *Beyond the Shadows*, a macabre Gothic tale set in the Actor's Studio milieu of the Village. A Svengali-like acting teacher (modeled on Lee Strasberg) assigns, to each of his students, a character that they must fully become — to his most promising student, a troubled young man, he designates the role of a vampire from a late 18th century Gothic novel. The student so fully immerses himself in the role that he becomes a serial killer, haunting the alleys of Manhattan, and finally turning on his mentor (and father figure).

While seriously lacking in the suspense department, the script nevertheless delivers an evocative portrait of the Village Hipster scene of the late fifties, much as his unfinished *The Hipsters* had done for the Paris Hipsters of the early fifties.

Like all of Southern's previous teleplays (save for *The Emperor Jones*), *Beyond the Shadows* went unproduced, as did his first foray into writing a screenplay for a feature film — *The Big Touch*, a rather gritty take on the traditionally exotic (in the cinema, at any rate) world of the jewel thief.

Southern recalled his inspiration in undertaking the project:

> I did get a letter one time from Jerry Wald saying, "I read your story in *Harper's Bazaar* and I think you have a very good cinematic quality. Would you be interested in writing for the screen...." I showed this letter to a friend of mine, Harold Meeske, who said, "Don't even answer the letter. The thing to do is write a screenplay and send it back. Like, am I interested? Dig *this*.... "[Note: this is a singularly awful piece of advice that Southern seems to have accepted unquestioningly.] "Okay, what's the story?" And he said, "I got it. This friend of mine is just coming out of Sing Sing; America's number one jewel thief. He's getting out Friday and we'll write a script based on his adventures."... Well, I moved in with them, and he moved in with them, and the four of us worked on the screenplay and then sent it in to Jerry Wald. No response. Never heard anything about it.[7]

The Big Touch remains notable for the way in which it foreshadows both *The Cincinnati Kid* and *Easy Rider*, as well as Southern's film adaptation of John Barth's *The End of the Road*. The jewel thief protagonist cuts himself off from love, and from everything else in life that will distract him from his one driving dream and vision (that is, stealing diamonds). And in the end, it is his vision which drags him down, into the watery depths — in a final image reminiscent of the dead bikers on the highway, or Steve McQueen standing in the New Orleans rain.

Southern's developing talents as a scriptwriter were bearing no fruit at this point, and his income from the book reviewing was paltry, but he was still honing his craft as a member of "the Quality Lit game." In the January/February 1960 issue of *Evergreen Review* (Volume 4, No. 11), the second installment of Southern's unfolding Texas Cycle appeared, "Red-Dirt Marijuana." In this story, picking up from where "A South Summer Idyll" had left off three and a half years before, Howard has now become Harold (or "Hal"), and we are first introduced to C.K., the black surrogate father who replaces Harold's ineffectual actual father as a true teacher and mentor.

Like "Idyll," "Red-Dirt Marijuana" is a vintage slice of Texas life in the thirties. But unlike the earlier story's violent bleakness, "Red-Dirt Marijuana" is suffused with a serene glow, a happy memory of Harold's introduction, via C.K., to the joys of smoking "mighty fine gage."[8]

Having discovered a marijuana plant growing in a cow pasture (by observing a cow's odd behavior after eating some of it), C.K. and Harold bring it back to the barn, where C.K. instructs Harold on how to store it properly, and the differences between various kinds of marijuana ("you don't swing with you heavy gage, you just goof"[9]). Harold never actually smokes any of it in the course of the story; he learns simply by watching C.K., and from asking questions:

> "How come it's against the law if it's all-fired good?" asked Harold.
> "Well, I used to *study* 'bout that myself," said C.K., tightening the lid of the

> fruit jar and giving it a pat. "It ain't because it makes boys like you *sick*, I tell you *that* much.... I *tell* you what it is," he said then, "it's cause a man *see* too much when he git high, that's what. He see *right* through everything ... they's a lotta trickin' and lyin' go on in the world ... well, a man git high, he see right through all them tricks an' lies, an' all that ole bull-crap. He see right through there into the *truth* of it!"
> "Truth of what?"
> "*Ever*' thing."¹⁰

If ever there was an explanation of why Southern developed the sensibility he did, and why he wrote the surreal tales that he wrote — it is here in C.K.'s lessons to Harold.

Thirty-one years later, when the stories of the Texas Cycle were collected, augmented, and published as the novel *Texas Summer*, a fuller significance and meaning for this tale is made evident. At the end of "Red-Dirt Marijuana," C.K. and Harold put the marijuana in the fruit jar. On the final page of the novel *Texas Summer* (Chapter XVI), we return to the scene where the story ended, with Harold left alone after the death of C.K.:

> In the open-end dirt floor shed, Harold sat in the same place where C.K. used to read his western story ... he fired until the bull's-eye was completely shot away ... but he continued shooting until the gun was empty.
> He was sitting cross-legged, the shell box and fruit jar of grass at his feet. Using the knife that had skinned the rabbit, and scooping with his hands, he dug a hole in the soft earth and put the two containers in it and covered them over. He gazed down for a long moment at the place where they were hidden. He knew they were buried deep enough not to be discovered, but not so deep that he couldn't get to them, if he should ever want to.¹¹

The marijuana is a tool for seeing; like Southern's prose itself, it is an explosive device that allows one to peer past the illusions and masks, past the flash and into the filigree. And though often forced underground, such tools are always there, available and waiting to help, waiting to be used, to destroy lies and limitations, allowing people to truly and fully see. The marijuana is of the earth and in the earth, lying in wait to well up and undermine a false culture.

The last of the Texas stories to appear in print before *Texas Summer* was "Razor Fight," which appeared in the magazine *Nugget* in October 1962. It is the third of a trilogy that began with the brutality of "A South Summer Idyll," continued through the peace and vision of "Red-Dirt Marijuana," and climaxes in "Razor Fight" with the horrific death of C.K.— the embodiment of kindness and benevolence, destroyed by the brutality of Texas. Before C.K. is cut to ribbons by his brother Big Nail, however, the story establishes an evocative portrait of the Deep Elum that Southern so often visited in his youth:

> The place was jumping — funky wailing blues and high wild laughter ... at last they would be in the dark interior itself, seemingly windowless, smelling of kerosene and liniment, red-beans and rice, cornbread, catfish, and possum-stew; and Harold would sit in the corner with a glass of water given him and maybe a piece of hot cornbread, while C.K. sat at the table, in the yellow glow of the oil lamp ... while on the stool against the wall where Harold sat, Blind Tom Ransom played his guitar.[12]

Big Nail arrives in the bar, knowing that his brother C.K. has been sleeping with his woman while Big Nail was in prison, and looking for revenge; they come at each other, each armed with a razor:

> So they came together, in the center of the room, for one last time, still smiling, and cut each other to ribbons.
> Blind Tom Ransom, sitting on a stool inside the door, only heard it.... "It's all ovah now," he said, "all ovah now."[13]

Harold's tutelage under C.K. is over, and when he finally breaks down, hours later, and cries over the death in his family's kitchen, the tears he cries are "not the kind of tears he had known before, but tears of the first bewildering sorrow"[14]; that is, of the realization that kindness is prey to the brutality of the world.

The story ends with Hal's family failing to comprehend his loss — his grandfather simply remembers Blind Tom as the best cotton picker in the state before he lost his sight. But years later, the novel lets us know that although C.K. is gone, his influence has not been stilled. It is embodied in the jar of red-dirt marijuana, and all that it represents; Harold places it into the ground and into his subconscious, in preparation for his move to New York and to Paris in *The Hipsters*— and for his work as a writer, making it hot for them. And should there be any doubt that *Texas Summer* is an autobiographical portrait of Southern, note that he changed his original title, *Youngblood*, to one whose initials correspond to his own name.

Meanwhile, Southern's voice as a journalist was being heard more often. *The Nation* seems to have offered him the greatest freedom and the greatest arena for creative growth in this field. His book reviews for *The Nation* were not the brief plot summaries that he offered *The Times* and *Observer*; rather, they were often extended, meditative essays. "Pellet of Nihilism," published in the May issue of *The Nation*, is an indictment of the recent execution of Caryl Chessman, and a response to an Australian paper, *The Sidney Sun*, which had described the execution as an act of "cynicism." Southern counters:

> [cynicism] is an attitude which always carries with it an awareness of certain values which *oppose* this attitude; an act of cynicism, then, is one in defiance of these values for the sake of the specific motivation; it is an act, in short, which is *con-*

> *sciously immoral* ... what *The Sidney Sun* is describing, however, is *nihilism*, or the complete absence of values. Here was an act in which apparently there were no values or emotions in play other than a kind of crippling interdepartmental spite.... The execution of Chessman ... was an act of insect-mentality, carried out in a moral vacuum ... What we must think about now is: where do we go from here?[15]

Chessman's executioners are akin to Candy's inquisitors, in Southern's eyes — by arguing that no morality is at play here, that this is the work of "an insect mentality," Southern is stripping away the façade of culture, again bringing his readers face to face with brute nature. Where can we go, the essay asks, but away from a culture of death, toward a culture that embraces "a new ethics?" This is a phrase that will be used again, in the title for his introductory essay to the collection *Writers in Revolt*, at least in manuscript; the essay there is called "Toward a New Ethics,"[16] questing as it is for one that acknowledges nature and resists a "morality" of death.

This essay can serve as testament against all those who have accused Southern's black humor itself of nihilism. Southern does not assault prevailing values to replace them with a universe of meaninglessness: his universe does have meaning, a meaning found in nature. This is not, however, a value shared by the status quo, by those in a position of power ... those who could kill someone like Chessman.

The essay "New Trends and Old Hats," a critique of several current novels, by writers such as John Barth, William Styron, and John Updike (among others), indicts what Southern labels "the cult of bigness," one that, in Southern's eyes, is dragging down the American novel, and rendering it culturally irrelevant. The cult, he says:

> ... is by now a well-annotated American disease.... The bloated format of our novels is most usually a panicked attempt to bolster the otherwise rather shaky impression that anything worth saying is being said.[17]

He goes on to criticize the novels for all suffering from this bloated quality, concluding with a brief dismissal of *Rabbit, Run* as:

> ... a story which has been told and retold a dozen times ... that kind of work in which the ingredients, including three ounces of earthy dialogue and a heaping big spoonful of compassion, are consciously added as though preparing a small stew, and the canisters from which they are drawn are the past works of a hundred hands. But there is more to life than literature, and surely there is more to creative literature than novels that suggest otherwise.[18]

This curt dismissal may account for Updike's snide comments about Southern thirty years later, in his introduction to the Henry Green collection *Surviving*.

Southern continues this assault on "the cult of bigness" in a later review, "Christ Seen Darkly," which appeared in the February 25, 1961, *Nation*.

When reviewing Peter Matthiessen's new novel *Raditzer*, he comments that "It is well enough for coarse works of yesteryears ... to pound along fat and tardy, but novels of contemporary form should enjoy, above all, sharpness of pace and event."[19]

Southern also offers warning to any who might seek to read his own novels as pure allegory when he observes, "Probably the weakest thing in literature outside the pun is the deliberate allegory, because it can never be more than that."[20]

He loves Matthiessen's new novel, particularly for the unpleasant character of the protagonist: "It is in certain ways as though a whole novel had been devoted to one [Nelson] Algren's sideline freaks, a grotesque and loathsome creature, yet seen ultimately, as sometimes happens in life, as but another human being."[21]

Just as it is the grotesque that attracts Southern in Matthiessen's work, so it is this quality that he finds most appealing in Henry Miller's novels as well. In an essay on Miller entitled "Miller: Only the Beginning," published in the November 18, 1961 *Nation*, he notes that:

> Miller's work is in the tradition of Whitman, Wolfe and Sandburg ... the tradition of *romantic agony*.... In its American species it has never, before Miller, been full-blooded — the negative has always been edited out of it, either after or before leaving the author's desk; and over the years it gradually became a lopsided, unbearable freak.... What we are seeing now in the new and popular work — as represented by that of Kerouac and Ginsberg — is a revival of this old form, almost at its purest. There is nothing mysterious about the national appeal of this literature, nor, certainly, is there anything merely voguish about it ... the reason one can stomach it in its present form is that, unlike that preceding it, it is now legitimately balanced: for every ounce of the ecstatic, there is an ounce of the morbid. It has become, or very nearly so, full-blooded.[22]

What Southern is praising in these writers is the Decadent — that is, the two American strains that stem from Emerson and Poe, seen side by side: the bounty of nature and its possibilities, and its harsh limitations as well. It is timeless in its appeal, and it is what his own work offers as much as (if not more than) the authors that he praises.

During his time as book reviewer for *The Nation* and other publications, he also made one very brief foray into the world of theater review. In the January 30, 1963, issue of the British magazine *Queen*, he became *Queen*'s theater critic, reviewing the Friedrich Durrenmatt play *The Physicist*; it is not hard to see why he was never invited back to review subsequent productions.

The review begins with Southern visiting a friend, "Young Lord X," in a swanky insane asylum somewhere in the English countryside, and describes in detail their conversation and lunch. This goes on for a good half of the review space, at which point Southern then segues into a description of a dinner sequence in the play itself. He has little to say about the specific play, and dismisses the actors as merely "competent"; but he concludes the review, after this dispensation with the duties at hand, by sermonizing on the notion of theater as an anachronism:

> A considerable number of people do not seem to realize that the fact that there was a Greek theater, and an Elizabethan theater, does not mean *anything* except that there was no cinema during those times ... with the advent of sound film, the theater should have passed quietly and gracefully, with a measure of dignity befitting its long service, from the scene, instead of hanging on like some kind of eccentric ... diehard, half deaf, half blind, ranting at top voice about "the good old days" ... it has no present basis in any conceivable scheme of aesthetics.... If a play could have been a film, then there is surely no excuse for its existence as a play ... its survival ... has been due solely to its keeping ahead of popular cinema ... in the ... work of Genet and others.[23]

This preoccupation with the cultural primacy of cinema carries over into Southern's final long form review in *The Nation*, "When Film Gets Good..."; an essay which serves, in retrospect, as Southern's farewell to the Quality Lit world, prior to his embarkation for Hollywood:

> Now, when Film gets good, Book is in trouble. Theoretically, it is not possible for a book to compete aesthetically, psychologically or in any other way with a film. Of sensory perceptions it is well established that the most empathetic are *sight* and *sound*. It is for this reason that to *see* someone badly hurt, for example, hit by a car, bleeding, crying with pain, is a totally different experience from reading about it in the paper.... Film, by its very nature, more closely approximates first-hand experience than does print. And there, of course, the advantage only begins.
> What these new developments mean in terms of the novel, is something which seems so far to have been ignored in literary criticism and, at least consciously, by authors themselves. It has become evident that it is wasteful, pointless, and in terms of art, inexcusable, to write a novel which could, or in fact should, have been a film.[24]

His excitement about the film medium was heightened at this time by the advent of the new wave of European film-makers, such as Bergman, Fellini, and Antonioni. Had Kubrick not given Southern the call to come to London to help on *Dr. Strangelove*, almost immediately after the publication of this essay (although it is unlikely that Kubrick ever read this piece), it is still highly likely that Southern would have found some means to have abandoned the novel for film, to have taken his cinematic prose to its logical next level.

In the very same month that the essay "When Film Gets Good..." appeared in *The Nation*, Southern's first satirical piece appeared in Paul Krassner's underground newspaper *The Realist*. Asked in an interview years later "What's your favorite piece of work that you've done?," he responded:

SOUTHERN: I know some of my favorite is stuff that's in *The Realist*.
INTERVIEWER: Because you're given complete freedom?
SOUTHERN: Yes. I think *The Realist* is the most important publication in America ... or maybe letters, some letters never published, and unpublishable I suppose.[25]

Peter Matthiessen also recalled that some of Southern's finest writing was in his private letters because, as he put it, "he could go off on a riff, just go with it."[26] The short story, the episode, the skit — these were Southern's strengths, not sustained large-scale works (no member of "the cult of bigness," he).

Paul Krassner afforded him the sort of freedom in public that previously (and subsequently) he only found available to him in private letters: the ability to take a joke and simply go with it, to see where it took him, not having to follow dictates of form or structure, or demands of public discourse. He created, in his *Realist* pieces, a new kind of pop satire, a *Mad* magazine aimed at adults that would come to influence subsequent publications and cultural institutions (*National Lampoon, Saturday Night Live,* et al., ad nauseam, in our currently satire-soaked culture).

National Lampoon grew out of the *Harvard Lampoon,* and one of Southern's first satirical sketches appeared in the Harvard publication *Hasty Papers* in 1960: entitled "Love Is a Many Splendored," the tale consists of three smaller pieces stitched together. "First [Splendored]: A *Call of Certain Import*," details Franz Kafka and his mother's torment at the hands of Sigmund Freud, who prank-calls their apartment: "VOICE (*Impatiently*): Now, look here, Franz, I need your help and I need it badly! Now, then, tell me this: Does ... desire-for-ejaculation *precede* state of erection? OR does state of erection precede this desire? Eh? Tell me that, Mister Franz Kafka! ... (*Laughs uncontrollably for a full minute ... Hangs up*)."[27]

The sketch ends with Franz wildly jiggling the receiver, trying to reestablish contact with Freud. From the obvious comedy of this conversation, we are plunged into the more sobering conversation of "Second [Splendored]: *An Orderly Retreat*," as one soldier tries to learn from another soldier what the situation looks like over the horizon:

> The fear of the infantry stretches out through time ... one bleak afternoon when inside the head, somewhere just behind the eyes: *the world pops open*....
> "Are you going to start that again, for Christ's sake?"
> "I'm not going to start anything, you son of a bitch."[28]

Leaving another conversation in which two people refuse to connect, the tale moves to "Third [Splendored]: *A Bad Mother-hubber*," in which a white man, in the midst of getting married at the City Clerk's office, accidentally dumps a can of white paste on the black minister who is performing the ceremony.

The minister, the black man inside white paint, turns out to be a sort of human chameleon, emitting from beneath the paste a variety of voices: German, Texan, Elizabethan and "reproducing almost exactly the last lines Michael Redgrave in the ventriloquist sequence of *Dead Night*." Finally, after assuming a bewildering variety of personae, the minister concludes by dancing to:

> ... the wailing funk of Ray Charles "*It's a Low-Down Liberal, Low-Down Liberal Shame.*"
> And then when the silence began to close in, somewhat like a shroud, he went "*Ooh-scubee-doo-bop*"— very softly, that's how hip he was.²⁹

What are we to make of this odd trio of vignettes? In each one, a bewildered protagonist (Franz Kafka, a World War II soldier, a man getting married) tries to interact with someone (Sigmund Freud, another soldier, a chameleon-like minister) who refuses to take part in a conversation, to give the response that is called for or the answers demanded. And in moving from an apartment in 1914 Prague, where Kafka has "just come in from his clerical job," to the trenches of World War II, to a contemporary clerical office, the reader is also bewildered, dislocated, with no common ground left below the feet.

"Love Is a Many-Splendored Thing" was a popular song that year (1960), a sappy pop ballad of banal cheer, and Southern's "Love Is a Many Splendored" is his own send-up of the song, each "(Splendored)" a verse in his own answer ballad. Though the sketches were perhaps written separately and then stitched together for publication, they all deal with the concept of love— and, like the dark side of his Geneva tales, the inability to ever truly connect.

The verses pull the rug out from under the banal idealization of love found in the pop song: Freud, obsessed with sex, torments Kafka, terrified of sex, and still living with his mother at age 33; that is the sexual face of love. Two soldiers in the trenches can't refrain from bickering: so much for love in the face of death, valor in the fields of combat, and the dignity and heroism of war. Finally, we have the white man and the black man unable to communicate, two races unable to love because one can only see the other through a veil of perceptions, through the masks he puts on the other, while that "other" can only respond by playing with those masks; no true contact is ever established.

Fear characterizes one interlocutor in each conversation, obtuse role-playing and games characterize the other. And that, Southern seems to be telling us, is the eternal truth underlying all the dances, and all the faces, of love—and so much for the easy pop song notions that sustain the pop song industry.

Two years later, in the June 1962 issue of *Nugget*, Southern returned to the triangle of "Dr. Freud" and "Franz and Frau Kafka," in a satirical script very similar to those Woody Allen would write a few years later, in such books as *Without Feathers* and *Getting Even*. The piece, titled "Apartment to Exchange," focuses on Franz Kafka: tense, dreamy, overly analytical; and his mother Frau Kafka, shrill, shrewish and practical. They wish to exchange their smaller apartment for a larger one — Sigmund Freud responds to the ad, bringing them to an apartment that turns out to be "a huge loft-like room bare of furniture except for a table, chair and a couple of mattresses,"[30] containing a booth in a corner and a large hole in the middle of the floor.

In the booth is a "young Samoan couple" that Freud has been observing for some time, jotting down his findings in a notebook. When Frau Kafka sees what is going on in the booth, she screams and falls backwards into the hole in the middle of the floor, which, Freud had told them, was for "waste disposal." Franz leaps in after her. Freud runs to the hole to help them out:

> *His expression changes from alarm to fascination; he quickly lays the rope aside, takes out his notebook and begins making notations in it as he peers into the hole; he speaks with terse excitement.* "Yes, yes ... that's it ... excellent! ... yes, yes, react!... REACT!"
> STAGE DARKENS, LEAVING ONLY THE BEAM OF THE FLASHLIGHT DARTING ABOUT IN THE CIRCUMFERENCE OF THE HOLE.[31]

Freud is obsessed with exploring turbulent nature, playing his flashlight around the interior of the dark hole. Kafka, terrified by it, clinging to his mother, is swallowed by it — as, in fact, he had been all along, living in his mother's shadow.

There's no great profundity to this skit; it's simply a joke piece. But it *is* notable for being awash in sexual imagery, focusing on different modes for *dealing* with sexuality, in an era when America and its popular culture was highly reticent to discuss sexuality at all. Such humor pieces, in such an era, are what gained Southern his cult reputation as a dangerous humorist.

Southern's next satirical humor piece to appear was his *Realist* debut, "The Moon-Shot Scandal," in which he lampoons the space race between America and Russia. The article is an expose, revealing that the American astronaut team was a gang of flagrantly effeminate homosexuals:

> It is generally presumed because of this apparent and completely above-board policy that everything which occurs in regard to these American space shots is immediately known by the entire public. Yet can anyone really be naïve enough to believe that in matters of extraordinary import an attitude of such simple-minded candor could obtain? Surely not. And the facts behind the initial moon shot of August 17, 1961, make it a classic case in point. Now the true story may at last be told ... the story, namely, of how the moon-bound spaceship, "Cutie Pie Two,"

was caused to careen off into outer space, beyond the moon itself, when some kind of "*insane faggot hassle*," as it has since been described, developed aboard the craft.[32]

What follows is a series of transcripts from the flight:

> MAJOR DOLL: Stop *what*? I was only calibrating my altimeter — for heaven's sake, Freddie.
> LT. HANSON: ...I'm talking about your infernal *camping*![33]

The piece reaches its climax when "Colonel Slattery raged out from his forward quarters like the protagonist in *Psycho*—in outlandish feminine attire of the '90s, replete with a dozen petticoats and high-button shoes"[34]—after which the ship spins off into outer space. While such a sketch seems tame by today's standards, it should be recalled that this appeared during the Kennedy Administration, at a time when the space race was taken very seriously, as was patriotism — such parody was hardly the norm (nor, for that matter, were straightforward references to homosexuality, even in a mocking tone).

Subsequent *Realist* pieces included "Red Giant on Our Doorstep!," Southern's idea for a musical comedy (this brief joke was a companion piece to Southern's more sustained and serious critique of Kennedy's venture in the Bay of Pigs, "Recruiting for the Big Parade," which appeared in *Esquire* at roughly the same time). The cast includes "Lenny Bruce as the friendly camp surgeon (*ostensibly* friendly, but actually in Red Castro hire)," a mad scientist who injects drugs into his soldiers' heads by night, and Castro himself, "played by Groucho Marx or Orson Welles in fantastic orgy scenes.... The purpose of the film would be to combat the notion of communism as an absolute or as a Russian monopoly, possibly even to suggest that there are instances of worse conduct."[35]

This was a dangerous point to make in the era of Kennedy-brand patriotism and optimism. Another parody piece, "Scandale at the Dumpling Shop," which appeared in the February 1964 *Realist*, was headlined in the original manuscript as "Spy's Corner," making it one in a series that also included the *Olympia* piece "New Art Museum in Hamburg Blown Up." Again, Southern plays the straight-faced observer of cultural outrage, this time taking on a story assignment...:

> At the behest of several irate American mothers.... After all, these are serious times. East and West locked in dynamic struggle, our own culture faltering, indeed at times floundering in a sea of cynicism and failing beliefs, youths desperately seeking values.[36]

After reviewing the "Little Cathy Curse Doll — Complete with Teeny Tampons," the piece concludes in a paroxysm of mock moral outrage at a children's doll that actually acknowledges nature and sexuality:

Have we really so depleted exploitation that it has come to this? And moreover, where then is it to end? ... Our presses and our staff stand ready to shoulder a man-size burden ... the cause of every right-thinking parent throughout this grand land.[37]

Southern's most memorable piece for *The Realist*, however, was not a joke that sprang from his imagination, but an actual interview with a male nurse from a city hospital. The article ("Terry Southern Interviews a Faggot Male Nurse"), was published in the September 1963 *Realist*. It manages to present a homosexual sans mockery, despite the politically incorrect tone of the title; but then again, a close friend of William S. Burroughs and Frank O'Hara was unlikely to be morally opposed to homosexuality. It also returns Southern to the territory of *Flash and Filigree*'s Dr. Eichner and *Candy*'s Dr. Krankheit — the critique of another bastion of cultural authority, the Medical Establishment:

> A. Well, they're sadists, a lot of them, especially in the mental wards. Big and insensitive. Well, you've got no idea what goes on in some of those wards. Animals, like apes ... they just sit around waiting for someone to blow his stack so they can slam him ... another kind ... work in hospitals ... so they can get morphine. They couldn't care less about hitting anybody, they just sort of step aside, I guess hoping the guy will fall out the window or something ... [the doctors are] like zombies, no feeling, none at all. They can't help the patient.[38]

This was the value Southern found in *The Realist*: not just the underground humor and sensibility, the outrageous critiques of government and culture through jokes and put-ons — the greatest value was in actual, documented exposure of the shocking conditions at institutions like these city hospitals and wards.

At that time, in the early sixties, only an underground magazine newspaper like *The Realist* would have offered the forthright, uncensored comments of a "faggot male nurse." And Southern, in being given the freedom to speak openly with this person, and to speak freely in his own parodic sketches, offered a pointed social commentary not found in his surreal novels and tales.

At the same time that his voice was being given free rein by Krassner in *The Realist*, *Esquire* magazine began to hire him as an investigative reporter; Southern had come to *Esquire*'s attention through the combined notoriety of his novels, his short stories, and the underground success of his *Realist* pieces. *Esquire*, however, had stricter demands in terms of presentation than *The Realist* did; and in combining the forthright social commentary and wild humor of his *Realist* work with the exquisite, painstaking care that he brought to his fiction, Southern helped create, in a short series of articles for *Esquire*, a new breed of writing: one that, in the next few years, would come to be known as New Journalism.

8

Hipster

In the 1950s, Southern was more likely to couch cultural commentary in the form of fabulation (such as the fairy tale adventures of young Candy Christian or Guy Grand, the Magic Christian); he fashioned children's books for adults, imparting existential moral lessons that ran in the face of conventional wisdom.

But in the early 1960s, trying to make financial ends meet (as he always was), he picked up some journalism grunt work for *Esquire* and turned in a handful of articles that Tom Wolfe later credited with jump-starting the genre of New Journalism.

"New Journalism" is ultimately as meaningless a term as "Black Humor"—the passage of time shows how dangerous it is to include the term "new" in a genre name, just as all humor contains an element of blackness, of subversion. As John Hollowell has pointed out, if New Journalism merely means writing journalism from a clearly subjective standpoint, then the genre cast list has to include Daniel Defoe and Stephen Crane along with the rest of the New Journalists.

It's best to look at New Journalism as the particular product of a specific moment in time—an equivalent to Pop Art, as Southern's earlier fabulation was. This is why he made the crossover so easily. The excitement generated by New Journalism was the excitement of seeing novels turn away from charting the inner life to once again charting the outer social scene, as Tom Wolfe points out in his introduction to his anthology *The New Journalism*.[1]

Some critics of the time charged the New Journalism blend of fictional technique and factual material with being what is today called "infotainment," warping objective facts to fit a subjective lens. Its defenders would say "precisely"—by foregrounding how this is done, reportage becomes more honest than when it aspires to a false tabula rasa "objectivity."

In his journalistic articles, Southern donned his familiar Jazz Hipster mask and plunged, this time, into milieus not fantastic or farcical but real, creating not a sideways commentary on society, but a vivid, as-is portrait. From racial unrest at a baton-twirling school in Oxford, Mississippi, to recruitment procedures for the Bay of Pigs invasion, Southern turned his coolly ironic eye on what was going on in early sixties America, creating a career formula for Wolfe and Hunter S. Thompson along the way.

However, his true love was the fantastic imagination, not just-the-facts journalism; and as revenue from film work began to fill his coffers, he (perhaps unwisely) turned his back on the one prose style that flourished in the sixties and seventies. He devoted his fullest energies to his beloved film, neglecting an arena of self-mythologizing writing that might have given him his greatest success, had he continued to cultivate his public persona with as much care as, say, Thompson.

However, as much as Southern affected journalism, journalism affected him. In his fiction of the later sixties, gone is the ethereal Hawthorne style that had marked his earlier prose, replaced by a harder, more violent, more naturalistic tone. Southern's greatest short story, "The Blood of a Wig," and his most ambitious novel, *Blue Movie*, are fusions of his previous work, the fabulist tale and the Hipster New Journalist combined to create a new entity.

Southern's professional relationship with *Esquire* had begun in August 1962, with the publication of his short story "The Road Out of Axotle." This was followed by two subsequent short stories in 1963: "You're Too Hip, Baby" and "Sea Change" (later included in the *Red-Dirt Marijuana and Other Tastes* collection under the title "A Change of Style").

In *The Nation* piece "Miller: Only the Beginning," Southern had given a perhaps too-generous assessment of the Beat form of "Romantic Agony" that had been flowering as a popular fad in America for the past several years, since the appearances of *On the Road* and *Howl* in 1956. Where Southern may have erred as critic, however, he was unfailingly on target as a creative artist.

"The Road Out of Axotle" is Southern's assessment of the whole Beat "On-the-Road" craze, and the serious visionary flaws in its unbounded Emersonian optimism. In this tale, we see a disciple of Poe shrewdly assessing the disciples of Whitman: finding that they are unbalanced in their assessment of nature, he demonstrates how their appreciation of only its bright side, and not its darkness, can result in dire consequences. Southern had observed, in his "Impolite Interview" with Krassner in *The Realist*, "There was a certain cloying sentimentality in *On the Road* that stuck in my craw, so to speak. But its significance as a moving force which has had these great effects seems obvious.... The Beat generation is the source or origin of the great wave of civil rights action."[2]

Southern was generous enough to grant the Beats credit as a positive social force, but his focus in "The Road Out of Axotle" is that "cloying sentimentality" is a view that does not have the proper respect for the darkness within nature in its more freakish aspects, for the dangers of freedom, for the terrors of the void.

What Beat sentimentality lacked was a respect for the dangers of nature, and that is a failure that "Axotle" sets out to correct. The tale is, in effect, a more surreal, Poe-influenced warm-up for *Easy Rider*, written only five years later — a film that would indict the same naïvety, in their Hippie descendants, that "Axotle" critiqued in the Beats.

Discussing Southern's critique of the Beats offers a good moment at which to discuss Southern's standing in literary histories of the era. Many accounts focus on the Beats; few, if any, mention Southern. He is never lumped in with that group because Southern was a Hipster, and for those "in the know" in that era, "Beats" and "Hipsters" were very different breeds of cultural outsider. Albert Goldman was a friend of Southern's, and in fact often resembles Southern's Doctor Warner — an academic trying to gain intellectual understanding of the Underground by associating with its denizens. In his biography *Ladies and Gentlemen — Lenny Bruce!!!*, Goldman discusses the difference between the two factions:

> The difference was drastic: The Hipster was your typical lower class urban dandy dressed up like a pimp, affecting a very cool cerebral tone.... The Beat was originally some earnest middle class college boy like Kerouac, who was stifled by the cities and the culture he had inherited, and who wanted to cut out for distant exotic places where he could live like "the people" ... while rhapsodizing about this great land of ours.[3]

Southern, who aspired to the Hipster lifestyle, turns his focus in "Axotle" on the "earnest ... college boy ... who wanted to cut out for distant exotic places, where he could live like 'the people.'" The tale, echoing *Pym* yet again, follows the narrator and his compatriots as they voyage ever further into the "weird":

> The way it happened, I was with these two friends of mine in Mexico City — I say friends of mine, though actually we'd met only a few days before. But anyway, we were together this particular night in their car — and the idea was to pick a town, such as the one we were in, and then just sort of drive away from it in the opposite direction, so to speak. I knew what they had in mind, more or less, but it did seem that in being this strong on just wanting to get away from, we might simply end up in the sea or desert.[4]

The narrator, on the road with his friends Pablo and Emanuel, is aware that there may be some dangers in simply running away, ending in the blankness of sea or desert — but he goes along for the ride anyway. This brand of opening sequence, with three friends looking for kicks out on the great highway, was familiar enough in this era of the Beat, but Southern soon veers away from this, into the Poe territory of "The Gold Bug":

> It was then, while I was trying to hold the book up and away to get more light, that something fell out of it.... What had fallen from the book was a map of Mexico ... it was not of the same school of mapmaking as were the maps in the guidebook. It was like something from another era ... the paper was extraordinarily thin — bible paper, but much stronger, like rice paper or bamboo — and it was hazed with the slightest coloration of age which seemed to give a faint iridescence to the soft colors.[5]

Following this map, the three friends leave the established, charted highways and go off into a bizarre night country, speaking a then-all-too-familiar Beat dialect:

> "Man, dig this ... road! ... it's *lions and tigers!! ... big ... pointy rocks!*" ... fairly shouting with laughter, he handed me another joint.[6]

They come across a fat Mexican tollkeeper, a character that fuses B. Traven with Southern's own M. Pommard (of "The Automatic Gate"); the Lovecraftean town of Corpus Christi (townspeople fill the square at midnight, all of them covered by enormous green bugs) — and finally, on a stretch of dark desert road, an enormous fence that stretches on and on, far into the darkness, giving no clue as to what it contains. It is a great blank:

> I had become obsessed by the mystery of it. What was it behind this fence in the vast area where one town used to exist and no town was supposed to? The fabulous estate of a mad billionaire? The testing ground for some fantastic weapon? Why had not the sign proclaimed the source of its authority? ... here was a case of security so elaborate, so resolved upon, that even the power behind it would remain secret. Whatever it was — was so dreadful, it was not supposed to exist.[7]

This is not Roswell, nor any one person or group of people excluding others: this is the inscrutable face of nature itself, the end of the road for man's pursuit of mystery and meaning. When the narrator tries to scale its walls and learn its secrets, nature strikes back:

> I had a sudden uneasiness of something very menacing nearby and moving closer and, as suddenly, I knew what it was ... through the snarls before they [a pack of wild dogs] caught me I could hear the teeth snapping as though they were so possessed by rage to bite even the air itself. I half stumbled and turned when the first one bit the back of my leg and clung to it in a loathsome way not unlike a tarantula.[8]

In exploring freedom, in exploring the benevolence of nature in "this great land of ours," the Beats must eventually come up against nature's other face, the hunchback that completes Candy Christian. This is what happens to the three protagonists here, on the road out of Axotle. Escaping the dogs, they turn away from the dead end of the road, returning to civilization.

There, the unnamed narrator leaves the reader with a warning: "So that was that; and the point of it all is they left me the map — that is, should anyone ever care to make it, I mean down to the big fence on that road out of Axotle."⁹

Eventually, in plunging into the great wide open, one will come up against a fence. Like *Easy Rider* a few years later, "The Road Out of Axotle" tells us that freedom has its dangers, nature its limitations, and in so doing shows us that the Hipster cosmology, in taking into account darkness and death, is more complete, more full — at any rate, more Decadent — than the naïve Beat philosophy. Poe trumps Emerson.

Southern's next appearance in *Esquire* was in February of 1963, with the landmark article "Twirling at Ole Miss"— it was accompanied by photographs taken by the author himself, already moving beyond the word, into visual media. Tom Wolfe, in introducing the piece in his anthology *The New Journalism*, noted, "It was the first example I noticed of a form of journalism in which the writer starts out to do a feature assignment ... and ends up writing a curious form of autobiography. The supposed subject ... becomes incidental. And if the writer has the wit to make his own reactions that fascinating, the reader doesn't care."¹⁰

Southern begins this first real foray into the world of investigative journalism with a mock-serious invocation of the beauty and joy of baton twirling:

> In an age gone stale through the complex of bureaucratic interdependencies ... it is a refreshing moment indeed when one comes across an area of human endeavor absolutely sufficient unto itself, pure and free, no strings attached — the cherished and almost forgotten *l'art pour l'art*.¹¹

Southern is striking the pose of the Existentialist Hipster, seeking to undermine a culture of limitations that is "aimed to converge into a single totality of meaning."¹² The reporter searches for freedom, for possibilities — he is also, in this piece, self-revealing in a way that he has not been before:

> In my case, it was the first trip South in many years, and I was duly apprehensive. For one thing, the institute is located just outside Oxford, Mississippi — and by grotesque coincidence, Faulkner's funeral had been held only the day before my arrival, lending a grimly surreal aura to the nature of my assignment.... Would reverting to the Texas twang and callousness of my youth suffice to see me through?¹³

He is uneasy at returning to the South, his personal locus of violence, but soon finds distraction. Ever the leering admirer of teenaged girls, Southern lovingly paints a pastoral portrait of pretty young things cavorting in skimpy costumes — but even this cannot hold him long. Like Hawthorne's *The Blithedale Romance*, the real punch and impact of the piece comes from conveying the menace that lies behind the bright façade, the pain that this paradise is built on: "Next to the benches and about three feet apart are two public drinking fountains, and I noticed that the one boldly marked 'For Colored,' is sitting squarely in the shadow cast by the justice symbol on the courthouse façade — to be entered later, of course, in my writer's notebook under 'Imagery, sociochiaroscurian, hack.'"[14]

In Brechtian style, Southern deconstructs journalistic pretensions to poetry, the propensity for finding haunting symbolic images — he still conveys the image, to be sure, but also distances himself from the manipulation necessary to get it across and make its cultural point. Still playing the detached Hipster as crusading journalist, Southern interviews the students, describes the lifestyle on the campus, and subtly evokes the racism that underpins the entire community: "*We* nevuh had no Negra problem heah," said one of them, shaking his head sadly ... then to the tune of *John Brown's Body*, the two graduate law students begin to sing, almost simultaneously: 'Oh we'll bury all the niggers in the Mississippi mud...' ... despite a terrific effort at steely Zen detachment, the incident left me somewhat depressed."[15]

The emptiness of the white culture at Ole Miss, and the callous indifference to the racial problems, eventually numbs Southern even to the attraction of the coeds:

> As the evening wore on, I found it increasingly difficult, despite the abundance of cutiepieness at hand, to string along with these values ... after lunch I packed, bid adieu to the Dixie National, and boarded the bus for Memphis. As we crossed the Oxford Square and passed the courthouse, I saw the fountain was still shaded, although it was a couple of hours later than the time I passed before. Perhaps it is always shaded — cool and inviting, it could make a person thirsty just to see it.[16]

The fountain that he is referring to is the one marked "For Colored," and after pointing a finger at the chilling emptiness of the white culture of the South, we are again reminded why the boy from Dallas would be attracted to Deep Elum rather than Pocahontas; why young Harold would grow up to become a Hipster emulating the black culture around him rather than the white; why the glare of Ole Miss would make one thirsty for the shade of the colored fountain.

Southern's next appearance in *Esquire*, in April 1963, again dealt with the difficulties of communication between white and black Americans. This time, it was a fictional tale: "You're Too Hip, Baby," culled from the same quarry that produced "Put-Down" and the rest of *The Hipsters*—that is, Southern's life in Paris in the early '50s, and the Hipster culture he was a part of there. And this time, the finger is pointed at himself.

Like Southern himself, the tale's protagonist, Murray, is enrolled at the Sorbonne. Murray is, in many ways, a dark self-portrait, following on the heels of, perhaps even spurred by, the perceptive self-portrait he gave in "Twirling at Ole Miss":

> The Sorbonne, where Murray was enrolled for a doctorate, required little of his time. Class attendance was not compulsory and there were no scheduled examinations. Having received faculty approval on the subject of his thesis—"The Influence of Mallarme on the English Novel Since 1940"—Murray was now engaged in research in the libraries developing his thesis, writing it and preparing himself to defend it at some future date of his own convenience. Naturally, he could attend any lectures at the university which he considered pertinent to his work, and he did attend them from time to time—usually those of illustrious guest speakers like Cocteau, Camus and Sartre, or Marcel Raymond, author of *From Baudelaire to Surrealism*. But for the most part, Murray devoted himself to less formal pursuits. He knew every Negro jazz musician and every club in Paris.[17]

In creating this portrait of Murray, Southern has etched a strikingly faithful self-portrait, right down to the subject and title of his thesis. Wolfe has identified the journalism of "Twirling at Ole Miss" as autobiography; the fiction of "You're Too Hip, Baby" is equally so. Murray befriends "the Negro pianist, Buddy Talbot" and his wife Jackie, who have just arrived in Paris to play at the clubs, and helps them ease into life in Montparnasse: "Murray was helpful in much more than introducing them to a good hash connection. Right away he found them a better and cheaper room, and nearer the Noir et Blanc.... He took them to see *L'Age d'Or* at the Cinematheque, to the Catacombs, the rib joint on Montmartre, to hear Marcel Raymond speak at the Sorbonne, to the flea markets."[18]

Almost a decade after leaving this scene in Paris, Southern lovingly recalls its sights, sounds, and smells in detail. But he remembers his own role there, his own pose as Hipster, with a sting.

Buddy and Jackie keep trying to repay Murray for his kindnesses in all sorts of ways, but Murray refuses everything. Jackie and Buddy each finally offer themselves sexually to Murray, and both are refused by him in this as well. Ultimately, Buddy confronts him: "'You're too hip, Baby. That's right, you're a *hippy*.' He laughed. 'In fact, you're what we might call a kind of professional *nigger lover*.' He touched Murray's shoulder as he moved to leave. 'And I'm not putting you down for it, understand, but ... like the man said, "It's just not a scene I make."'"[19]

The tale ends with Murray alone, seated in a café. He orders coffee:

"Noir, Monsieur?" asked the waiter in a suggestively rising inflection.

Murray looked up abruptly at the man, but the waiter was oblivious, counting the money in his hand.... "*Oui*," he said softly, "*noir*."[20]

From his boyhood visits to Deep Elum, to his Paris visits to the jazz cafés, right up through the journalistic expose of casual racism in Oxford, Mississippi — Southern's work had been concerned, time and again, with bringing black American culture, its vitality and its troubles, to the attention of white American culture.

But on the heels of his visit back to the South of his youth for "Twirling at Ole Miss"; in revisiting (in his imagination) the Paris culture that formed his Hipster sensibility; Southern, in painting this portrait of Murray, makes a serious and damning self-appraisal. It is not only the smug self-complacency of other Americans, of a "Swiss machine" like Dr. Eichner, that Southern wishes to smash: it is his own, the self-satisfaction of the Hipster, that he wants to destroy as well.

Southern's next piece in *Esquire* was a return to journalism, following on the success of "Twirling at Ole Miss": an article entitled "Recruiting for the Big Parade," it was a detailed indictment of the Bay of Pigs invasion. Again, Southern settles into his role as crusading journalist by striking the pose of Hipster's Hipster, master of the deadpan put-on:

> One night not long ago I was sitting around the White Horse Tavern in New York City's colorful Greenwich Village having a quick game of chess with a self-styled internationally famous blitz chess champ. Six snappy ones and I pretty well had the game sewed up when the champ suddenly said: "Say, see that guy at the bar — he was in the Cuban fiasco."
>
> "Cut the diversionary crap, Champ," I countered, not bothering to look around, tapping the board of play instead, "and face up to the power." I had slapped the old De Sade double cul-de-sac on his Lady — and as Bill Seward says, that's a rumble nobody can cool.[21]

The "Bill Seward" he references here is William Seward Burroughs, the one Beat writer that Southern unequivocally admired — probably because Burroughs was, properly speaking, more a Decadent writer than a Beat. He is far more pessimistic in outlook than Ginsberg or Kerouac, and more in keeping with the tradition inaugurated by the father of modern Decadence, the Marquis De Sade — who is referenced in the previous line.

Southern finally meets the man pointed out to him (his real name was Boris Grgurevich, though this is not revealed in the article); he invites him over to his apartment, where Southern interviews him. What follows is a record of how the CIA openly recruited people looking for work in Miami, and shipped them off to a camp in Guatemala, where they were trained to invade Cuba.

The man granting the interview (Grgurevich) was trained at the camp: his account of the training inspired Southern's musical comedy parody in *The Realist* ("Red Giant on Our Doorstep!") and a later, fuller account of the training ("Fiasco Reverie") written in the eighties and still unpublished. "Fiasco Reverie" reads like a detailed film treatment, and ends with a wildly farcical, slapstick depiction of the actual invasion, including the fat commander falling on his face on the offloading ram, trampled by his own fleeing soldiers.

What distinguishes "Recruiting for the Big Parade" from Southern's other treatments of the whole Bay of Pigs fiasco is the voice and tone of his interview subject: the savvy, knowing Hipster thrown into the middle of an inept government project. His story becomes the antithesis of the typical Hollywood boot-camp saga (sloppy, dissolute men fashioned into a crack fighting unit for the glory of God and country); there is no glory, for Southern, to Cold War war stories. In this world, the dissolute recruits are far superior to the incompetent governments they fight for. And the entire Cold War stance that fired the patriotism of the Kennedy Era, the opposition of America to the "Communist threat" of its neighbor Cuba, is revealed to be a farce; the Cubans emerge from the whole conflict with far more dignity.

After indicting Southern racism and puncturing Cold War patriotic zeal, Southern turned, in his next assignment for *Esquire*, to the Quality Lit crowd. "I *Am* Mike Hammer!" is a portrait of pulp fiction legend Mickey Spillane, master of the hard-boiled detective novel. Spillane had gone to London to star as his own hero, Mike Hammer, in a film version of Spillane's novel *The Girl Hunters*, and Southern opens and concludes the article with meditations on what could happen if other authors got the same idea:

> If Spillane's undertaking is a successful one, and it appears quite possible, will it not definitely signal a new trend in creative fiction?... an irate and astonished director shouting "Cut! Cut!" is apt to have precious little affect on chaps like Mailer and Kerouac once they are swinging.... But of course the real coup will be when some enterprising producer signs up grand old Henry Miller — providing, natch, that Hank is given free reign and the books are done *right*, without your usual cinematic compromise.[22]

Despite the tongue-in-cheek tone of the piece, it is impossible not to see that Southern does indeed admire Spillane: "For someone like myself, with a Café Flore and White Horse Tavern orientation — where the whole point was not to write a book but to *talk* one — speaking with Spillane in regard to the lit game was refreshment itself."[23]

Written only a few months before *The Nation* article "When Film Gets Good...," "I *Am* Mike Hammer!" is a further indication that Southern was himself eager to get out of the Quality Lit game and into the film industry — to quit being a "loser" and become a "winner"[24] (Spillane's terms).

Southern published one more short story in *Esquire* in 1963, "Sea Change" (later retitled, when included in the *Red-Dirt Marijuana and Other Tastes* collection, as "A Change of Style"). The piece is evocative of Roald Dahl in tone and style, with an elaborate setup, stretched over several pages, leading to a wry, ironic twist in the final line. It focuses on the dreams and musings of a bored Los Angeles housewife as she leaves a beauty parlor where she has had her hair bleached, and heads home to greet her husband, imagining his pleased reaction: "She takes the hat from her lap, tries it at a tentative angle. Amazing. Who would have guessed that blonde hair could make such a difference — all the difference in the world. What will Ralph say? Ralph had always wanted a blonde and now he would have one. Perhaps it is true, after all, that men do prefer blondes!"[25]

With only a few deft strokes, over only three pages, Southern artfully evokes an entire world: the empty landscape of the fifties suburban cocktail set. Grace, it becomes apparent, has grown distant from her husband Ralph; she has had an affair with Harry, but has ended the affair and now, she only wants to make her husband happy:

> And Grace Owen finds herself in love with her husband all over again.... She hears the door swing open behind her, his footsteps on the threshold, and then the abrupt stop. She thrills to the sharp catch of his breath, the husky, unfamiliar panic — and something more — just before he says,
> "For Christ's fucking sake, Elaine, I told you never to come here!"[26]

It's an easy joke, to be sure, but what makes the piece linger in the memory is the evocation of Grace's hollow, vacuous existence, akin to that of the coeds at Ole Miss. With one quick, contemptuous sketch, Southern turns his Hipster gaze on the suburban scene that obsesses such contemporaries as John Cheever and John Updike, and quickly dismisses it.

In reviewing Vonnegut's *Cat's Cradle* for the *New York Times* in June of 1963, Southern had noted: "Like the best of contemporary satire, it is work of a far more engaging and meaningful order than the melodramatic tripe which most critics seem to consider 'serious.'"[27] The brief span of "Sea Change" is all the time Southern can waste on the "melodramatic tripe" that fills so many of the other American novels of the era, and with the ghoulish glee of Dahl, he smashes their dreams and illusions, and moves on.

After this, Southern would move on from *Esquire* as well. He returned only once more, in 1968, when *Esquire* sent him — along with Burroughs, John Sack, Ginsberg and Jean Genet — to cover the 1968 Democratic Convention in Chicago; one last New Journalism hurrah for the man who started it all. Over the course of a year, from late 1962 to late 1963, Southern had given *Esquire* six pieces (three short stories and three articles of investigative journalism) that did more to build and bolster his reputation in American popular culture (as opposed to underground culture) than anything else he wrote — that is, prior to the publication of *Candy* in the U.S. the following year, coupled with the release of *Dr. Strangelove*. Southern was on his way to becoming a star.

Meanwhile, as his professional reputation was growing, his private life had changed dramatically, as well.

9

Beyond the Beat

In 1960, Terry and Carol purchased a twenty-nine-acre farm: it consisted of a 1756 Colonial house complete with large barns, fields and river (the chickens and sheep came later, along with Black Angus steer). This was done using an inheritance from Carol's mother, as Southern himself still was making no money.

It was located in the Berkshires, and situated on the banks of the Blackberry River, in the town of East Canaan, Connecticut; Southern promptly (and unsurprisingly) dubbed it "Blackberry River Farm." All of his subsequent manuscripts, anything written from the mid-sixties until the end of his life, are stamped with this address. The boy from Texas, after detours into Bohemian life in Paris and Greenwich Village, had finally arrived at his permanent home, in the heart of Melville and Hawthorne Country. When asked by *Life* magazine in 1964 whether his life as a country squire indicated that he was "going square," he simply replied, "I need the isolation."

Later that year, Carol gave birth to their son; they named him Nile, although Southern would continue to refer to the child for the next several years by the affectionate term "Inf," his shortened Hipster take on "infant." A letter from Terry to Carol during this period offers a touching portrait of their life at this time. Dated "Sunday Night" and addressed to his "True Darl," he tells her that:

> Winter has come. I had forgotten to feed the animals this afternoon since everything seemed so different with the snow. So I just went out now and there are huge geese tracks everywhere. They are excited about the snow and rushing around it. The silly chickens are sleeping in their tree and getting covered. Also, a little while ago Inf fell out of his crib ... there he was in the dark on the floor *under* his crib.... He hardly woke up — wasn't he dear?[1]

This is quite another persona from that of the cool, sarcastic Hipster; this is the face of the man who wrote *The Donkey and the Darling*, protector of "the smallest and dear" ("Show the infant a letter from Da-da: 'Letter Da-Da!' You must shout it at his funny head!"[2]) Southern's star was on the rise professionally, and he had found joy in his home life.

At the same time, two important and influential friendships were being cemented. The first was with the consummate Hipster Comedian, Lenny Bruce. Bruce and Southern were kindred talents, both bringing the cynical, scathing humor of the jazz underworld into popular consciousness. Southern had been an admirer of Bruce's since the late fifties, as both Carol Southern and Peter Matthiessen noted. And when *The Magic Christian* was published in paperback, Bruce came out as an ardent Southern fan, supplying the blurb on the back cover: "Hosanna. In only one printing Southern has achieved Second Coming. Funniest book I ever read."[3]

Southern and Bruce became close friends in the early sixties, in a period when Bruce had risen to superstardom and was beginning to suffer serious harassment by the authorities, due to his use of "profanity" on stage. Albert Goldman, in his biography of Lenny Bruce, offers a vivid portrait of the relationship between the two: "What a team, Bruce and Southern! Terry is sitting there in the tape room, slumped heavily, flaccidly on a bed, his face covered by a thick scruff of beard, his eyes shielded by dark glasses, hair tousled, blue shirt hanging out of dirty gray-white pants, a beat Charles Laughton."[4]

Goldman conveys a sense of the close friendship that had developed between these two great purveyors of African American humor to the Anglo-American public, while also offering an eyewitness account of the substance abuse that began to grow more frequent, and more debilitating, as Southern's fame and success increased. Right now, Southern was riding the crest of a wave — but soon enough (as was already becoming true for Bruce), the toll would become apparent.

Speaking of substance abuse, the other great friendship that developed in this period was his relationship with William S. Burroughs. Southern had first been exposed to Burroughs' work by Gregory Corso, on one of Southern's visits to Paris when discussing the publication of *Candy* with Maurice Girodias, during the time that he was living in Geneva:

> Our most frequent cafe in those days was the Saint-Germain des Pres, opposite the Flore. It was there one winter's morn, while Mason and I were having our customary *grande tasse*, that a certain Greg E. Corso, author of the epic poems "Bomb" and "Gasoline," and the novel *American Express*, presented himself at the table. He plopped a manuscript down and said in his usual gross manner "Now dig this...."
>
> It turned out that the ms. was, of all things, *Naked Lunch*.... Mason and I set out to convince Gid that it was worthy of his distinguished imprimatur.[5]

Southern and Hoffenberg ultimately succeeded in convincing Girodias to publish *Naked Lunch*—but only when they lied to him, persuading him that the title was American slang for sex in the afternoon.

When *Nova Express* was published in America, Southern wrote a laudatory essay about Burroughs' work in the November 8, 1964, issue of *Book Week*, an essay titled "Rolling Over Our Nerve Endings" (original manuscript title, "The Burroughs Express"[6]). Southern describes Burroughs' humor and vision in terms that are equally applicable to his own:

> It is an absolutely devastating ridicule of all that is false, primitive and vicious in current American life: the abuses of power, hero worship, aimless violence, materialistic obsession, intolerance and every form of hypocrisy ... it is poetry of the most consummate control ... for those who fail to see "form" in this, and are disturbed because of it, one may only conclude that they see in life itself a "form" which has eluded philosophy from the beginning of time. And may God help them.[7]

That is to say, "those" do see form, but that form is a false prism—life through a skewed perception, a veil of illusions, one that the humor of Burroughs (and Southern) strips away. In the nineties, Victor Bockris, a close friend of both Southern and Burroughs, remembered that "Southern and Burroughs together could almost have been a vaudeville team."[8] In his book *With William Burroughs: A Report from the Bunker*, Bockris describes a typical evening that Burroughs and Southern would spend at Burroughs' apartment, located in the Bowery in lower Manhattan:

> At Burroughs' apartment, Ter emptied the bag of drug samples onto Bill's big parlor table. And as I turned on the tape and fired up the bomber, Bill motioned us to fix our drinks, donned his reading glasses and settled in for a good scrutiny of the dope labels, using a magnifying glass like a jeweler examining precious stones.
> BURROUGHS: Now, then, what is all this shit, Terry?
> TERRY SOUTHERN: Bill, these are pharmaceutical samples ... anything that won't cook up, we'll eat.[9]

As with the Bruce vignette, this anecdote, while amusing, offers a disquieting revelation of the substance abuse that would lead to the loss of focus, the dulling of perception, the loss of vision in the years to come. But as with Bruce, it is not difficult to see why Southern and Burroughs became such close friends, sharing their kindred vision.

Like Southern, and unlike the Beat companions with whom Burroughs' work is normally lumped, Burroughs' writing displays a pessimism and savagery that connotes a fuller appreciation of nature, an American writer's vision more in the tradition of Poe than Emerson. And like Bruce on stage, and Southern on the page, Burroughs also did not offer sustained plots, well-structured story arcs—his novels, like Southern's, were collections of comedy skits that displayed Hipster lingo and an affinity with the Hipster sensibility, while undermining commonly shared perceptions of American culture. Burroughs himself said of his work: "I just make up these little skits, that's all. I am sick of having this heavy thing laid on me where I just make a little slapstick and someone comes up on me with this 'Oh, God, he's rejecting everything' shit."[10]

He rejected the negative label because, like Southern and Bruce, he simply refused to accept, as Southern pointed out, "all that is false"; he *did* embrace possibility rather than limitation, fullness rather than half of the truth. That vision that Southern, Burroughs and Bruce shared (hopeful at its core, yet refusing to shy away from the negative aspects of American culture) was explicitly delineated by Southern, in his best attempt at a serious scholarly tone, in his essay "Toward the Ethics of a Golden Age" (original manuscript title: "Toward a New Ethic"[11]). This essay served as the introduction to a collection he edited (along with Richard Seaver and Alex Trocchi) called *Writers in Revolt*, published in 1963, before Southern knew he was on the cusp of super-stardom.

Seaver had been co-editor (with Alex Trocchi) of *Merlin* back in the early fifties, and was now one of the co-editors of *The Evergreen Review*. Trocchi, still moving back and forth between New York and Paris, still refusing to settle down (though he had a wife and child), was only drifting further and further into heroin addiction, though he had experienced some degree of success with his novel *Cain's Book*.

The original idea for the anthology (and its original title, *Beyond the Beat*) was Southern's. All of the new prose material supplied for the volume, the general introduction and the introductions for the individual authors, is also by Southern; it is safe to assume that, despite the credit given to his friends (and perhaps one or two suggestions from them) the volume is almost entirely the work of Southern (another indication that the volume is solely, or at any rate largely, Southern's doing is that it is dedicated to his lawyer, Seymour Litvinoff).

As its original manuscript title, *Beyond the Beat*,[12] demonstrates, Southern wished to introduce readers to writers in what he had termed the "romantic agony" tradition — and in particular, writers who embraced a fuller vision of that tradition. This is a vision that he had begun to describe in his "Miller: Only the Beginning" essay — that is, a Decadent vision that embraces nature, both in its positive and negative characteristics, its freedom and its limitation.

The volume serves as a primer for the Decadent Romantic tradition in the nineteenth and twentieth centuries, beginning with Sade, who began his own career in reaction to Rousseau, a writer whose outlook is more closely allied with that of the Beats. It then continues through such writers as Baudelaire, Hesse, Celine, Miller, and on up through the Beat visions of Ginsberg's *Howl* (Parts I and II) and Burroughs' *Naked Lunch*. By including Burroughs, Southern also offered him his first U.S. publication for *Naked Lunch*, one year before the Supreme Court cleared the novel of all charges of obscenity.

Southern begins his introduction — his manifesto — by asserting that "In existentialist thought, the death-of-God concern is not with the wisdom of abandoning the God idea, but the acknowledgment that the role of this idea is no longer one of dynamic force in Western cultures." Going on to ask "...What is the principal force ... from which we attempt to draw our ethics and our sense of values?,", Southern replies that "The answer ... is psychology."

Since, he goes on to assert, "Freud, as is well known, left no ... ten commandments ... it is evident that we are searching for a new system of values, and to find it, we must swim with the tide."[13] The best art, he therefore concludes, is art that deals in ambiguities — this accounts, he says, for the:

> ... sudden advanced critical interest in the deceptively oblique novels of Henry Green. It is significant too, that where statement is made, simple and direct, it is invariably iconoclastic.... The implication is not that statement or ambiguity, is an end, or of value per se; it is rather the logical effect of assaulting established canons, now deemed suspect, if not totally inadequate.... The writer still struggles for the freedom to use his tools — language — without restriction.[14]

Southern explains his assaults on cultural authority and rants against censorship — he's still feeling the sting of having "The Accident" tampered with all those years ago. Having established that the artist, in this day and age, must detach himself from existing values that are no longer adequate; that he must resist concrete assertions, but rather imply; he then concludes:

> What is required then is the deliberate avoidance of lip service to assumed values, and adherence instead to deeply personal impulse, as well as the active response to the most private value inclinations. For it is in this way alone that the great hollow symbols by which cultures pretend to live, are given faith in substance, the dead-lips color, warmth, and perhaps in the end, something meaningful to say.[15]

With this volume, Southern has established a tradition which, by implication, he himself belongs to; it stems from Sade and culminates, via the introduction, with Southern himself. He may have been a rebel against the status quo, but with this volume he demonstrated that he was the product of a long and distinguished lineage — the kinship with Sade would become apparent again later, with the publication in 1970 of Southern's novel *Blue Movie*, a latter-day version of Sade's *120 Days of Sodom*.

Having discovered his voice, having discovered his lineage, and now feeling the yearning to move beyond the confines of the printed page to the more "immediate" form of film, Southern was offered the chance to begin this passage when *Esquire*, which had given him his most visible public platform in America up to this point, offered him a new assignment as investigative journalist—an assignment he never completed. It is complete in manuscript form, but was not published at the time, for unknown reasons. Nonetheless, it helped to inaugurate the next phase in his career. On the heels of his interview with Mickey Spillane, exploring the connections between literature and film, *Esquire* asked Southern to interview a young American director named Stanley Kubrick.

This turning point came not long before the writing of what is perhaps his greatest short story: "The Blood of a Wig" (ultimately published in *The Evergreen Review* in 1967). This tale is the culmination of Southern's heretofore schizophrenic career as both fiction writer and journalist, for it is an artful fusion of the two strains in Southern's work: a story with serious aspirations, an expose of life on a men's magazine staff, and a *Realist*-style put-on, all rolled into one.

When Southern collected his favorite short work for the *Red-Dirt Marijuana and Other Tastes* collection, he selected "The Blood of a Wig" to be the concluding entry, while "Red-Dirt Marijuana" opens the anthology. They are perfect bookends: twin recipes for vision, for truly seeing. One is innocent, one hip; the unnamed narrator of "The Blood of a Wig" could be the grown Hal of *The Hipsters*, returned to New York after Paris.

The narrator has gone to work for a magazine called *Lance* ("The Mag for Men"); the details of his tasks as fiction editor are culled from Southern's own very brief experience as fiction editor at *Esquire* in 1962–1963, though the magazine itself seems to be patterned more on a low-end skin magazine like *Nugget*, rather than the high-end *Esquire*. At the magazine, the narrator reads through the manuscripts sent in for publication consideration: "It was a source of irritation and chagrin to my secretary when I first told her to read '*all* unsolicited manuscripts, and *no* manuscripts from agents.' ... I have this theory about the existence of a *pure, primitive, folk-like* literature ... whereas I knew the stuff from the agents would be the same old predictably competent tripe."[16]

Southern, as arbiter of taste, pits his pulp fiction against the offerings of the Quality Lit crowd, and Lovecraft's weird tales again find more favor than Updike's suburban angst.

The narrator and the other staffers are all drafted, by the editor-in-chief, to try their hand at an article on the Kennedy assassination conspiracy theories (this less than a year after the assassination). Searching for inspiration in a drug store on Sheridan Square, he meets a character straight out of his unpublished early fifties story fragment "The Pusher." The young pusher offers him "the blood of a wig" as a drug offering — that is, the blood of "Chin Lee ... a famous East Village resident, a Chinese Symbolist poet who is presently residing at Bellevue in a straightjacket."[17]

When administered, the blood grants the narrator visions of what really happened at the JFK assassination ("NECK-ROPHILIA!"); after a night of frantic, visionary composition, he submits his article to the editorial staff the next morning. They react with outrage — shades of the classroom reaction to Southern's earliest Poe pastiche, back at Winnetka Elementary all those years ago.

The narrator, in defending himself against the insults of an angry colleague, tells him "...about an insight I had gained into Vietnam, Cassius Clay, Chessman, the Rosenbergs.... He couldn't believe it. But, of course, no one ever really does — do they?"[18]

Ron Rosenbaum, in his *New York Observer* column "The Edgy Enthusiast," wrote an appreciation of Southern shortly after Southern's death. It focused on two Southern tales ("The Blood of a Wig" and the later "Heavy Put-Away"), describing the pair as "ugly parables of Art." In analyzing Southern's approach to art, he likens him (surprisingly enough) to Sir Philip Sidney. In Sidney's "An Apologie for Poetrie" essay, Rosenbaum explains: "[he] defended art as a bittersweet pill, a delectable exterior conning the reader into swallowing difficult inner truths. Terry Southern's defense of art is a kind of inversion. The pill is bitter on the surface and the promised sweetness at the center a con, but there are some who still can't resist the taste for it."[19]

The message that Rosenbaum finds in "The Blood of a Wig" is that art "drives some to court madness and the Muse by taking the blood of a wig as a sacrament." I agree with Rosenbaum in seeing that the primary focus of the story is not an evocation of worklife at a men's magazine, nor is it a parody of JFK assassination conspiracy theories, although that accounted for much of the story's notoriety in the sixties. It can also be argued, however, that Southern's focus in the tale is less art itself, than it is the *means to create* art.

The story opens with the account of the inadequacy of all manuscripts that the narrator receives as editor; this is done in order to counter these worthless writings with the insight gained by the ingestion of the blood of a wig. It is significant that the drug that is taken is not Dexamyl, nor alcohol, cocaine, or heroin; it is *blood*, human blood — which is to say, the very sap of nature itself.

Nature doesn't cause insights into the "essential I," the true self, as LSD does; it causes *obliteration* of it. Persona is just another mask, another cultural manifestation, powerless against teeming, bloody, chaotic ("wig") nature. Only an infusion of nature allows one to evade the self (and, therefore, bad writing stemming from the lies of the self). In this way, the artist sees through all the cultural deceptions that surround him or her, from the JFK assassination, to Vietnam, to the execution of Caryl Chessman (a lie Southern had previously explored, and exploded, in his *Nation* essay "Pellet of Nihilism").

The art that is created after taking "the sacrament" is important, and certainly more valuable than the art described at the opening of the tale; the editor searches for a "primitive, folk-like" writing, something of the earth, but fails to find it. But it is the very nature of the sacrament that is of most significance: this is "the blood of an art," to repeat the phrase employed by Southern in his unpublished essay from the early fifties, "The Bird Is Gone."

"The Blood of a Wig" is a Hipster variation on the opening of Keats's poem fragment "The Fall of Hyperion"; what is significant in this tale is not the vision achieved through taking the sacrament from the Muse, although that is far more significant than the visions achieved by those who refuse the sacrament. What is of most value is the sacrament and the Muse itself, for they are one and the same.

This tale is Terry Southern's greatest hymn to pagan nature.

Conclusion to Part One: Bedtime Stories

And so we find him on the cusp of new fame and new fortune in the films, which makes this a fine moment to step back and reflect on the "Quality Lit" years, and also begin to gauge what lies ahead.

Southern's was an essentially cinematic imagination, no matter the medium that he chose to work in. His unique perspective was a composite of three main strands of influence: the Texas Blues and Southwestern humor he was steeped in as a child, the cultural milieu that he developed in; European and American literature (his tastes in American literature stem from Poe, who is more European than American in sensibility, which may account for why Southern is never lumped in with his compatriots the Beats, who trace their lineage to the more avowedly American Whitman and Emerson); and finally, American and European film.

What is central and important to an understanding of his vision is the prose: the novels, the short stories, the essays and journalism. His work in film is arguably irrelevant to any serious study of what he had to say, but that "arguably" is there due to the fact that he is remembered at present largely because of what he did in film.

And so his work in Hollywood, though less purely "his" than what he contributed to "The Quality Lit Game," must be studied: it is the source of his enduring fame, and it was the medium he most loved; for as he explained in his essay "When Film Gets Good...," it is the art form that most fully synthesizes all other art forms into a perfect whole.

Of course, it is less instructive to follow his career in Hollywood because, by and large, the work he did was contract work (just as it was for his spiritual forefathers Faulkner, Chandler, and West): others gave him the plots, the themes, the actors; the vision was compromised.

Still, it was what he did with the given themes that render these screenplays interesting. Southern with other people's plots was like Davis or Coltrane with someone else's song: yes, the standard was in there somewhere, giving a base and structure ... but look what was done with it, how it was expanded into new shapes, how new possibilities were opened up.

Take *Dr. Strangelove*: it started life as a hackneyed Cold War melodrama by Peter George, and there's still much of that melodrama in the finished package, framed by Kubrick (note his gritty documentary realism in the bomber sequences, the emerging Kubrick voice in the War Room set, both those features predicting *2001* a few years later)—but Kubrick knew how inadequate George's scenario was.

So he handed his and George's work to Southern, like one might hand a recording of Julie Andrews singing "My Favorite Things" to John Coltrane. The result? A melodrama reborn as something else, a farce infused with the manic glee of the purest black humor.

No doubt the original laughter at *Strangelove* was a trifle hysterical in the wake of the Cuban Missile Crisis—a landscape of fear and dread is where Black Humor flourishes, as it did during the celebrated Black Humor Wave that Southern rode in the early sixties.

That is the humor that Terry Southern practiced, with an artistry reminiscent of Poe: it is a humor that arises out of a dissatisfaction, or downright disgust, with the human (as was the case for, say, Swift) or the social condition—and this was Southern's concern. Just as for music, so there are different modes for humor: the soothing, the confrontational. A genteel humorist like P.G. Wodehouse delights in the idiocies of modern culture; Southern regarded them with, for lack of a better phrase, fear and loathing (a phrase trademarked by one of Southern's artistic progeny, Hunter S. Thompson).

Southern's career in Hollywood must ultimately be considered a tragic (if hardly surprising) failure—the efforts of an artistic Don Quixote in Lotus Land to remake Hollywood in Antonioni's image; or, for that matter, the image of any of the other European surrealist filmmakers he so loved: Fellini, Bergman, et al.

It was a project doomed from the beginning: despite the social earthquakes of the sixties, and an attendant generation of Baby Boomers with cameras descending on L.A., the John Ford populist tradition of linear narrative was too firmly entrenched. Such a method of composition, of storytelling, was anathema to Southern—his skill was the moment, the aphorism, and his creed a philosophy that couldn't accommodate to the strictures of linear three-act plot, nor the comforting messages that Hollywood demanded.

So what is left from Southern's extended time in Hollywood? Traces of a ghost in the Hollywood machine, still haunting the fringes of Independent Film. There is a reason, after all, that it was Steven Soderbergh who purchased The Terry Southern Archives, then donated them to the New York Public Library: a contemporary giant of American Independent Film recognized Southern as a worthy forerunner in his own chosen tradition.

This revolutionary sensibility is still fleetingly glimpsed and heard, and left us the indelible imprints of *Dr. Strangelove*, as well as a handful of others. Take *The Loved One*— try connecting this rude cosmic farce to Waugh; Southern adds whole new dimensions. Or *The End of the Road*— the same goes for John Barth's parochial novel. *Barbarella* turns a French comic strip into a space-age *Candy*, though Carol Southern maintains that the long-lost first draft was a far sweeter fairy tale. Of course, there was also all the anonymous script-doctoring work, on forgettable comedies like *Casino Royale* and *Don't Make Waves*. And there are his memorable twin portraits of breakdown in the Big Easy, *The Cincinnati Kid* and *Easy Rider*; the unpublished "Brothel Sequence" from *Easy Rider*'s first draft demonstrates just how close these screenplays originally were, both stylistically and thematically.

That's what Terry Southern has left behind, from his time in Hollywood: a legacy of other people's tame plots, transformed by the alchemy of his surreal vision into enduring existential statements of despair and black joy.

On the face of it, Southern's output is bewilderingly varied, seeming to lack any consistent style, vision or voice. He swings seemingly at random from genre to genre, from fiction to journalism, to screenplays to poetry; from the serious to the comic; from realism to surrealism. Adhering to the principle that consistency is the hobgoblin of little minds, Southern assiduously avoided assuming one defining voice or method. In an unpublished fragment from his fifties journal, he begins to explain why he did so:

> It used to be that the Young Writer ... was instructed first and foremost, to "*develop a style.*" ... One must take care, as the English novelist, Henry Green, so aptly put it, "not to become trapped in one's own clichés"; and he went on to illustrate how the work of Henry James, for example, through an ever more relentless refinement of style, finally became quite meaningless.
>
> An informative analogy may be recognized, I believe, when considering the work of a great *actor*— Brando or Olivier, for instance.[1]

Southern saw the writer as comparable to the actor, which explains his strong ear for styles of speaking, his knack for dialogue, the cinematic style of his prose, as well as his easy adaptability to the demands of screenplay writing. The act of writing was, for him, the art of putting on and taking off a series of masks; but underneath the play with personae, a consistent vision endures.

In understanding Terry Southern's ultimate significance in the context of the development of post–World War II American literature, it will be even more helpful to compare the Novel with Painting in the same period. If the High Modernist novel, difficult and often forbidding at first glance, can be likened to Abstract Expressionism in its inward gazing, then Southern can be seen as a Pop Artist. He returned the novel to a direct communication with the commercial culture around it: in his work, Southern carefully selects and rearranges pieces of popular culture as the tools whereby he constructs his vision. Albert Goldman has called *Candy* "the prototypical Pop novel,"[2] and Southern himself claimed, in an interview with *Life* in 1964, that Pop Artists "say essentially what I think."[3]

So if Southern's tales, novels, journalism, and screenplays can be viewed as literary Pop Art, what are we to make of other labels that have been applied to him, and how can any of these tags help illuminate exactly what it is that he is trying to "say?" Is there a cohesive vision uniting his disparate styles and media? Or is he simply a mimic, lost in a fun house of warped mirrors?

The term "Black Humor" is vague and meaningless (all humor is "black" to some degree, as Southern himself observed), and the label "Satire" carries far too much specific baggage to accurately apply to Southern; or, indeed, any American writer—it's doubtful that America is a culture that could spawn true satire. It is, and always has been, a relatively permissive culture, which renders satire nearly impossible.

Southern is no satirist—what he wrote was surreal, fantastic, and Decadent comedy in the tradition of Lewis Carroll. Carroll's strange wonderland presented a distorted reflection of Victorian British society, one in which rules of decorum were cut loose from any foundation or justifying reason. Southern's American wonderland of innocents and monsters, grotesques and con men, is an existential looking-glass reflection of mid-to-late twentieth century America, and its own peculiar rules of conduct.

Like Lenny Bruce and William S. Burroughs, Terry Southern was a Jazz humorist, a pure product of his era (the late 1950s and early 1960s), bringing the Hipster sensibility of the Jazz underground culture, of artists like Charlie Parker and Miles Davis, to the attention of mainstream America—a sensibility rooted in alienation, spawning a sense of humor fueled by sarcasm, irony, and the art of the put-on.

Southern is less a satirist than a satyr, going back to satire's primal roots—he is, to borrow imagery from Camille Paglia, a high priest of pagan nature. Guy Grand, his clearest alter-ego—next to Hal in *Texas Summer*—is Pan, god of chaos, come to 1950s plastic America as an embodiment of chthonic nature, with the sole purpose of cracking the carefully preserved mask of social artifice.

The few critics who have tried to bring any sort of scrutiny to bear on the marvelous fairy tale of *The Magic Christian* have usually asked all the wrong questions: is Grand God? The Devil? Is he a social anarchist or Situationist? Back in Southern's day, when any "dirty" book with serious aspirations appeared, defenders were always quick to point out how "moral" it was (see William Styron's blurb on the Grove edition of *Candy*). But Southern, a die-hard existentialist, offered his loyal readers and movie viewers no moral system, save Decadence.

And only a Decadent criticism, of the sort that Paglia helped pioneer in *Sexual Personae*, can properly understand a Decadent artist like Southern. Chapter Ten of *Candy*, the only truly essential portion of the novel and the seed from which the rest of the book sprang, is an absurdist vision of Judeo-Christian culture conquered by Pagan nature. This is the central conflict that has driven Western culture over the last two millennia — and it is here disguised as a luridly hilarious encounter between a sweet, pretty coed and a monstrous, hunchbacked dwarf.

Decadence does not *loathe* culture and extol the virtues of atavistic nature, of course — Carroll and Wilde loved Victorian artifice, and Southern is certainly enamored of American Pop (not to mention Candy Christian). But it does remind us of the (often horrific) power of nature, and the fact that culture is never rooted in Absolute Truths, only arbitrary ones.

The children's tale is Southern's proper storytelling medium (as it was Wilde's, Carroll's, and Poe's), but the only true "moral" of his bedtime stories is that nature always wins out, in the end, over culture — and that the hypocrites who pretend otherwise, do so only to grab on to power, and abuse it.

Southern's Pop Art novels (and tales, and journalism, and screenplays, etc., etc.) — like Warhol's Pop Art paintings — are carefully selected mosaics of junk culture, placed in new contexts to create new meanings. They are also an American version of a certain "mad tradition" in English literature that includes Carroll, Woolf, and Southern's beloved Henry Green. And like his fellow New Journalists, but in his own inimitable fashion, he pointed out a fruitful direction for the novel: back to direct conversation and conflict with the culture (and nature) all around it.

The American Grotesque tales of Southern show us that the Invisible Republic isn't dead, nor is it some archaic, long-lost realm only visited by cultural archeologists. It is a well, a source of renewal and replenishment, as Bob Dylan seems to have discovered in his later career. "The Old Weird America" is alive and can always serve to affect, even transform, America.

Southern played with masks, poses, styles — hence his sense that a writer is like an actor. But he did so with less success as the years wore on, and the jetset lifestyle wore him down. In time, his star faded. Americans hate the stink of failure, and Southern refused to burn out; rather, he faded away. So America forgot him.

If he had found the self-discipline that Zen meditation afforded his friend Peter Matthiessen, perhaps he would not have slipped into the wasteful destruction of his health and his talent — but that is conjecture best left to those who knew him. A reader, however, can offer certain conclusions based on the work. And it seems, in retrospect, that one of his greatest strengths was also ultimately one of his greatest weaknesses, and was responsible for the stilling of his voice — and I speak not of his dependence on alcohol and drugs, but his philosophy as expressed in his art.

We are all, in this life, pilgrims on the road to wisdom — that road out of Axotle that we all take, with varying degrees of success. We are here to learn, and hopefully make the world a little better by doing so; wisdom is composed of equal parts intelligence and compassion, and Southern's work is filled with compassion for the innocents, as well as warnings against those monsters who lack it. One can certainly find a groping towards wisdom in these tales, a movement in the right direction, and therein lies a great deal of their power, even all these decades later.

Existentialism is an important step on that road to wisdom — a point where you take off all of the baggage of accrued cultural ideas and values, and examine it with a detached and clinical air. Sooner or later, however, one has to decide which baggage has value in the journey. You then put it back on, and move on down the road — or you run the risk of remaining stuck in that one spot, forever uncertain which way to turn, what you can take and what you can leave behind, as you strive to make a better world.

This is the state of current academic humanities departments, crippled by the extreme existentialism of deconstruction and warring ideologies ... and this, I suspect, was one of the most crucial artistic dilemmas for Terry Southern. Existentialism awakened his voice when he arrived in Paris, learned from the lectures by Sartre and Camus that he regularly attended. The high priest of nature was exhilarated by existential critiques of accepted cultural values — his voice was set free. And there, the trap was waiting. Without making moral choices that could create a new culture rather than simply critiquing the old, that freedom eventually comes to a dead end, as surely as the road out of Axotle did for his protagonists.

Nature, in Southern's vision, was his means of exposing the lies of a corrupt culture — but where do you go from there? This is the question his work fails to answer. It can be argued that this failure, as much as the substance abuse, accounts for why his great seven-year cycle of artistic productivity came to an end, and little of substance followed.

However, this philosophical flaw was compounded by another weakness in Southern's artistic vision — a structural weakness that was exposed by the very nature of film as a storytelling medium, when he made the leap from page to screen. And this will be discussed in the section that follows, as we follow Southern from the realm of Quality Lit, into the new frontier of Hollywood.

PART TWO: THE MOVIE YEARS

Introduction to Part Two

I. "Whatever Happened to Terry Southern?"

The preceding section of this book, focusing on the early, book-oriented phase of Southern's career, was written several years ago, as was the original draft of this second section, which focuses on the later phase, which is almost entirely devoted to his film work.

In the time since the first draft was completed, I have been working in the film and television industry, a business of which I had no first-hand knowledge when I initially studied Southern's work. The knowledge I have gained from that experience has greatly altered how I gauge both the strengths and the weaknesses of Southern's film work, and has led to substantial revisions of this second section.

What's more, in revising the original draft, I believe that I may have finally solved the mystery that first compelled me to write this biography. This previously unanswered, simple question was asked by so many people I spoke to while researching this book. It's a question pondered by those who knew him, puzzled over by admirers of the books and the films. The question is simple: "Whatever happened to Terry Southern?"

How did this literary bright light get extinguished so quickly, and so fully? I think I do know the answer now, and attempt to explain it in the second section — both the silencing of his voice, and the vanishing of his reputation.

It is a realization that led me to see his early work in a new light as well, but the assessment of that earlier work is not invalidated. It is, instead, altered, by adding to it a new layer: the realization that Southern's failure in his later career is inextricably linked to a fundamental flaw in his artistic vision. The latter is caused by the former. In seeing what is the strength of his early tales, we can also see where he stumbled further on down the road.

II. Working the Muscle

In 1998, Mark Singer published a *New Yorker* article on the genesis of the *Easy Rider* script, in which allegations were examined that Dennis Hopper and Peter Fonda had poorly used Terry Southern—his was the script, theirs the credit and profits. The article was titled "Whose Movie Is It, Anyway?"[1] It's a question that the article never definitively answers, and this is not a slight against Singer's article. Such a question can never be answered.

The brutal fact is that film is always far too much of a collaborative process to sustain any real auteur theory, especially for a screenwriter—if that screenwriter also directs his own scripts, we might detect a cohesive vision from film to film, and suspect that the story told is the story he wanted to tell.

Unfortunately, Southern never did direct—nor even, for the most part, did he inaugurate projects, at least ones that were actually made. He is known for projects in which he was brought on board to pitch in ideas; often the story was well along in the planning stages—Kubrick had his Cold War apocalyptic melodrama, Fonda and Hopper wanted to make a hippie biker *On the Road* (or more properly, *Huckleberry Finn* and the umpteen American road stories that have followed in its wake). Did Southern add spice, clever dialogue and scene ideas? Undoubtedly—but to call any of these scripts uniquely *his* is simply wrong—he was adding decorations on houses that were already well under construction when he came along. None of these stories are his alone—the scripts are all better for his input, but only the fiction and journalism can be said to be truly indicative of his vision and talent.

So why did he do it? He said, when asked, that he was "hooked on the bread,"[2] but that's hardly a satisfying answer. Most others do it to support their "bread" habit as well—but they also make up their own stories, because there's far more bread in originals than in adaptations or script doctoring, however lucrative such jobs may be.

He didn't abandon books for movies purely in the interests of money—he did it, I believe, because he had nothing else to say. His films, however celebrated, are not his, not truly—his work was window dressing. Every job he took showed, on some level, a creative well that had run dry—but as long as folks like Kubrick and Hopper brought him on board to spice up their stories, he could not only make money but also hide the fact that he had no stories of his own to tell.

Southern *had* a vision in his early career, as I have tried to systematically demonstrate in the previous section. But a vision, a philosophy, does not guarantee a strong story — and film is merciless when narrative is weak. It simply does not work without a strong story spine.

Southern abandoned the field of novels, which in its "Quality Lit" aspect had likewise abandoned narrative, some time before; he also abandoned journalism, which relies on ideas, but also reportage, a labor that seemed to hold little appeal for Southern. He then went to the one medium that would expose his greatest flaw as a writer: his lack of narrative sense, of story structure, of spines and dramatic arcs.

Film has far more in common with pulp fiction than it does with Quality Lit — even the "quality" films *need* strong story structure. For instance, Robert McKee's "Story Spectrum" (as explained in his screenwriter's manual *Story*) allows for the sort of "story" that Southern told in his novels, which would, under McKee's criteria, fall under his label of "Antiplot." However, McKee warns that the "meat, potatoes, pasta, rice and couscous of world cinema" (p. 46) is found in what he calls "the Archplot," the "Classical Design" that shapes Hollywood's classic three-act structure: protagonist in search of a goal, who faces conflicts along the way.[3] This is the spine and skeleton of Hollywood film, the shape that pulls in audiences and investors. This is the type of plotting that a Hollywood scriptwriter must practice.

Faced with this challenge, Southern dug in his heels and refused (some might say perversely) to create strong visual stories — and the work stopped coming. Perhaps it's not fair to say he refused, but perhaps more kind than saying he simply *couldn't*, although I frankly suspect the latter.

Film exposed the flaw that his earlier work could hide: to put it bluntly, Southern simply wasn't very good at making up stories, as opposed to moments, to gags, to sketches. Coming face to face with this realization (slowly, over the course of about ten years, from the mid-sixties to the mid-seventies) seems to have mortified him, frozen him in his tracks. It's as if he lost all of his confidence, even for the forms (short story and journalism) where he had shown real promise, and had made a real impact.

Gripped with stage fright, he lost the ability to write, retreating into drugs and alcohol, endlessly rehashing his "greatest hits" when called upon to write anything new, and desperately trying to score big and simultaneously hide his inability to write any more by nailing down an adaptation of somebody else's work — so gripped by fear and uncertainty that he even bungled all of these, finding no sure thing in hiding behind someone else's story work.

Prose of the non-pulp variety no longer values narrative highly — film values little else. Film showed Southern what he couldn't do — tell a compelling story — and he never recovered from the blow. Even his greatest story of the late period, "Heavy Put-Away," was given to him: an actual anecdote related to him by John Calley, that he then polished into a cold hard diamond of nihilism.

That's my take on the mystery of what happened to Terry Southern, literary darling for a day or so in the late fifties and early sixties. Others maintain that drug and alcohol abuse were the prime culprits, but I think they were solace from the real problem — maybe I'm wrong.

Maybe I'm wrong as well in theorizing that film gave him stage fright by exposing his artistic weakness — maybe he'd already realized it for himself, knew that his well of ideas wasn't deep enough. Marvin Barrett's article "The Southern Way of Death," written in 1965, notes a worrying tendency already present in Southern to rehash his best bits — but again, I think *Strangelove* may have already started Southern in thinking that there was trouble, and in *The Loved One*, we see the first manifestations of that fear. In retrospect, his greatest popular success was also the moment of his undoing.

Southern's vision of nature overthrowing culture was strong — it lent his voice and his tales a unique vitality. And yet he could not or would not master the basic storytelling techniques and mechanics that would enable him to encase that vision in sturdy, long-running vehicles that would capture the attention of story-hungry America (just look at our seemingly insatiable appetite for films and television — we are gluttons for story). William S. Burroughs was fortunate to have associates such as Jack Kerouac, Allen Ginsberg and James Grauerholz, willing to mold his sketchy vignettes into cosmic science-fiction epics. Southern had no such partners in crime, and going it alone artistically, he didn't make it. This aspect of the fading reputation — having a caretaker to preserve the legacy, as Burroughs did — will be discussed more fully in a later chapter as well.

Stephen King might be correct, in his book *On Writing*, when he says that storytelling is a muscle like all the others.[4] Keep exercising it and it gets easier to use; and it's not as if Southern didn't realize this. He and Allen Ginsberg conducted a decades-long correspondence arguing the merits of careful composition versus Beat spontaneity, with Southern reminding Ginsberg in one letter that "surely there is, in almost any endeavor, such a thing as acquired skill and craft."[5] So why did it get harder and harder for Southern to apply the skill and craft he'd worked so hard to master?

Again, who truly knows? This is all supposition based on long study and rumination about the works and circumstances, but the more that I test my theory against his writings and life, the sturdier this supposition seems: Southern had a vision of nature's supremacy over culture, and thought that would be enough to sustain him. But in the end, culture bit back, revealing the lopsided quality of his vision.

Without the rigors imposed by the cultural vehicle of Story, the chaotic nature — literally — of his vision overran the banks, diffusing and dispersing in an unfocused career, dabbling in a medium completely unsuited to such a vision and such a visionary. Nature, uncontained by culture, consumed him, and he sank. Southern, in his tales, favored nature over culture — it's as if he missed the point of his hero Sade, who was lampooning Rousseau, not agreeing with him. The truth is, nature and culture need each other, endlessly sparring in a necessary dance, instinct incomplete without rationality, and vice versa. This is one lesson that Southern's career can teach us ... if we choose to see it that way.

This will be discussed more fully in the context of the second half of Southern's career, in the pages that follow. The screenplays and stories that fill The Terry Southern Archives (and that even occasionally leak out into public view, as the years go by) give us a self-portrait of the artist in decline, as the culture transformed around him. Caught in the double bind of needing the order of art to present his triumph of nature, he was also faced by the disappearance of the culture he attacked, while he was being attacked by that cruel aspect of nature known as aging. It was a further ironic turn of the screw that he needed a culture to focus his vision ... a vision that was being gradually sapped by nature.

All of this is what makes the later work, the writings of The Movie Years, so fascinating ... as well as heartbreaking.

10

The Great Stanley K.

Southern's *Esquire*-generated interview with Kubrick "took place in the New York office of Harris-Kubrick Productions,"[1] and is surprisingly straight by Southern's normally outlandish *Esquire* standards. There is no put-on opening, but rather an adulatory homage by Southern to a director who has "created a body of work ... as richly diverse as it is subsantial."[2] As it survives in manuscript, it's a straight transcript of the taped interview — or so Southern claims.

In fact, the interview had begun a few months before, but the manuscript, which remained unpublished for the next forty years, was fine-tuned while Southern and Kubrick were collaborating on *Dr. Strangelove*. What remains interesting in the interview as it survived is their discussion of the (at that time) recently completed *Lolita* — and in particular, Peter Sellers' role in it:

> INT: This role, the role of Peter Sellers as Quilty and his disguise throughout the film seems unique. I don't recall any other instance in movies of such an elaborate combination of the Comic-Grotesque.
>
> KUBRICK: Well, that aspect of the picture interests me very much — I've always thought, for example, that Kafka could be very funny, or actually is very funny — I mean, like a comic nightmare. And I think that Sellers, in the murder scene and, in fact, in the whole characterization, is like something out of a bad dream, but a funny one. I'm very pleased with the way that came off, and I think it opens up an avenue, as far as I'm concerned, of telling certain types of stories in ways which haven't been explored in movies.[3]

The "avenue" that Sellers' role opened up was the avenue of The Grotesque, which Southern and Kubrick would then explore together in their subsequent collaboration, *Dr. Strangelove*. Though *Esquire* had assigned Southern to interview Kubrick, it was Sellers who truly brought them together as a creative team. Sellers had first been exposed to Southern's work through their mutual friend Jonathan Miller, who, in addition to being a practicing medical doctor, was also a comedian of sorts, being a member (along with Dudley Moore, Peter Cook and Alan Bennett) of the British satirical revue Beyond the Fringe. Southern later recalled:

> ... During the fifties, I was friends with the English writer Jonathan Miller. I knew him for quite a while before I discovered that he was a doctor — that is to say, the kind of doctor who could write you a prescription for something like Seconal — at which point I besieged him to become my personal physician and perhaps suggest something for my chronic insomnia. To encourage his acceptance of me as a patient, I gave him a copy of my recently published novel *The Magic Christian* ... Miller was impressed, at least enough to recommend it to his friend Peter Sellers. Peter liked it — to the improbable degree that he went to the publishers and bought a hundred copies to give to his friends on their birthdays, Christmas and so on. One such friend, as luck would have it, was Stanley Kubrick.[4]

It's likely that the normally reclusive Kubrick only agreed to be interviewed by Southern in the first place because of his favorable impression of the novelist's skill, after reading *The Magic Christian*. Subsequent to being interviewed by Southern, and to the release of *Lolita*, Kubrick then set to work on his next film: a straightforward, melodramatic thriller about imminent nuclear war called *Red Alert*, based on the novel by Peter George.

Kubrick had been working with George, struggling to make a suitable screenplay out of the novel, when one morning he "woke up and realized that nuclear war was too outrageous, too fantastic, to be treated in any conventional manner."[5] Realizing that the only proper way to deal with the threat of nuclear war was as "some kind of hideous joke"[6] — that is, the sort of joke epitomized by the then-current vogue for Black Humor and the Absurd, as practiced by such individuals as Lenny Bruce, Samuel Beckett, William S. Burroughs and Terry Southern (the Black Humor trend will be discussed more fully below).

So Kubrick put in his call to Southern at Blackberry River Farm. Years later, Southern was asked in an interview how he got into the screenplay writing trade. He recalled:

> I was supposed to be doing an interview with Stanley Kubrick for one of the magazines — *Esquire*, probably — in New York, about 1962, after he had finished with *Lolita*. He was on his way back to London and was just here a few days. Well, it turned out that he'd read *The Magic Christian* and dug it, so somehow or other we get into this rather heavy rap — about *death* and *infinity* and the *origin of time* — you know the sort of thing. We never got through the interview, but the point is we met a few times, had a few laughs and some groovy rap ... and then about three months later, he called from London and asked me to come over and work on *Strangelove*. So that was how I got into screenwriting....[7]

In a subsequent interview, when asked what it was like working with Kubrick, Southern recalled:

> Well, at the time, I very aware of the novelty of it, working in the medium and that kind of situation. It was the first time, I think, in my life that I'd gone any-

where with a sense of purpose. I mean, I'd always traveled, I'd made about ten trips back and forth, but just aimless, with no justification except having the G.I. Bill and using it as a means to be there. It was the first time I'd gone anywhere and paid for it. It was just the principal of the thing — very satisfying, very interesting and almost unbelievable to be moving about like that.[8]

Years after these interviews, when recalling this decisive event — as the opening paragraph of the opening chapter of his memoir *Making It Hot for Them*— he vividly recalled Kubrick getting in touch with him and requesting him to come to London to work on the film:

> A death gray afternoon in early December and the first snows of the New England winter had just begun. Outside my window, between the house and the banks of the frozen stream, great silver butterfly flakes floated and fluttered in the failing light. Focusing beyond the stream past where the evening mist had begun to rise, it was possible, with a scintilla of imagination, to make out the solemnly moving figures in the Bradbury story about the Book People (*Farenheit 451*); in short, a magical moment — suddenly undone by the ringing of a telephone somewhere in the house. And then, closer at hand, my wife's voice in a curious singsong:
> "It's Big Stan Kubrick on the line from 'Old Smoke.'"[9]

Southern claims, in the next paragraph, that when this call came, he had never met Kubrick, which of course is not true, as he himself stated in previous interviews. But he was always first and foremost a fiction-maker, and this certainly works as a dramatic moment.

Even more curious and telling, in the passage quoted above, is how he conjures a magical moment of stillness on the farm, suddenly undone by the harsh ring of the telephone. Looking back from the vantage point at which he wrote this piece (the mid-nineties), after almost thirty years of disappointment and failure in the film industry, the reader cannot fail to detect a hint of nostalgia for what that pastoral evocation represents: a time when he was a rising star in the literary firmament, full of focused creative fire, before the lure of Hollywood Mammon destroyed that concentration, and broke that wave forever.

Why else that mention of "Bradbury's book people," those characters in *Farenheit 451* who protected books against those who would destroy them? Carol Southern recalls Terry telling her, near the end of his life, "I never should have given up writing books." She saw his subsequent career as a tragedy of talent and promise squandered when he forsook the writing of books for the making of movies — nearly all of which were never made.

Southern, it would appear, saw it the same way — and he saw, in the moment of this late December afternoon, not only the start of his involvement in his most famous project, but also the end of his greatest phase as a writer.

But that darkness was down the road: when Kubrick called, his biggest popular success was immediately before him. A series of letters to his "True Darl" (that is, Carol) written on the fly from the Pennsylvania Railroad Station, from the airplane, from the Mount Royal Hotel in London, convey not only a touching love for True Darl and "Inf," not only concern for the farm ("You are doing such fine work with our fencing, etc. I am sorry I did not leave you with more firewood..."),[10] but also tremendous excitement over his new job — which, as he said, gave him a sense of purpose for the first time in his life: "Things are going well here, but very busy the first two weeks on complete revision of the script — necessary to complete in order to get best actors to accept parts."[11] Little wonder that he continued to seek renewals of this experience, pursuing subsequent film projects rather than returning to the loneliness of his book writing.

Upon arriving in London, after a brief stay at the Mount Royal Hotel, the production crew found Southern a flat in Knightsbridge, not far from Kubrick's own home. In an essay entitled "Memories of *Dr. Strangelove*," written to commemorate the twentieth anniversary of the film (published in the July 1983 issue of *The Movies*), Southern recalled their working method together:

> Dark London winter mornings, and I would get to Kubrick's place in Knightsbridge at about five A.M., then we would be in the back seat, but it was more like a small room than a seat — of this grand old Bentley, for the long ride to Shepperton Studio. Outside it was pitch black, cold and fantastic with the all-enveloping fog. Inside it was warm, glowing with peach-color Bentley sconce light from the corners behind, and the script pages spread across two table tops which folded out in front of us. With the driver's partition closed, we could have been in a cozy compartment on the Orient Express, working on a scene to be filmed that morning — already written, of course, perhaps many times rewritten — but never really perfect. It was a magical time.
>
> "Now then," Kubrick might begin, perhaps only half in jest, "what is it we're trying to say with this scene?"
>
> "A comment about some poignant aspect of *la condition humaine*?" I might venture. "Just a shot in the dark, of course..."[12]

Southern would suggest an idea for the scene, a comment by one of the characters:

> I crossed my fingers. Would Stan go for it, or was another tongue-lashing on tap? I watched in excitement as his great chess-playing poet's brow furrowed in considering the madcap turn of phrase:
>
> "Hmm," he mused, "Yes ... yes, I believe he would say that, wouldn't he?"
>
> Hats off to the grand chess-playing poet of this big twentieth — may the force be with him still![13]

Kubrick was fanatical in his zest for chess — when Southern first met him, Kubrick was at the desk in his office, playing against his German computerized chess opponent, with a plate indicating that the game had progressed to the "Grand Master Level." "I have perfected my endgame to such a degree that I can now elude the stratagems of this co-called 'opponent,'"¹⁴ Kubrick told Southern, who marveled at Kubrick's tightly organized manner of thinking, so different from his own.

Despite the differences, they got along very well. As Southern later told an interviewer:

> Stanley himself is a strange kind of genius.... I'd always had a notion that people in power positions in movies must be hacks and fools, and it was very impressive to meet someone who wasn't. He thinks of himself as a "filmmaker"—his idol is Chaplin—and so he's down on the idea of director. He would like, and it's understandable, to have his films just say "A Film By Stanley Kubrick." Anything that is exterior to that is intrusive, fucks up the ideal of the filmmaker. Even though he's very conscientious and generous in other regards, he has this kind of perfectionist feeling that a movie should be the work of one person, and he tries to cover the whole thing from beginning to end.¹⁵

This raises, again, the thorny issue of collaboration, the problem that plagues discussion of Southern's film work—and what Southern is here referring to is Kubrick's desire to be recognized (however falsely) as the sole creative force behind his films. It is an issue that eventually drove a wedge between the two men.

When *Dr. Strangelove* was released in 1964, the advertisements billed it as coming "From the Writer of *Candy*." Strange it may seem now, but at that time, Southern was a more famous figure than Kubrick, and the producers were eager to capitalize on his brand recognition. The campaign brought on Kubrick's wrath, and after a heated exchange of letters between Kubrick's lawyers and the studio, the ad campaign was dropped. According to Carol, Southern "was mortified,"¹⁶ not wanting to offend Kubrick in any way and only too glad to have the ads terminated. Though Southern and Kubrick remained friends until Southern's death, the incident threw a certain chill into their relationship that never quite dissipated.

As Kubrick's biographer John Baxter noted: "To Diane Johnson, Kubrick summarized Southern's contribution as 'Terry would drive by in a cab and toss out a few pages.' Asked why he gave him credit at all if his contribution was so minor, he told her, 'I guess I was being generous ... but I thought it might help him get more work if he wanted it.' Southern later countered this by claiming: '...What he neglected to say about his completed script is quite simple: it wasn't funny'" (p. 194).¹⁷

To this, Baxter responds: "Southern's assertion that the first script of *Strangelove* wasn't funny rings more than true. Kubrick is not known as a generator of laughs." Moreover, he goes on to argue that Southern's contribution to the film "was crucial, beginning with its retitling (from *Two Hours to Doom*) as *Doctor Strangelove, or How I Learned to Stop Worrying and Love the Bomb*, an adaptation of the facetious mock–Edwardian titles pioneered in *Esquire* and quickly picked up by Hollywood" (p. 177).[18] Southern would later go on to employ the "mock-Edwardian" title on several occasions, such as "Heavy Put-Away, or, A Hustle Not Wholly Devoid of a Certain Grossness, Granted," published in *The Paris Review* in 1975, and "Tito Bandini, or, Doggy Dope Run," published in *High Times* in 1978.

Baxter also tells us:

> ... The intellectual and physical similarity of Adam (Ken Adam, the film's set designer), Southern and Kubrick became more apparent. All three preferred severe black clothing and a conversational style of reticent understatement. All shared the same dark hair, heavy eyebrows, and hawk-like profile, as did Peter Sellers; visitors to the set said that Kubrick, Southern and Sellers might have been brothers.
>
> Adam ... was less enamored of Southern (than of Kubrick), especially when the writer, after his first look at the giant War Room set in January 1963, drawled, "It looks great, Ken — but will it dress?" [pp. 179–180].[19]

Sellers eventually played three roles in the film, but was originally slated to play four, the fourth being the role of Major "King" Kong, which was ultimately played by Slim Pickens, a former rodeo clown from Texas whom Kubrick had met on the set of the film *One-Eyed Jacks*. In an attempt to master the Texas twang necessary for the part, Sellers asked Southern to record all of Kong's dialogue. Sellers listened to the tapes every day with headphones, playing them over and over, yet failed to ever master the drawl, forcing him to finally relinquish the role to Pickens.

The film originally concluded with a sequence devised by Southern — a giant pie fight in the War Room. However, in 1995, Southern told an audience at Yale that Kubrick cut the sequence because "everyone was having too good a time."[20] Though the filmed sequence was lost, it stuck with Southern, who eventually retooled it for the climax of *Grossing Out*, an unproduced 1980 screenplay about the arms race that was commissioned by Sellers and director Hal Ashby.

Grossing Out concludes with a group of generals, in a set reminiscent of *Strangelove*'s War Room, gleefully opening weapons packages like children on Christmas morning. On reading it, one has to conclude that, obvious as it is, Kubrick was right to excise the similar *Strangelove* conclusion.

Kubrick desired sole authorial credit, but nothing in his career before or after even faintly resembles *Dr. Strangelove*, while it has distinctly Southern touches throughout, and though it can never be clearly established who wrote what, certain elements of the screenplay are unmistakably Southern-style contributions, touches far more reminiscent of the author's work than

Kubrick's: Kong's Texan dialogue, character names like "Burpelson" and "General Jack D. Ripper" (not to mention Major "King" Kong), and even more so the speeches about "precious bodily fluids" and "pre-versions."

All these smack of Southern, making this screenplay the best film translation of Southern's vision, the most clearly representative of Southern's authorial voice in its "high speed" mode. Unfettered by any creative interference from others, the film clearly shows Southern playing his jazz improvisations on Kubrick's melodrama — it was "Red Giant on Our Doorstep!" sprung to life, imagined on the screen much as Southern sought to work his own changes on the Bay of Pigs invasion in the pages of *The Realist*.

Though it gained a reputation as political satire, it in fact said very little about the politics of the day — it is, rather, broad farce, with a cast of rampaging generals and doddering presidents, rather than cheating husbands and shrewish wives; that such talented actors as Sellers and Sterling Hayden could imbue their roles with such depth, and that Kubrick's visual sense could imbue the burlesque with such stark, shadowed beauty, does not alter the fact that the script is far more Feydeau than Joly. This is not weakness but strength: it is the very quality that makes it timeless, still delighting audiences long after the end of the Cold War.

Besides *Dr. Strangelove*, two other events that took place during the filming bore later fruit for both Southern and Kubrick. Southern arranged a screening of a pornographic film for the conservative Kubrick, in the privacy of Kubrick's own home. A group assembled to watch the film, after which Kubrick observed to Southern that "It would be great if someone made a movie like that under studio conditions."[21]

This planted the seed of an idea in Southern's head, one that would fully flower a few years later as the novel *Blue Movie*, in which the protagonist is clearly modeled on Kubrick — and Kubrick himself almost filmed the novel. That is, until Kubrick's wife read the novel and announced to her husband, "If you film this, I'll never speak to you again."[22] Exit Kubrick as director. Southern, disappointed in Kubrick for backing out, ruefully observed that "It turned out he has an ultraconservative attitude to things sexual" (p. 248).[23]

The other incident that had repercussions down the line was that while in London for the filming, Southern read a new novel called *A Clockwork Orange*, by Anthony Burgess. Highly enthused about it, Southern gave copies to Kubrick and to William S. Burroughs, both of whom likewise became fervent admirers of the novel. Southern optioned the rights to the novel and collaborated on a screenplay with the photographer Michael Cooper (intending it as a vehicle for Mick Jagger) — but at the time, although he read the completed script, Kubrick wasn't interested in making the film. It was only years later, after completing *2001*'s utopian vision of the future, that Kubrick became more amenable to Burgess's dystopian vision.

At this point, Southern's option had lapsed — and though he offered to collaborate with Kubrick on another draft of the screenplay, Kubrick refused, stating that he wanted to write it by himself. The resulting Kubrick screenplay, it should be noted, is striking in its similarity to the Southern/Cooper draft.

Despite these ups and downs, Southern and Kubrick stayed in contact and remained friendly through the ensuing years — in fact, immediately after completion of *Strangelove*, Kubrick indicated, in a letter to Southern, that he was open to the idea of another collaboration right away:

> August 1st, 1963
>
> Dear Terry,
>
> Thank you very much for the check. All goes very well here. Cutting proceeds smoothly. Harry Salzman is still tumulting. I haven't come up with any brilliancies yet for a new story.... For Christ's sake, if you see anything you think might be good, do let me know. Atomic warfare, science fiction, mad sex relationships — something along those lines — possibly all three might be fun! What are you working on now? Where do we stand on *Esquire*? How is Carol and the lad?
>
> Regards,
> Stanley[24]

In the early eighties, Kubrick tried to entice Southern into another collaboration, hoping to partner up for a film adaptation of Arthur Schnitzler's novel *Traumnovelle*, which he eventually filmed in 1999 as *Eyes Wide Shut*. After reading the novel, Southern responded in writing with a screenplay fragment reminiscent less of Schnitzler than *Flash and Filigree*, focusing on a maniacal, sex-crazed gynecologist attacking his patients. Kubrick didn't even bother responding to that effort, merely looking elsewhere for his collaborator on the project (the job eventually went to Frederic Raphael).

During the filming of *Strangelove*, Carol and Nile had come to live with Terry in London, where they were frequent guests at the Kubrick home. They had left America in obscurity. Now, the family returned to Blackberry River Farm, to find Southern nearly a household name.

11

Riding the Black Humor Wave

Candy had finally been legitimately published at home, as part of the 1964 Supreme Court ruling on obscenity that also at last permitted publication of *Ulysses*, *Tropic of Cancer* and *Naked Lunch*, among others. For six years, after its 1958 publication in Paris, *Candy* had only been smuggled into the U.S., to be distributed among friends or sold under the counter at the Gotham Book Mart. Now legal, it shot to the top of the *New York Times* bestseller list, where it remained for over thirty weeks—not that Southern made any money from it:

> ... just before the six-month royalty statement was due, Girodias made a deal with some fellow for a pirated edition, so the royalties were held up indefinitely ... it was one of those things where if a book in English is first published outside the U.S., you have to apply for something called an ad interim copyright, which is good for six months, then has to be renewed every six months until it's published here. Well, we knew nothing about this, but I guess Girodias did, because a whole swarm of paperback publishers started putting it out fly-by-night.[1]

Though it made no money for Southern, it certainly expanded his reputation, as he and Hoffenberg had dropped the "Maxwell Kenton" pseudonym and taken full credit for the novel. According to Southern, they had originally used the nom de plume because "Mason ... had an attack of conscience and said 'Man, I've decided I don't want my mother to know about this book....'"[2] Having overcome this "attack," Southern and Hoffenberg's names rode up the best-seller lists.

When it appeared, it caused a minor sensation. Many reviewers dismissed it—but Alfred Chester, in *Book Week*, warned that "...what the reader should be on guard against is that posture now being assumed in some dubious American circles (*Time Magazine* is a case in point) which pretends very noisily and very frequently to be already bored with sex in literature. This pretense of boredom is, in fact, a concealment of outrage for a sexually free people."[3]

Michael O'Donoghue, later the editor of *National Lampoon* and one of the original stable of writers for *Saturday Night Live*, was working as a clerk in Brentano's bookstore in Manhattan when *Candy* was released. Southern was O'Donghue's self-professed idol, and *Candy* was a book he relentlessly promoted in the store, sometimes to the dismay of his customers: "Older women would come in and say, 'I'd like a book for my niece/daughter.' And I'd say, 'How old is she?' 'About sixteen or seventeen.' So I'd say, 'Oh, I have just the book. It's about a girl her age who has all sorts of adventures and stuff, and she'll just love it.' And then I'd sell them *Candy*, by Terry Southern. One woman came back livid with rage, but I know that book changed some girls' lives forever."[4]

Candy—and *Strangelove*—became part of a cultural wave that was breaking in 1964: a pop culture phenomenon that came to be known as the "Black Humor Wave," an evolution of the "Sick Humor" phenomenon of the fifties that had already produced such curious cultural artifacts as "dead baby jokes" and the career of Lenny Bruce, dubbed by the press "The Sickest of the Sick." Bruce was still riding high in 1964 (although drug and legal troubles were catching up to and would soon overtake him), and his fellow "Black Humorists" now included such novelists as Kurt Vonnegut, William S. Burroughs, Thomas Pynchon and Joseph Heller, whose first novel, *Catch-22*, had also just been published.

In May of 1964, the *New York Times* hailed Black Humor as "the one genuinely new post-war development in American literature,"[5] and even staid *Time Magazine*, perhaps feeling chastened by Alfred Chester, gave its approval of the wave by early 1965. Robert Scholes's study *The Fabulators* appeared in 1967, giving the academic blessing with a scholarly analysis of the Black Humor "Genre," a group of novels that included (besides *Candy* and *Catch-22*) such novels as *Slaughterhouse Five*, *Cat's Cradle*, *V.* and *The Magic Christian*.[6]

But it is Conrad Knickerbocker's essay "Humor with a Mortal Sting" that remains the pivotal essay on the Black Humor phenomenon of the early sixties. Appearing in the *New York Times* Book Review of September 27, 1964, it continues to map the terrain that Southern began charting the year before, in "Toward the Ethics of a Golden Age." The Existential Everyman novel that was all the rage in the fifties, perfected by such genre stalwarts as Saul Bellow and Bernard Malamud, was dying out as a popular fad—as a result, "certain critics," Knickerbocker warns:

> ... may tell us the spirit of alienation — a vitalizing force in much of our best literature — is dying, and that American fiction is moving into a period of accommodation with things as they are.... As always, trying to hear what has already sounded,

critics tend to ignore new thunder on the horizon.... The Black Humorists have become keepers of conscience, strident, apt, they challenge the hypnotists and hysterics, they urge choices on us. Amid the banality, the emptiness and excess, they offer the terrors and possibilities of self-knowledge.[7]

Knickerbocker moves beyond the confines of Southern's essay, which focuses solely on literary figures — Knickerbocker connects the Black Humorists with such popular culture phenomena as "the Pop Art put-ons of Roy Lichtenstein and Andy Warhol." This would help clarify a somewhat obtuse comment from *Life* magazine's profile of Southern, included in a photo caption: "In Manhattan gallery, Southern discusses Lichtenstein's Pop-Art painting, which he admires. 'Pop Artists,' he says, 'say essentially what I think.'"[8]

In 1964, Knickerbocker praised the Black Humorists for their "morality"; in 1995, Steven Weisenburger found less in that area to commend. In his book *Fables of Subversion: Satire in the American Novel 1930–1980*, he buries the Black Humorists with his memorial chapter "What Was Black Humor?"[9]

In the chapter, Weisenburger chastises them for failing to ever develop any social scheme to counter the prevailing social agendas they attacked. It can be argued that the phrase "social agenda" is merely the liberal nineties equivalent of "morality," which would find Knickerbocker and Weisenburger at sharp odds regarding the moral stance of the Black Humorists.

Albert Goldman's essay "Boy-Man Schlemiel" also surveys the Black Humor phenomenon, noting that in *Candy*, Southern's "satiric strategy is identical with [Lenny] Bruce's. From beginning to end, this novel is a rollicking revenge on mass culture illusions" (p. 185).[10] Goldman wasn't always so kind to *Candy*: in his essay "Pop Is Mom," he finds the novel "a giant step along the current road of cultural regression" (p. 335).[11]

So why all the schizophrenic double-takes?

Where Goldman's first essay traces Black Humor's roots in Jewish humor, his second essay goes down Knickerbocker's road, trying to find a "useful analogy between Pop Art and writing" (p. 333), and thereby explain Southern's cryptic pronouncement to *Life*:

> To my mind, the literary equivalent of the Pop-Artist's refusal to respect cultural values and to give his work "meaning," his isolation of a subject and intensification of its energic essence — all this equates with a writer's decision to treat violent, perverse and criminal actions in a style of such illusory detachment that the reader is unable to react morally or sympathetically, but is invited instead to respond amorally and empathetically, almost, but not quite, the way he responds to the lower case "pop" of detective thrillers, gangster movies, horror comics and the most explosive animated cartoons. The manic intensity of the comics and cartoons, their "cheery nihilism" (to borrow a convenient phrase of Susan Sontag's), is, in fact, characteristic of several recent novels; chief among them is Terry Southern and Mason Hoffenberg's *Candy*— the prototypical Pop Novel [p. 333].[12]

Goldman goes on to compare *Candy* and *Naked Lunch*, deciding that "Burroughs writes as a sinister voyeur, Southern and Hoffenberg as hysterical exhibitionists. But both are buffered by the use of fantasy and humor, which disarm the reader's moral judgments."[13]

Ultimately, Goldman faults *Candy* because "The authors of *Candy* found a formula for safely violating the taboos of civilization by treating perversion in a childish manner appropriate to its psychological origin and infantile sexuality.... Though written in 1957, its absolute contemporaraneity can be gauged from current sales of 2.5 million copies" (p. 334).[14]

In other words, the controversy over *Candy* can be divided into two camps: those who, like Knickerbocker, found in Southern's Pop Art a living morality to counter the prevailing desiccated morality of what they used to call "mass culture"; and those like Weisenburger, who found the novel lacking any moral or social scheme, and, also like Goldman, found it childishly evasive of taking any such stand. And then there were readers like O'Donoghue, who treasured the novel simply for its shock value.

All of them missed the point, which is that Pop Art is Decadent. As such, it neither evades nor embraces morality, but simply perceives morality and social schemes as part and parcel of a cultural artifice that seeks to evade or conquer nature. Decadence pits nature against culture and knows that, in the end, nature is always the winner.

It would seem, however, that not many literary critical readers in 1964 were viewing *Candy*, or any of Southern's other work, from a Decadent perspective — only card-carrying fellow Decadents like William S. Burroughs and Keith Richards could appreciate Southern's vision for what it was, without decrying a lack of social agenda, or insisting that it was at heart a reassuringly moral lesson he was teaching us, after all.

Goldman comes closest to discerning Southern's Decadent tradition, even as he damns the novel, when he observes that "*Candy*, far from being another *Candide*, turns out a Terry Toons version of the Marquis De Sade, in which even the most insane acts of sexual cruelty have the exhilarating effect of good, clean fun" (pp. 333–334).[15]

He's very nearly perceiving what Candy is, yet he's still disappointed that it is Sade, not Voltaire — scorning its cartoon nature, like a literary critical variation on Dr. Warner.

The unresolved "morality" debate failed to keep the book from selling, however — the Black Humor Wave had arrived, and Southern was riding it to his moment of glory: because hot on the heels of *Candy*'s publication, *Dr. Strangelove* was released.

12

The Southern Cult

Dr. Strangelove's release in February 1964 kicked off what was indisputably Southern's greatest year, in which he became a genuine pop culture celebrity, no longer just an underground figure. Suddenly, everything gelled: all the long years of hard work and obscurity paid off with his name on movie marquees and book best-seller lists. He was being profiled by *Life*, *Newsweek* and *Time*: Southern was the hipster's hipster, a superstar finally getting his fifteen minutes of fame.

The director Tony Richardson, fresh off his tremendous success with the film version of the Henry Fielding novel *Tom Jones*, was now in Los Angeles, working on a film adaptation of Evelyn Waugh's novel *The Loved One*, collaborating on the screenplay with British expatriate Christopher Isherwood. Isherwood, a friend of Henry Green, was aware of Southern's work — and with the release of *Dr. Strangelove*, so was Richardson.

Isherwood sensed that this seeming heir apparent to Nathanael West might offer invaluable input for enhancing and updating Waugh's 1930s send-up of Los Angeles lifestyles, and so he suggested to Richardson that they bring Southern out to Los Angeles, as a third collaborator. Richardson readily agreed.

With the extraordinary success of *Candy* and *Dr. Strangelove*, 1964 was as good as it got: a happy home life with Carol and Nile, a proliferation of well-received journalism in *Esquire* and *The Realist*, and now, the promise of Hollywood fame and fortune on the horizon. Little could Southern have guessed that his fifteen minutes were soon to be up.

Los Angeles, with its promise of easy money and widespread recognition for his work, would ultimately prove to be his undoing. His arrival there in 1964, at the height of his powers, would precipitate a long decline from which Southern would never recover. Southern had concluded his unpublished Kubrick interview with the question, "Will Success Spoil Stanley Kubrick?," to which Kubrick had tersely replied "Fifth Amendment."[1]

12. The Southern Cult 141

Success and the seduction of Hollywood most certainly did spoil Southern, but all that lay in the future.

So Southern packed up and boarded a train for Los Angeles; he was accompanied by an old friend from Paris, the novelist William Styron, who recounted their cross-country journey in his memorial essay about Southern, "Transcontinental with Tex" (published in the spring 1996 issue of *Paris Review*, part of the portfolio of memorial essays for Southern).

Styron felt that one of the reasons their friendship endured through the years was that:

> Like me, Terry was an apostate Southern Protestant, and I think that one of the reasons we hit it off well together was that we both viewed the Christian religion — at least insofar as we had experienced its Puritanical rigors — as a conspiracy to deny its adherents their fulfillment as human beings. It magnified not the glories of life, but the consciousness of death, exploiting humanity's innate terror of the timeless void. High among its prohibitions was sexual pleasure, and contemplating Americans stretched on the rack of their hypocrisy, as they tried to reconcile their furtive adulteries with their churchgoing pieties, Terry laid the groundwork for some of his most biting and funniest satire [p. 224].[2]

Styron had not seen much of Terry since Southern had left Paris for Geneva:

> ... but back in the States, Terry was very much a part of the Quality Lit scene in New York during the next twenty years, frequenting places like George Plimpton's and later Elaine's, where I too hung out from time to time. He had great nighttime stamina, and we closed up many bars together [p. 218].[3]

It was Southern's idea to take the train because, as he pointed out to Styron, "...it would be a precious slice of Americana soon to be foreclosed to travelers in a hurry, and [Styron] thought it a fine idea" (p. 219). Southern, Styron and Styron's wife, Rose, stopped off in Chicago to meet up with their old friend Nelson Algren, author of the novels *The Man with the Golden Arm* and *A Walk on the Wild Side*, amongst others, and described by Styron as "one of the original hipsters, [who] had been telling stories about junkies and pimps and whores and other outcasts while Kerouac and Ferlinghetti were still adolescents..." (p. 219).

Algren took them to visit a prison in Chicago, where they met an inmate named Witherspoon, "a mountaineer transplant from Kentucky ... (and known in the press as the 'Hillbilly from Hell')":

> Witherspoon himself had a preacher style. "I hope you two good writers will proclaim to the world the abominable injustice they done to me. God bless you both."
> "Mr. Witherspoon," Terry deadpanned, "be assured of our constant concern for your welfare" [p. 222].[4]

Concluding their visit with Algren, the trio set out from Chicago on the Super Chief train of the Santa Fe line:

> One clear memory I have is of Terry in the lounge car, musing over his Old Granddad as he considered the imminent demise of the Super Chief, and with it a venerable tradition. His voice grew elegiac, speaking of the number of "darling Baptist virgins aspiring to be starlets" who, at the hands of "panting Jewish agents with their swollen members," had been ever-so-satisfactorily deflowered on these plush, softly undulating banquettes.
> In fact, he had a fixation on the idea of "starlets," and it was plain that in Hollywood he would be looking forward to making out with a gorgeous ingénue from MGM and embarking on a healthy and erotic adventure.
> Toward the end of the trip we stayed up all night and drank most of the way through Arizona and southern California, watching the pale moonscape of the desert slip by, until morning dawned, and we were in Los Angeles [p. 225].[5]

Before parting, they decided to visit Forest Lawn Memorial Park together; this monument to Hollywood Tack served as the inspiration for Waugh's Whispering Glades in *The Loved One*:

> It was inevitable, I suppose, that the studio had arranged to put Terry up at that decaying relic the Chateau Marmont. For me, it was an unexpected bonus to catch a glimpse of the mythic Hollywood landmark before heading out to Whispering Glades.... [At the cemetery] Terry said he felt a little ill. We all agreed to go our separate ways.
> "A bit of shuteye and I'll soon be in tiptop shape," he assured us as we embraced.
> We left him standing at the taxi stop. He had his hands thrust deep in his pockets and he was scowling through his shades, looking fierce and, as always, a little confused and lost — but in any case, with the mammoth American necropolis as a backdrop, like a man already dreaming ideas [pp. 225–226].[6]

Styron's vision was prophetic: Southern did meet an "MGM ingénue" in the person of Gail Gerber, who was working as a dancer in the Elvis Presley MGM vehicle *Harum Scarum*, which was filming on a lot adjacent to Southern's own *The Cincinnati Kid* (his next film project after *The Loved One*); and Los Angeles did prove a necropolis of sorts, for Southern's career. As Carol Southern remembered it: "...he sort of snapped off his friends when he went to Hollywood.... And I would say 'You can't do that...' [but] he wouldn't want to hear about it. He was interested in Hollywood and he was really taken in ... Hollywood used him up and threw him away, and he couldn't get back on his feet ... we were driving through Beverly Hills and he said, 'Isn't it beautiful?' and ... I thought it was a horror ... this was a serious rift between us...."[7]

But at the moment of Southern's arrival, things looked good. It was Tony Richardson who first thought of updating Evelyn Waugh's thirties satire to the sixties, riding the crest of the Black Humor Wave, influenced as much by Lenny Bruce as by Jessica Mitford's *The American Way of Death*. As Richardson recalled in his autobiography, *The Long-Distance Runner*: "I talked to Christopher Isherwood. He was keen to work on the project and to work with Terry Southern, and so, with lots of laughter along the way, we progressed towards a script..." (p. 195).[8]

Richardson recalls one amusing incident during the prep period for the film, when Southern employed the services of Richardson's then-wife, the actress Vanessa Redgrave, in doing some hands-on research at Forest Lawn:

> She even made one hilarious expedition with Terry to Forest Lawn, which had, of course, imposed an edict of total non-cooperation with the film. Terry needed some research for a scene, so he made an appointment for him and his young British wife (just arrived, and unused to the customs of the country) to see the managers there, to discuss with them how to handle her mother, who was dying of some incurable disease, and whom his wife wished to be transported there when dead, so she could be near the remains.
> Each time he hinted at this, Vanessa burst into a flood of tears, and Terry comforted her with a "Now, my dear, we must bear up, be a soldier." It was, Terry claimed, one of Vanessa's finest performances [p. 201].[9]

During production, Southern kept notes for a planned "making-of" book about the film, eventually published as *The Journal of The Loved One*, accompanied by the set photography of William Claxton. Even critics of the film found the *Journal* entertaining; unfortunately, one particularly good bit in the manuscript was cut from the published version. Southern attended a luncheon for the director, the stars and the screenwriters, at which Vivien Leigh was also present. Southern spent the luncheon trying to enlist Leigh to play Aunt Livia in the film version of Candy, and mortified her when he began to reminisce about how she fuelled the erotic fantasies of his adolescence.

It was Southern's turn to be mortified, however, when an increasingly drunk and pugnacious Robert Morse — the star of the film, and the only other American present — began loudly and belligerently insisting that it's the duty of actors and entertainers to make the audience happy, not to horrify them. Apparently, Morse was growing uneasy about Southern's brand of humor as the screenplay developed.[10]

As work progressed on *The Loved One*, Southern moved from the Chateau Marmont to a rented house in Beverly Hills — and the accolades and attention from the popular press kept pouring in. Both *Life* and *Newsweek* came to interview Southern at the house, where he was now living with Carol and Nile. He told Jane Howard, the interviewer from *Life*, that:

> "The important in writing ... is the capacity to astonish. Not shock — shock is a worn-out word — but astonish. The world has no grounds whatsoever for complacency. The *Titanic* couldn't sink, but it did. Where you find smugness, you find something worth blasting. I want to blast it."
> And so blast away he does, currently from the bastion of a rented Beverly Hills

mansion, which has an electric gate and a swimming pool visited once a week by a gardener, who fishes out the five or six leaves that might have fallen into the water. His helper is Nile Southern, now three and a half....

One of his friends says: "He has a checklist of all the things we get choked up about, like war, sex, the military, medicine, American womanhood. He knocks them down one by one." For Southern, there's cold, hard purpose in his madness:

"Ours is not a physical search for the fountain of youth, but an inward one," he says. "We have no understanding at all of death, infinity, or the origin of the universe. We ought to try to understand. There ought to be no barriers."[11]

This was heady stuff—the hashish-fuelled, Left Bank existential raps from *The Hipsters* were being eaten up by the All-American weekly pop news outlets, and Southern was only too eager to provide material. His observations were approvingly quoted by Conrad Knickerbocker a few months later, in an essay for the *New York Times*, elaborating on Knickerbocker's earlier rave review for Candy:

> Terry Southern is a new kind of best-selling novelist, a comic pornographer with a profound moral sense. Sometimes, it is so profound that hostile critics claim it is undetectable, but it is there.
>
> And he can write. Modeled in his boyhood on the stories of Poe and Hawthorne, his prose now has a weirdly old-fashioned grace, like antique gold filigree, in which his radical new ideas glow like blood-red stones. An idea man unconfined by any ideologies, Southern is a sort of hip social anarchist. He never seems to get mad at what he tries to destroy.... When he arrived in Los Angeles, Southern was at the top of his trade. *Candy* had risen from ninth to seventh place among the nation's top ten novels, and is continuing to sell "like hot cakes." The first three printings (10,000 copies each) had all gone. And the fourth printing (15,000) was going fast.... A director of great distinction and present shyness has taken an option to put *Candy* on film. He will emerge from anonymity when—if—Southern solves the difficulties of expurgation without self-betrayal.... John Calley, the producer of *The Loved One*, plans to film another Southern novel, *The Magic Christian*....[12]

Southern recalled in the *Newsweek* interview how he had been a pre-med student at Southern Methodist:

> "It was very inhuman and abstract—not the friendly country doctor kind of thing. It was just chemistry and biology, without girls."
>
> But doctors have figured prominently in his writing, especially in his first novel, *Flash and Filigree*.
>
> "Doctors are the most powerful people in our society today," he said, "except for teachers of Method Acting, who have a more dedicated, more intelligent following."[13]

When making this last odd pronouncement on Method Acting, Southern perhaps had in mind his unproduced screenplay *Beyond The Shadows*. At any rate, the article ended with Southern's optimistic predictions for the future: "'I think this is a golden age for creative work of any kind,' the long-haired, unpressed, unbuttoned, chain-smoking Southern said."[14]

Compare this portrait to *Life*'s slightly earlier picture: "He looks like a walking hangover: his suit, shirt and tie are in rumpled disarray. He drags intensely on his cigarette and stares at you through puffed lids. Ask him a question and he may give you an utter banality for an answer...."[15]

Though it was *Life*'s evocation that probably fuelled David Levine's memorable caricature drawing of Southern from this era, it is clear that a short time in the California sun had loosened up Southern considerably, and the newly laid-back Southern held forth with his vision of what lay in store for Western civilization: "The people who go all out will make it. We've only scratched the surface of our Freudian heritage. We are undertaking an exploration of the mind, and we're making some interesting discoveries. We have discovered the value of not being prejudiced. The assumption has always been there that there have been no limits, but we now know that there are no limits."[16]

Southern's grandiose statements—one can even go out on a limb and call them pretentious—show that he was aiming to be in synch with the scent of change in the air: it was 1964, the Beatles were coming to America, Bob Dylan was talking about changes in the wind, revolution was in the air. If Southern had stuck to the printed page, or even gone into uncharted territories like pop music (however unlikely a scenario that is), perhaps he would have found that Golden Age he detected on the horizon—as the rock musicians did, in this era.

Instead, he stuck to the film industry in Hollywood—the one area of the arts that, in the sixties, would discover plenty of limits. Old Hollywood was in its death throes, the New Hollywood yet to be born, and whatever was happening in Europe, American film was, in this decade, irrelevant (like the novel, unfortunately, which had quickly fallen from the place of prominence it held in the fifties).

Still, the kudos for Southern kept pouring in—and one of the most insightful came from the friend Southern had visited in Chicago, Nelson Algren. The essay, "The Donkeyman by Twilight," was published in the May 18, 1964, issue of *The Nation*, and may even have been spurred into existence by Southern and Styron's visit. In it, Algren refers to "Red-Dirt Marijuana" as "one of the best American short stories of the past twenty-five years," and calls Southern's own literary criticism in the pages of *The Nation* "indispensable."

This is all very flattering to a friend, but the essay is at its most valuable when this fellow craftsman brings his own critical skills to bear on Southern's novels. Unconsciously connecting adherents in The Mad Tradition by likening *Candy* to Carroll's *Alice in Wonderland*, Algren observes that: "Her search for the father, through a setting as changeful as Alice's, is really a journey through the country of America's sexual myths. Before it is concluded, I'm afraid, Henry Miller will be startled to find *Tropic of Cancer* in the same league as *The Good Earth*. After *Candy*, sex in America is never going to be quite the same."[17]

Algren proves most incisive in finding the tradition in American letters that Southern belongs to (as noted in this volume's Introduction), and then vents his anger on the American literary establishment that has ignored Southern (and, it should be noted, that continues to ignore him, right up to the present moment of 2009): "His work has been evaded here by critics too obsequious to damn ... too dull to catch his mockery, or too timorous to touch the anger beneath it. People don't want even a president to make it hot for them, much less a small-town boy from a Texas whistle-stop...."[18]

He concludes his appreciation by noting that:

> Southern is the only contemporary American novelist, among our very best novelists, who is not dependent upon a single well — and a single bucket — for his sources.... Saul Bellow keeps bringing up Herzog. Mailer had World War II — do we have to get a third world war to get another good novel from him? Styron's almost flawless classic *Lie Down in Darkness* was followed by a work of "Literature with a Capital L." Southern's personal flexibility, like Lincoln Stephens,' yields him an infinity of wells and various buckets. He will continue making it hot for them.[19]

"The Donkeyman by Twilight" left readers with the idea that Southern's talent was inexhaustible and limitless — but an essay that appeared the next year, anticipating the imminent release of *The Loved One*, worried that the limits of Southern's talents were already becoming all too visible. In "The Southern Way of Death," published in *The Reporter* on November 18, 1965, author Marvin Barrett observes that:

> ... a Southern Cult has found expression in recent years.... The faithful ... are devout indeed. All the more so, it would seem, because their faith is based on so little....
> One problem is that Southern's vision, clear or dim, is hypnotically contemporary. It deals with current idiocies and has no interest ... in the foibles of even the recent past.[20]

Where Southern actively sought to abolish limits, to create new possibilities, Barrett (among others) faults Southern for this very tack — because, he argues compellingly, satire cannot work without a firm, clearly delineated moral stance to oppose what is being criticized.

Barrett has a particular problem with elements in the film such as the grotesque Mrs. Joyboy, the leering leader of Whispering Glades, and the homosexual Air Force chiefs.

Barrett then goes on to criticize Southern's most recently published book: *The Journal of The Loved One, the Production Log of a Motion Picture*.

This was basically a merchandising tie-in, a scrapbook compiled by Southern and his friend, the jazz photographer William Claxton, who took several candid photographs on the set of the film during production.

Barrett concludes this unfortunately spot-on analysis of Southern's recent work by noting that:

> Terry Southern has obviously become the beneficiary — or victim, depending upon how one looks upon it — of a post-war American phenomenon that might be called the "irreversible reputation." Whatever his failures ... he is held stonily in veneration....
>
> He has started to quote from himself, often a sign of failure of artistic nerve. And he seems to take himself dreadfully seriously, or at least not to discourage those around him who do....[21]

Barrett was one of the few observers at the time to note, in an articulate and convincing fashion, that Southern's artistic nerve had already failed, even at this peak moment of fame. Barrett was already seeing through the emperor's clothes, discerning that the great period of productivity was over; and he seems to have been the only public voice at this point to pick up the trouble signs. Having failed to master the art of storytelling itself, this storyteller was coasting on fumes, and Barrett realized it.

It can be also be argued, however, that to a certain degree, Barrett was missing the point with *The Loved One*. Isherwood, like other long-time British expatriate Los Angelenos such as Aldous Huxley, resented Waugh's parochial snobbery in the novel — they had come to California out of disgust with England, and Isherwood wasn't going to allow his countrymen to get off as easily as Waugh had done. He was as determined to send up British culture as much as Californian, and when collaborating with a proponent of nature like Southern, it's easy to make all cultures, all socially accepted moralities, seem lacking.

When Southern and Isherwood make these two cultures collide, they are making the point that both cultures are at fault and are ultimately in collusion — it is a conspiracy consisting of Whispering Glades, the U.S. Air Force and the British actors that sends its joint madness into space at the end. Waugh's parochial satire has gone cosmic, and Southern's second foray into screenwriting remains the second best screen representation of his vision, showing clearly his own unique take, an unfettered riff on another's song.

Mrs. Joyboy is the grotesque heart of the film, a nightmare personification of American consumerism run rampant. But she has her equivalent in the British Robert Morley; driving home this point, Southern had even intended for Morley to appear in drag at one point in the film, but Morley refused, telling Richardson that "his public"[22] wouldn't stand for it. As always in the universe of Southern, all cultures are cruel — those who ultimately pay the price are the poor innocents caught in their crossfire, like poor Aimee Thanatogenous.

Barrett may have failed to perceive Southern's "moral stance," such as it was (nature good/culture bad, not to put too fine a point on it), but he was alarmingly on-target about the other danger signs for Southern's output. As the *Life* and *Newsweek* interviews amply demonstrate, Southern was indeed taking himself "dreadfully seriously." Certain contributions to the *Loved One* screenplay were inarguably retreads of earlier bits, contradicting Algren's optimistic forecast of a bottomless well of creativity inside Southern.

Even Southern himself, in the years immediately after *The Loved One*'s release, judged the film harshly: "as a totality, it seemed pretty shaky and uneven and eccentric"[23] (though in later years, shoring up his fragments, he would protest that it was also "the most underrated film I've worked on"[24]).

Despite these storm clouds on the horizon, the work assignments kept on coming.

13

The Hollywood Kid

Southern's next job was again with MGM, providing a rewrite on Ring Lardner, Jr.'s, screenplay adaptation of Richard Jessup's novel *The Cincinnati Kid* (released in October 1965, two months before *The Loved One*, though Southern worked on it subsequently). In contrast to his earlier film efforts, this tale exercises the less grotesque, quieter side of Southern's vision, the storyteller who gave us "Razor Fight" and "Red-Dirt Marijuana," portraits of Southern violence and racism — elements explored in *The Cincinnati Kid* as well. As Southern recalled:

> Sam Peckinpah was the original director of *The Cincinnati Kid*. There is a sequence in the beginning where Slade, a wealthy Southerner played by Rip Torn, is at home with his wife and two children. He is shown to be a sanctimonious family man; in a subsequent scene, he is shown in bed with his mistress.
> Well, it was obvious that the full irony of this hypocrisy, in this citadel of Southern virtue, New Orleans, could only be attained by her being black. So that's how it was written and that's how it was shot with Peckinpah, of course, in enthusiastic agreement.
> When the producer saw the dailies, he freaked. "We're not making a message picture," he said, and replaced Peckinpah pronto with Norman Jewison, who said something like, "Hey, you guys must have been nuts to try that."[1]

Only one year later, Southern dismissed *The Cincinnati Kid* as "hack work,"[2] which, along with the interracial love scene designed for an MGM movie, probably did not earn him any new friends in town. But he was responsible for the evocative final shot, which also didn't endear him to the powers that be:

> Norman said "Okay, let's create an atmosphere of really devastating loneliness, maybe Steve walking along an empty street, you know, putting an emphasis on a solitary situation. Think that will do it?"
> "Yes," I said, "if it's at night."
> That gave Norm pause. "A night shoot? Very expensive, Ter. Well, I guess we can manage it."
> "Well, if you really want to max it for loneliness," I said, "it should really be raining as well."
> "A night shoot in the rain? Holy Christ!"

So there we were with a couple of blocks in midtown New Orleans cordoned off at night, with big rain machines letting it pour.... Of course, Big Mort Ransahoff, the guy who had fired Peckinpah, freaked out completely. "Are you guys out of your gourd?" he kept shouting. "You're killing me, you're killing me!"[3]

This anecdote, and Southern's nickname for him, indicates that Ransahoff probably served as the primary role model for the character "Big Sid Crassman" in *Blue Movie*, which Southern was already in the process of writing at this point.

The filming of *The Cincinnati Kid* is also where Southern first met the actor Rip Torn, who remained a close friend for the rest of Southern's life. Southern was growing chummy with many leading lights of the film community — the hipster superstar from Manhattan had unsurprisingly fallen in with the hipster crowd, such as it was, of Los Angeles, spending time with the likes of young actor Dennis Hopper.

He profiled Hopper and Hopper's then-wife Brooke Hayward for a fatuous fluff piece in the August 1, 1965, issue of *Vogue* (accompanied by Hopper's photographs and Joan Didion's photo captions). The article displays a disturbing amount of self-satisfaction and adoration for the Hollywood jet-set on Southern's part, and a degree of sexism that may not have sat well with the *Vogue* readership: "[Hopper] is now morassed in a creativeness that is almost as hopelessly complete as that which spread and drowned the great Cocteau.... Speaking of Brooke now, it should be of interest to girl and lady readers to know that here, at last (hats off!) is a woman who has given her 'all for her man!'...."[4]

Then again, perhaps the sexism is tongue-in-cheek; Southern was at this moment also writing a screenplay adaptation of the John Fowles novel *The Collector*, for director William Wyler. Southern proposed a new ending in which the captive, played by Samantha Eggar, turns on her captor (played by Terence Stamp) and triumphs — an abrupt departure from the novel, and one of the few times when Southern's own instincts seem more in tune than the producer's with commercial tastes. Uncredited for his contribution to the screenplay, his proposed ending was also not used, and the film ultimately adheres more closely to the novel.

However, it was while working on that film in newly Swinging London that he found a booming social scene spurred on by the pop music of The Beatles and The Rolling Stones, and the films of Tony Richardson and Richard Lester, to name some leading lights. Excited by it all, and eager to be a part of the renascent British film industry, Southern began traveling regularly between Los Angeles and London.

His next London job after *The Collector* was also not credited — Peter

13. The Hollywood Kid

Sellers hired him to rewrite all of his dialogue (and his dialogue alone) for the disastrous James Bond parody *Casino Royale*: "After I got the script, I rewrote all of Sellers' part and turned it in and got the money — about 25,000 pounds, which was an enormous amount for work which I essentially did overnight."[5]

The speed with which Southern performed his job shows in the final product, as Sellers' scenes in *Casino Royale* remain some of the actor's most spectacularly unfunny, dead-on-arrival material ever committed to film. However, the blame for this can't be entirely laid at Southern's feet, as this was a period when the notoriously unstable Sellers had decided he no longer wanted to be a comedian but, rather, a suave leading man in the Cary Grant mode. The results of this creative decision, on display in *Casino Royale*, were not good.

The movie money was a lure in the city, but equally so was the London cultural scene, revolving around hotspots like Robert Fraser's famous art gallery (Fraser would design the cover for the *Sgt. Pepper* album in 1967):

> I knew about Robert Fraser's gallery, because friends of mine like Claes Oldenberg, Jim Dine, Larry Rivers and others would show there. He was an extraordinary guy. Kenneth Tynan lived on Mount Street, near the gallery. He used to take me to a lot of places like that. Fraser's gallery became very common knowledge in the industry. One day, Tynan said I had to see this friend of his, Colin Self, who had done this extraordinary sculpture which was like the Strangelove plane. They wanted me to pose with it at Fraser's gallery — this was my first actual trip there. While I was there, Michael Cooper, the photographer, came in and said, "You must come over for drinks, Mick (Jagger) and Keith (Richards) are going to be there. Robert used to have this very active salon at his flat, so I went over and got to know them in a very short time."[6]

So began enduring friendships with the Rolling Stones and the talented young photographer Cooper, who was a star in his own right: Antonioni based the lead character in his film *Blow-Up* on Cooper. He and Southern soon began collaboration on the *Clockwork Orange* screenplay, intending it for Jagger; and shortly before his death, Southern provided the text for *The Early Stones*, a collection of Cooper's photographs from this period (Cooper died of a heroin overdose in the early seventies).

It was also during this period that Southern wrote screenplay adaptations of both *Candy* and *The Magic Christian*, originally both for producer John Calley. In both cases, the screenplays adhere far more closely to the novels than the eventual film versions did — especially in the case of *Candy*. Southern later recalled to Lee Hill that:

> ... The first plan for *Candy* was for David Picker, who was the head of Paramount at the time, to produce, and Frank Perry to direct. Perry had just come off *David & Lisa*, so he was big. We were going to get Hayley Mills to play Candy — she was

perfect. John Mills, her father, wouldn't let her do it. We were still in the process of trying to persuade him to let her do it when David Picker lost his position.

Then my good friend Christian Marquand, the French actor who was trying to break into directing, and was certainly competent enough to direct at the time, begged me to let him have the option for two weeks for nothing, so he could put a deal together. So I did, and sure enough, Marquand immediately got [Marlon] Brando, because he was his best friend. They were lifelong friends to the extent that Brando named his first son after Marquand.

So, on the basis of getting Brando, he was able to get Richard Burton. And having gotten those two, he was able to get everyone else. Then he disappointed me by casting a Swedish girl for the lead role, which was uniquely American and Midwestern. [Note: It doesn't seem to have bothered Southern that Hayley Mills was unmistakably British.] He said this would make *Candy*'s appeal more universal — that's when I withdrew from the film.

The film version of *Candy* is proof positive of everything rotten you ever heard about major studio production — they are absolutely compelled to botch everything original to the extent that it is no longer even vaguely recognizable.[7]

It seems odd that Southern would "withdraw" from such a potentially lucrative project, not to mention one so close to his heart, as his fame rested almost entirely on the shoulders of *Candy*. And lucrative it was — perhaps it was a disaster artistically, but the film was financially successful when it was released in February of 1969, ultimately grossing almost $8 million, a huge haul at the time (and three million more than *Dr. Strangelove* made).

Whatever the reason, he did withdraw, and was replaced as screenwriter by Buck Henry. Southern never criticized Henry, but one can detect some lingering bitterness under the surface of his later comments: "I didn't know him at all at the time. I wasn't even aware that he had written a script of *Catch-22*; I just thought he was the creator of *Get Smart* ... I mean, situation comedy, what could possibly be creatively lower than that?"[8]

All of Southern's novels presented problems to the screenwriter seeking to adapt them, due to their random, episodic natures — but *Candy* at least contained some modicum of narrative momentum in terms of the heroine's global travels. *The Magic Christian*, on the other hand, contains no real plot, no conflict to be resolved or narrative arc of any kind. To remedy this problem and accommodate the classic three-act structure of Hollywood screenplays, Southern provided Grand with a wife, a mother — and most importantly, a son named Youngman Grand.

The dramatic conflict comes in the form of a generation gap (then a timely subject) between Guy and Youngman. The son does not approve of his father's jokes, and the story, such as it is, revolves around Grand's attempts to win his son's love and admiration, to make him understand why he behaves in the way that he does — one can speculate that this story take had its psychological roots in Southern's feelings of guilt, as his skyrocketing career necessitated further travels, further time spent away from Nile.

The screenplay culminates with reconciliation between father and son, as Youngman finally joins in his father's mission to make it hot for them. They walk off into the sunset, arm in arm, heading for a missile silo in the distance — implying that the world can only expect bigger, more explosive pranks out of the reconciled Grand family. The film failed to be made by Calley, and only traces of this father/son relationship would survive in the eventual British film version, made a few years down the line in 1969.

In 1967, after finishing work on *Casino Royale*, Southern did uncredited script-doctoring work on Alexander MacKendrick's *Don't Make Waves*, a send-up of the Los Angeles lifestyle circa 1967, starring Tony Curtis. MacKendrick had directed several of the classic Ealing comedies in Britain in the early fifties, and recalled the week spent collaborating with Southern as his only pleasant experience during this disastrous foray into American filmmaking.

Southern's next credited project to reach the screen (it was released in October 1968) was his screenplay for Roger Vadim's film version of the French science-fiction comic *Barbarella*, made at the Cinecitta Studios in Rome: "I was living at the top of the Spanish Steps, in a good hotel there. It was good experience working with Roger Vadim and Jane Fonda (Vadim's wife at the time). The strain was Dino De Laurentiis; he was just this flamboyant businessman. His idea of good cinema was to give money back on the cost of the picture before even going into production. He doesn't even make any pretense about the quality of aesthetic."[9]

Southern's comment about De Laurentiis clearly display the naïve, frustratingly blind eye that he continually displayed towards the "business" side of show business — the attitude that, more than anything else, set him up for failure in the film world. De Laurentiis was even trying to get Southern to pen the script for a musical version of *Roman Holiday* in this period, but Southern passed on the project, dismissing the idea as "dopey." It's a shame that he couldn't find some way to work compatibly with a "businessman" like De Laurentiis, to ensure not only future jobs with a proven moneymaker, but also some degree of artistic control over the resulting film.

Carol Southern recalled that Southern's original screenplay adaptation of the soft-core comic was actually "very sweet; it was a fairy-tale...,"[10] but laments that little to none of that version wound up on the screen. Any screenplay draft that might corroborate that tantalizing story doesn't survive, unfortunately.

Though in many ways Vadim's film resembles a science-fiction version of *Candy* (rather than "The Donkey and the Darling," as the lost early draft might), there is little to distinguish this as a uniquely Terry Southern work. Unlike the previously noted elements in *Strangelove*, *The Loved One* and *The Cincinnati Kid*, there is nothing here that exhibits his distinctive voice. Undeniably entertaining as this camp extravaganza is, anyone could have cranked out the workmanlike screenplay adaptation — the flair lies entirely in the direction and the original source material, not to mention the over-the-top acting.

Southern, although dismissive of the film, recalled that "Vadim is a lot of fun with a discerning eye for the erotic, the grotesque and the absurd.... The movie has developed a curious cult following, and I am constantly getting requests to appear with the film at some very obscure, weirdo place, like in Wenk, Texas, or a suburb of Staten Island."[11]

Years later, very near the end of his life and no longer in a position to turn down jobs, Southern wrote an unproduced screenplay, at the request of De Laurentiis, for *Barbarella 2*:

> He [De Laurentiis] was looking for a way to do a sequel — "on the cheap," was how he expressed it, "but with plenty action, and plenty sex!" Then he went on with these immortal words: "Of course, Janey is too old now to be sexy, but maybe her daughter. *On verra*."
>
> But nothing, perhaps fortunately, came of it.[12]

Barbarella is not nearly as satisfying a screen representation of Southern's voice as *Dr. Strangelove* or *The Loved One*— however, this job did lead to better things, when Peter Fonda came to Rome to visit his sister. While there, he told Southern that he was starting work on a low-budget biker movie, and would appreciate any screenplay assistance from Southern.

The stage was set for *Easy Rider*.

14

Excessive Verbiage

As noted above, there is a never-ending debate between interested parties as to who did what in the matter of the *Easy Rider* screenplay. Near the end of his life, a bitter Southern offered his own view of the "collaboration" between himself, Fonda and co-star/director Dennis Hopper:

> I did the only writing on it, and Peter Fonda was the only working actor in the group. Dennis Hopper wasn't really into acting at this time. He was a photographer and art collector.... Peter Fonda had been in several of these really low-ball biker movies for AIP [American-International Pictures]; he was in a couple of those and had a contract for one more of a three-picture contract. Dennis had this idea: instead of doing one of their B-Picture dumb-bell movies, under the guise of doing a biker movie, they could do a movie that might be more interesting. And he [Dennis] would be able to make his debut as a director in one fell swoop.
>
> It seemed possible, under these auspices, whereas otherwise, he couldn't get arrested. Because of the setup where Peter Fonda owed AIP this picture, it would be possible to get this different approach in, under the wire. He persuaded Peter to go along with this: "We'll get Terry to write the script...." That was through this guy Bert Schneider, who made a deal for the distribution rights. He wasn't involved during the production; he made some kind of deal with Dennis and Peter. Peter as the nominal producer, so that was the situation when they came to my place in New York.
>
> They said, "We want you to write this and we're going to defer any money in exchange for splitting ten percent three ways." I wasn't financially in a position where I could defer, so they said, "You can get $350 a week for ten weeks in lieu of that." So I had to do it that way. So I never had a piece of it, which turned out to be very lucrative.
>
> Anyway, so I had the story. They told me the basic notion of two guys that were fed up with the rat race of commercialization of America ... [but] they're not writers. Neither of them are writers. They can't even write a fucking letter.[1]

Southern was later to claim that "...it would be difficult to exaggerate the underhanded and really shitty, crooked behavior of theirs..."[2] but at the time, he felt swept up in the sixties notion of community:

> For a while, I thought it [film-making] could be done on a co-directing basis ... [with] people whose values you trust and so forth — but too often, it turns out you've allowed your friendship for them to exaggerate your notion of their talent,

and you find yourself right back, if one may coin, where you started — the same old six-and-seven pearls before a swine.[3]

Southern may also have been thinking at this point of his old friend Aram Avakian, with whom he made (and many say co-directed) the film version of *The End of the Road*. This too was a collaboration that ended badly, with the dissolution of their long friendship — but the majority of his bitterness in later years was reserved for Hopper and Fonda, due to the amount of money he felt he was swindled out of.

Since he freely admits even here to making a bad deal out of financial necessity, he clearly has no one to blame but himself, from a legal standpoint, for the inarguable fact that he made a great deal less money off of *Easy Rider* than either Fonda or Hopper did. What pained him most was the emotional wound of what he perceived as a friendship betrayed.

Hopper, Fonda and Southern met regularly for story conferences, at Southern's Manhattan office on 55th Street. Southern told his biographer Lee Hill that Hopper and Fonda "were writers only in the sense that they could talk up a storm,"[4] so the conferences consisted of Southern asking the pair questions, making suggestions and taping their conversations. A secretary would then type the transcripts of their meetings — and she herself found her way into the final screenplay in a roundabout manner.

Decades before *The X-Files*, Southern's housekeeper was obsessed with UFOs, entertaining the trio with long discourses on flying saucers and secret bases in New Mexico; Southern taped these as well, and one monologue found its way into the film as Jack Nicholson's campfire soliloquy.

What this proves yet again is the intensely collaborative nature of film, and the impossibility of ascribing sole authorship of the screenplay to any one party. It's likely that Southern worked alone in harnessing the mass of raw material culled from these meetings into a workable script — *Easy Rider* does, after all, tread similar turf to earlier works like *The Cincinnati Kid*, "Red-Dirt Marijuana" and "Razor Fight," while it bears little resemblance to later work from either Hopper or Fonda. A quick glance at IMDb shows that despite their long, distinguished acting careers, their writing credits could generously be described as sparse, both before and after *Easy Rider*.

Neither Hopper nor Fonda disputes the notion that the title was Southern's idea, a bit of Southern slang remembered from the writer's youth: an "easy rider" was a man who lives off the earnings of his lover, if said lover is a prostitute. Southern also credits himself with the creation of Jack Nicholson's character, which he based on "Gavin Stevens," a sensitive small town lawyer who appears in several tales by William Faulkner.

Southern had conceived the part for his friend and *Cincinnati Kid* collaborator Rip Torn—unfortunately, Torn wasn't able to appear in the film due to a prior commitment on the New York stage. Before it became clear he couldn't work the film shoot into his schedule, Torn met with Hopper and Southern for dinner in New York—an unpleasant encounter that ended in a fight between Torn and Hopper.

Decades later, during an appearance on *The Tonight Show*, Hopper told Jay Leno that Torn "came at me with a knife" during the fight.[5] Torn successfully sued Hopper for libel—and some say that the suit was brought after Torn made a promise to the ailing Southern that he would demonstrate to the world that Hopper was a liar.

It's not as if Torn was unaware of the longstanding feud between Southern and his collaborators: as far back as 1973, in a profile of Torn that Southern wrote for *Saturday Review of the Arts*, Southern managed to work in a swipe, noting that an event transpired "When I was working on the script for *Easy Rider*—and practically unassisted, despite any moronic notions to the contrary...."[6] If the story is true, it's touching to think that Torn may have been carrying on his friend's ancient grudge match with the collaborators, fighting the battle even after Southern was laid in his grave.

Southern also claimed that it was his idea to kill Captain America (aka "Wyatt") and Billy the Kid, the two bikers, at the end of the film. According to Southern, Hopper was for a time very much against this notion, claiming that to "kill 'em both," Southern must have been "outta [his] gourd...."[7] As has been noted above, the film's bleak conclusion echoes "The Road Out of Axotle" in showing the impossibility of finding freedom through escape on the road—more evidence of Southern's guiding hand in the screenplay.

The key difference between *Easy Rider* and "Axotle," worth noting here, is that where "Axotle" finds a darkness in nature, which the naïve hipsters come up against, the main characters in *Easy Rider* (like those in *The Hipsters*) find the darkness within themselves, as well as without. True, it's the ignorant rednecks (representatives of a culture of limitations) that finally kill the bikers, but as Captain America—supposedly representative of a culture of freedom—has already realized, "We blew it."

This is an echo of Ken Kesey's observation at the conclusion of Tom Wolfe's then-recently published New Journalism epic *The Electric Kool-Aid Acid Test*: the failure lay not in the stars of this generation but in themselves, a failure vividly suggested in the first scene of the film, as Captain America places the coiled tube of drug money in his bike—the serpent is already in the garden as they set out for Eden.

It seems fairly certain that Southern's original screenplay provided a solid blueprint from which the structure of the final film emerged—but the fragments of first drafts that do survive show quite a difference from the finished product. In fact, they offer a tantalizing glimpse of the film that might have been, had Southern actually been afforded more artistic control and input.

An example: the New Orleans "Brothel Sequence," as it is labeled in the so-called "55th Street Draft" contained in the Terry Southern Archives. There is some debate as to who wrote this sequence — some claim this segment was in fact written by Peter Fonda. But if we trust to Southern's assertion that the actors did very little, then it can be attributed to Southern — and it certainly reads as if it comes from his hand.

In this original screenplay fragment, the sequence is quite long, with a great deal of dialogue and a detailed evocation of a New Orleans brothel — it reads like a lost segment of a Faulkner novel, such as *The Reivers*:

> INT. WHOREHOUSE
>
> Wyatt and Billy are led down a long staircase into a huge room without windows. There are only doors. Giant mirrors hang at slight angles, their gold-leaf glittering in the soft light. The mirrors are draped in red velvet which clings and falls to the floor; they are crowned by giant gold-leaf antlers. Potted bamboo poles rise toward the ceiling, adorned at the top with the peacock feathers....
>
> The Pimp gestures for them to be seated, turns and snaps his fingers toward the end of the stage. Out of the darkness emerges a giant Negro, dressed in a turban and white satin.
>
> NEGRO
> What can I get for you gentlemen?
>
> ... The Pimp smiles hatefully and nods, staring at Billy. He slowly turns, walks down the stairs and into the shadows....[8]

Nearly all of these details and actions, and many more besides, are gone from the finished film: the long dialogue between The Pimp, Billy and Wyatt, between Billy, Wyatt and the whores — as well as the rather staid evocation of an acid trip that follows. In the film, the scene is whittled down to a few terse words in the brothel, followed by a psychedelic montage of sounds and images as they take acid and experience Mardi Gras in the city.

It's a matter of conjecture who had the final say as to what wound up on screen for *Easy Rider* — some say it was the director, some the editors. What seems indicated from Southern's screenplay is that if he had been given more control, the film would have been far more conventional than what *Easy Rider* became — closer to *The Cincinnati Kid* than the experimental breakthrough that it was.

Nonetheless, the process of transformation from script to film here seems a case of subtraction rather than augmentation — what wound up on the screen came from this draft, so that it can be argued that Southern provided Hopper and Fonda with a wealth of material culled from his Southern childhood, which they then pared down in order to produce the film that they wanted.

Another weakness in Southern's argument that he was solely responsible for the screenplay is the admitted fact that he was rarely on set. By the time that *Easy Rider* was in production, Southern's focus had moved on to other projects that consumed his full attention, and was busy shuttling back and forth between The Berkshires in Massachusetts (where he and Avakian were filming *The End of the Road*) and London (where *The Magic Christian* was finally going into production).

Southern later claimed that his main reason for absenting himself from the *Easy Rider* set was that he could no longer tolerate Hopper. Southern claimed that Hopper's massive drug intake, coupled with complete creative freedom, allowed him to indulge in childish, manic rages — he insisted on complete, dictatorial control over all facets of the film's production, but Southern says this rendered him incapable of doing little more than scream at the cast and crew. As he recalled to Lee Hill, Southern was ultimately forced to chastise him in front of the entire crew, admonishing him that "Your excessive verbiage ... is driving me to distraction."[9] After that, the set visits ceased.

Upon the film's release, it was a massive success, earning $17 million, a very impressive sum at that time (compare this to Southern's biggest previous success, *Dr. Strangelove*, which had earned $5 million). Of course, Southern had already signed away his points in the initial agreement, but he still tried to appeal to Hopper's sense of charity.

In a letter dated December 5, 1970, Southern wrote to his old "collaborator":

Dear Den,

I'm very sorry to bug you, Den, but I'm in a terrible bind — completely strapped. An inch, maybe less, from Disasterville. If I were alone I would never hit on you (not my style, Den) like this, but I have Nile and Carol to take care of — in the face of recent monstro-financial reverses and no relief in sight. In view of such circumstances, and of our (yours and mine) solid ancient friendship and of great success of *ER*, could you please put a single point of its action my way. I'm aware there may be a difference in our notions of who contributed what to the film (memory flash highly selective in these cases) but the other day I was looking through a copy of the original Fifty Fifth Street script that we did together and was amazed at the amount and strength of the material which went from there intact to Silver Screen. Please consider it, Den — I'm in very bad trouble. Thanks.[10]

Apparently, the letter never got a response.

15

The Epic Sensibility

While Hopper, according to reports, was still running amok down on *Easy Rider*'s New Orleans set like some hippie Lear on the heath, Southern and his old friend Aram Avakian were quietly creating a film of their own up in the quiet Berkshire Mountains of Massachusetts. The two friends collaborated so closely on the project that the resulting film, *The End of the Road*, represents the closest thing to an actual directing job by Southern — the path he should have chosen, had he wanted to gain control of his material and his career in the film industry.

Southern and Avakian had been friends since meeting in Paris in the late forties. The reason why they now decided to collaborate on *The End of the Road* was simple:

> He [Avakian] had a kind of renaissance quality, so he just got interested in films.... I had just read this John Barth novel (*The End of the Road*); Al had read it on my recommendation. We simultaneously agreed that it would make a good movie.... In the late summer of 1968, we scouted locations around East Canaan, in Connecticut, and Great Barrington, in Massachusetts. We found this fantastic old button factory in Great Barrington, which is perfect as a soundstage....
>
> We tried to give the film a full-on sixties flavor — student unrest and so on — which seemed inherent in the book. A very good book, and, I like to believe, a most faithful adaptation — with a little something extra in the form of Dr. D's theories.[1]

"Dr. D" was played by James Earl Jones, reuniting with Southern several years after his role as "Lieutenant Lothar Zogg" in *Dr. Strangelove* (Jones's first film). Jones delivers a tour de force performance here, in a role created for him by Southern.

Southern's screenplay, despite being an adaptation of the Barth novel, can also be seen as a companion piece of sorts to such earlier Southern stories as "Put-Down," or even "A Change of Style" and the recent "Plums and Prunes" (discussed below). These tales were unusual in Southern's body of work for the object of their focus: contemporary white American middle-class culture, the stuff of so much "melodramatic tripe" that Southern deplored in many novels of the era, by the likes of John Updike.

So what was it in Barth's novel that called out to Southern? On the surface, *The End of the Road* seems not far removed from the concerns of *Rabbit, Run*, which Southern so curtly dismissed in the pages of *The Nation*. It must have been that "sixties flavor" that Southern found "inherent in the book — a larger cultural, social dimension against which the lives of the three protagonists are played out."[2]

In his best work, Southern was never terribly interested in intimate character studies — his concerns were with the bigger societal picture, the culture pitted against nature. The independent film scene that developed after his era, and which might have offered him an alternative to the Hollywood Studio System that had no place for him, seems almost solely reliant on such small character studies as their stock-in-trade; Southern would probably have found no safe haven in that arena, either. Even though *The End of the Road* is an early example of authentic independent American film, it strains against its "intimate character study" confines.

Comics writer Grant Morrison once commended the film version of *The Magic Christian* for being "the only British film possessed of an epic sensibility," and however much that film may have strayed from Southern's script, the "epic sensibility" that appealed to Morrison was derived from Southern. That same sensibility is on display in *The End of the Road*.

In a fashion similar to Southern's adaptation of Waugh's *The Loved One*, his screenplay for *The End of the Road* gives a cosmic scope to the intimate drama being played out in the main narrative. Footage of student demonstrations and astronauts ascending into space imply that this is not merely the end of the road for two college professors and the woman involved with both of them, but for a culture as a whole — the world that they belong to, a culture cut off from feeling.

Viewed back-to-back with *Easy Rider*, the two films reveal themselves to be of a piece, each half of the pair complementing the other. Where *Easy Rider* focuses on the counterculture, *The End of the Road* examines the dominant culture, Nixon's "Silent Majority" — and the double vision of the two films sees both sides coming to the end of the road, crippled by the serpent in the garden, the darkness or void within.

The "little something extra" that Southern speaks of is Dr. D, who does not appear in the novel. This character is a familiar figure in Southern's work: an African American voice glimpsing other possibilities, other cultures — he's C.K. with a medical degree. He's also a complement to the Gavin Stevens variant that Jack Nicholson played in *Easy Rider*, the white man sympathetic to the African American perspective. But like the bikers in *Easy Rider* (and unlike Harold), the protagonists in *The End of the Road* refuse to listen.

The End of the Road stands as the best example of what a "Terry Southern film" would have looked like had he ever pursued a career as a director; from all reports, he was indeed the co-director, constantly on set and supervising all aspects of production, though he allowed his friend Avakian to take sole credit. He is solely responsible for the screenplay, despite generously allowing Avakian a co-writing credit (as he had done with Fonda and Hopper on *Easy Rider*)—as well as another man named Dennis McGuire. Apparently, McGuire had absolutely nothing to do with the screenplay—but he did own the rights to Barth's novel, and insisted on being cut in for credit as part of the deal.

Southern loved the medium of film, but seems to have lacked the drive or will to direct—and as a shy man who loathed confrontations, "co-director" was as close as he allowed himself to get to the director's chair. It's baffling why he wouldn't push himself in that direction, since he maintained that "...with the exception of *Strangelove*, of the films I've worked on there isn't one which would not have been infinitely improved by the absence of the director.... In his present role the director is wholly superfluous, an interfering parasite. His proper function ... has been taken over entirely by the Director of Photography."[3]

And yet despite this griping, Southern never bothered to halt that interference. And after *The End of the Road*, no other director ever offered a similar collaborative venture again. However, with this film we come tantalizingly close to seeing what could have been, had Southern ever fully freed himself from the comparatively helpless role of "screenwriter," and assumed as much control on the screen as he exercised on the printed page.

16

Come and Get It

After completing *The End of the Road*, and making a short trip to check out the madness on the *Easy Rider* set, Southern headed to London to see how filming was progressing on *The Magic Christian*. Peter Sellers had finally gotten his beloved pet project off the ground, and even managed to sign on a Beatle as costar: now that his band was disintegrating, Ringo Starr was trying out acting, essaying the none-too-demanding role of Youngman Grand.

Granted, this wasn't the first time Starr had taken on a Southern role, since he'd already graced screens (if "graced" is indeed the word) as the Mexican gardener Emmanuel, in the film version of *Candy*. But that role was little more than a cameo, mercifully; here, for the first time, he was cast in a leading role, without the support of his band.

The Beatles had already come out as Southern admirers by putting him on the Robert Fraser–designed cover of their album *Sgt. Pepper's Lonely Hearts' Club Band*, standing tall among the elite that comprised The Beatles' selection of "people we like"; some of Southern's companions there included his friends Lenny Bruce and William S. Burroughs, and, right next to Southern, his beloved Poe.

Prior to the start of production, Southern was highly enthusiastic about the coming film adaptation of *The Magic Christian*. One interviewer asked if Southern was bothered that the story's setting had been changed from America to England when "It seemed such an American book," but Southern replied that "…it works as well set in England, because the materialism which it treats is just as strong there."[1]

He was also filled with optimism due to the fact that this was his first collaboration with Peter Sellers since their triumph with *Dr. Strangelove*, aside from the uncredited work on *Casino Royale*— and Sellers nearly convinced Stanley Kubrick to come along for the ride again, as this letter from Southern shows:

> 15 December 1968
> Dear Stanley,
>
> I was delighted beyond all expressing to learn, from mercurial Pete Sellers, that it may be CAMEOVILLE for a certain Stan-The-Man K in the boat race fix of *Magic Chris*! I can only say that, since hearing that grand news, I have been doing my level best, scribewise, to beef up a decent vehicle for you. Let me ask you this, Stan: how would you feel about flashing? Now hold on, if you're concerned with heft, don't be — you'll have ample time to "work up" a darn good heft while we're lighting the stock, and/or can be assisted in same by one of the Nifties we shall have just off set for that very purpose.... Ringo Starr has promised a spritely tune ("Oh, I flash a thrusting heft from my Mac and jock!" Etc.), so our feeling is that with any luck at all, the scene could become a little showstopper.[2]

Kubrick failed to be lured in front of the camera, unfortunately, and the role was eventually played by Richard Attenborough, in a scene substantially rewritten by John Cleese and Graham Chapman.

When Southern arrived on the set in England, he discovered to his chagrin that the script he had written in 1965 had been largely jettisoned in favor of new material by British comedians, and that the mood here was nearly as chaotic as on the set of *Easy Rider*. His comments on the changes are some of his most revealing insights into his own creation; they also show a rare burst of anger towards his film collaborators:

> When I finally got to the set, I spent a lot of time doing damage control.... It was probably due to Sellers' insecurity, or a manifestation of that. Although he loved the original script and it was the key to getting started, he also had this thing where he would run into someone socially, like John Cleese or Spike Milligan ... and they ... would come in and make various changes, sometimes completely out of character, from my point of view ... these scenes, a couple of which had already been shot, seemed to be the antithesis of what Guy Grand would do.
>
> They were tasteless. Guy Grand never hurt anyone; he just deflated some monstrous egos and pretensions, but never like slashing a Rembrandt, which they had in there ... defacing this painting which you know was a great painting. Guy Grand would never do that. It was gratuitous destruction; wanton, irresponsible bullshit which had nothing to do with the character of the statement. It was very annoying....[3]

The director of the film was Joseph McGrath, who had met Sellers when McGrath was Richard Lester's assistant on *The Running, Jumping and Standing Still Film*, and had then gone on to direct several sequences for *Casino Royale*. McGrath reunited with Southern in 1992 when McGrath hired Southern to write the screenplay for *Festival*, a satire of the Cannes Film Festival, but the film was never produced (it is discussed below).

Southern later claimed that it was McGrath who pressured him into creating the part of Youngman Grand after seeing Southern socializing with Paul McCartney, and wanted to cast a Beatle in a starring role — however, this reminiscence doesn't quite gel with the fact that Southern had created the Youngman role when he wrote the screenplay back in 1965, in Los Angeles.

Casting a Beatle, however, did provide Southern with a lifelong friend in Ringo Starr — for a time in the early seventies, Starr owned the film rights to *Blue Movie*; the sleeve for his 1974 album *Goodnight Vienna* even advises the listener to "Buy Terry Southern Books!"[4]

And despite Southern's protests that the film version of Guy Grand behaves out of character — which is undeniably true, in a few inane bits like the aforementioned Rembrandt slashing — Sellers' performance is actually more faithful to the novel than Southern's own screenplay had been.

In the final film version, Grand is no longer married, nor is his mother present — although his two aunts are converted into unmarried sisters. Youngman is not his biological son, but a hippy Grand meets in the park and adopts on a whim, training him as an apprentice who will one day take over the family business of making it hot for them. Isolating Grand from a nuclear family unit was a wise move, emphasizing his magical aura.

Most interestingly, Sellers' performance is nothing less than a portrait of Southern himself, right down to the hair, the guffaws and the mock-English accent Southern loved to affect. Sellers' voice here captures that quality in Southern's own that led George Plimpton to describe him as sounding "not unlike Goofy ... if he were born an earl."[5] Sellers recognized that Grand is a self-portrait by Southern, and his performance is an affectionate tribute to his friend.

Paul McCartney wrote a theme song for the film, "Come and Get It," but audiences failed to heed his advice. Released in April 1970, *The Magic Christian* proved to be Southern's least successful film at the box office — but then again, by that point, he hardly considered it to be "his" film at all.

A few months later, *The End of the Road* was released to an even more dismal fate. Due to the graphic abortion sequence, the film received the dreaded "X" rating — which severely limited the number of theaters it could play in, ensuring that virtually no one saw it. Despite being Southern's most heartfelt, deeply involved film effort, it sank without a trace. It would mark Southern's final produced movie work until the ignominious final curtain call of *The Telephone*, eighteen years later. As abruptly as it started, the movie party was over.

Various reasons have been offered for the abrupt termination of Southern's career in the film industry, including the theory I put forward at the beginning of Part Two, which (needless to say) I find the most satisfactory explanation. But undeniably, there were other factors at work as well, compounding the central issue of his artistic failure of nerve.

Carol Southern recalls that he angered many people in the business, especially agents, due to his refusal to work in traditional channels — he was wont to simply accept money and commissions upfront, often without letting his agent handle it, and simply with a handshake deal — agents were routinely dropping him as a client for this, and such careless handling of money accounts for his constant financial woes, even with the big paydays in the late sixties. But if the films were hits (and many of them were), it seems likely such behavior would be forgiven in a business where box-office performance is all that matters on the résumé.

Lee Hill, who also got to know him well in the last years of his life, believes that Southern angered the Hollywood establishment through his independent production style, years before independent filmmaking became a commercial force in Hollywood: *Easy Rider* was produced on location, with stars no studio would bank on, for instance, while *The End of the Road* was filmed on location in the Berkshires, employing New York stage actors rather than Hollywood stars. But again, most in Hollywood probably couldn't care less how the film was produced if it made money — and in the case of *Easy Rider*, it certainly did, and changed the way Hollywood made films.

Others say that Southern's subversive style and sensibility were simply going out of fashion as the sixties waned, and this is certainly true. The Black Humor Wave had long since crashed and receded, and after all the social ugliness of the era, most audiences looked to film for reassurance, not more rocking of the boat.

All of these factors contributed, no doubt, to the decline of Southern's career in film — along with Southern's increasing substance abuse, which rendered his work habits (and the work itself) erratic. The one inescapable fact is that as the Swinging sixties geared up in 1964, Southern came into his own. And as they collapsed into the seventies, so too did Southern.

17

King Weirdo

Carol Southern lamented the fact that Southern had allowed his friendships back east to deteriorate when he'd gone west to make it in Hollywood; unfortunately, their marriage disintegrated as well, when he became involved with a young dancer named Gail Gerber, whom he met during the filming of *The Cincinnati Kid*.

Elvis Presley was filming his musical *Harum Scarum* on a nearby soundstage — when he heard that the author of *Dr. Strangelove*, one of his favorite films, was working next door, The King promptly summoned Southern into his presence. It was there that Southern met the woman who was to be his companion for the rest of his life.

Nile Southern remembers that his father had been gone from Blackberry River Farm for well over a year — he returned one day in the late sixties, sporting long hair and a beard, transformed by his new lifestyle; Nile didn't know what to make of him. An abashed Terry exclaimed, "Son, don't you know me?"[1] He had become a stranger in his own home — but from that moment on, Southern was an extraordinarily attentive and loving father, making a close relationship with Nile a top priority in his life, as if wishing to avoid the mistakes his own father made with him.

Hollywood success had brought many changes, both personal and professional — but Southern still kept writing, for himself as well as for films; unfortunately, he pursued his "Quality Lit" vocation with markedly less focus and discipline than before.

In 1967, the collection *Red-Dirt Marijuana and Other Tastes* appeared; the dust jacket boasted a shadowy William Claxton photograph of a suave and mysterious Southern embracing his *Barbarella* star Jane Fonda (that film was released at roughly the same time as the collection). Selected and arranged by Southern himself (not chronologically, but according to theme), it provides a good "Greatest Hits" package of Southern's short works — many of which, having been published in obscure literary journals of the previous decade, were now impossible to find.

The collection begins with the innocent child's first foray into "sense derangement" via red-dirt marijuana, and concludes with the ultimate hipster dissolution of self via the blood of a wig. Along the way, it demonstrates, through fact and fiction, the need for such alterations of perception: to counter and cope with a world awash in brutality and deceit.

By juxtaposing his forays into fabulation and journalism, it also demonstrates what a remarkable culmination "The Blood of a Wig" truly is, creating a realm in which the line between fact and fiction is completely blurred. Even more than pieces cited by Wolfe and Thompson (such as "Twirling at Ole Miss" and "Recruiting for the Big Parade"), this astonishing exercise in the American Grotesque stands as the first true piece of Gonzo Journalism.

It was noted, in an interview with Southern conducted in the seventies, that:

> ... Hunter S. Thompson would seem to have based his entire mature oeuvre on your "Twirling at Ole Miss"—and a few others. Perhaps you would discuss how you formulated this journalistic approach?
>
> Southern: There are some Edgar Allan Poe stories—particularly one called *The Adventures [sic] of A. Gordon Pym*—where he uses a narrative style which has a strangely authentic documentary quality; I mean, in the light of its time, natch. Anyway, I think I first picked up on it there from the great E. Poe. Then, of course, there was Henry Miller; he used the first person SO convincingly in the *Tropics* and his other sex adventure stuff that most people still don't realize it was 95 percent fiction.
>
> So that is it—roughly, to be sure—the genesis of it. The idea is to describe something in such a way that you truthfully convey the essence of it without being boring.[2]

Again and again throughout his career, Southern returned to *Pym* as his touchstone, the source and inspiration for his vision, whether the vision was fact or fiction. In an interview with *Paper Magazine*, conducted only days before his death, Southern again recounted with relish his rewrite of *Pym* for his classmates back in Texas.

Pym is his Bible of the American Grotesque; it formed his breed of New Journalism—and through him, that of his "heir," Hunter S. Thompson. Thompson took his own version of the Grotesque on a slightly different course, towards the violent, while Southern would swerve his variant towards the sexual. This is an angle that Thompson assiduously avoided, again proving Leslie Fiedler's maxim that all true American literature is boys' fiction, but Southern's bedtime stories demonstrate this fact just as well.

In 1968, Southern crafted a long essay devoted to the novel, titled "Trib to Pym." He wrote it not for any editor or event, but purely for himself—perhaps sensing that he was losing touch with his vision, his focus going adrift in the film business:

17. King Weirdo

Knocking around in the quality-Lit Game, you're bound to meet a wiseacre or two who will express surprise to learn that Ed Poe wrote a novel — and indeed, beyond surprised, almost chagrined, that they with all their crypto, heavy-Lit backgrounds were quite unaware of it. These so-called "quality-Lit Cowboys" (or "butterflies" as they're known around Longhorn Cafeteria down at the U. of T.) should not be taxed too severely in this particular, for here is a work which does not appear on any reading-list at any school in the country — by virtue of its extreme weirdness. "Too hot to handle!" seems to be the cry of dons and department-heads alike, "Christ, he must have been absolutely *bonkers* when he wrote *that* piece of swill!" *Officially*, of course, an effort is made to present a somewhat lower-key, more common-sense type profile when confronted, claiming the work to be of "inadequate format." "Too darn short for a novel," snaps Jack Hollander, of New Haven's Yale U, *par example*— but I'm afraid this won't wash, since word-wise it comes in at a strong 77 thou, making it longer than *Madame Bovary* (42 thou) and *Miss Lonelyhearts* (27 thou) put together — though not, natch, necessarily in that order. Thus, one is forced to the sad conclusion that such a blatantly absurd "reason" for the systematic exclusion of this longest and very ambitious work of the most celebrated author in the history of the country smacks a little too strongly of the old *papiers pentagoni* gestalt — if you follow my drift. It is a heinous conspiracy, in short, to suppress public knowledge of that with which they are unprepared to cope ... preferring instead that the image of "The Divine Edgar" remain essentially that laid down by the late great Chuck Baudelaire and the rest of the *soi-distant* "Frog Elite"—(specifically Rimbaud, Mallarme and Valery ... with the incredible Verlaine abstaining — though *not*, scholars please note, through gayness alone). It is an image, that is to say, of Poe as "master craftsman" and "prince of supernatch"— instead of "King Weirdo, *not for the squeamish.*"[3]

Southern next recounts that memorable first exposure to the novel as a child — this is its only appearance in his prose, but the memory would become a fixture in interviews: the teacher's description of Poe ("...elaborately avoiding any mention of his teeny-bop bedmate..."[4]), the loving recounting of the novel's most grotesque elements, and the astonished, horrified reaction his writing produced in his friends.

The essay was never published. This was written for Southern alone — a love letter to the Grand Master of the American Grotesque, defending the seemingly forgotten work that inspired Southern's entire crusade as an artist. It is as if the essay was designed to reorient Southern's own sense of who he was, and what his own writing was truly about, why he was writing in the first place — not for the "bread," but for something else. It ends, as does the novel, with this quote from the novel's postscript: "I have graven it within the hill, and my vengeance upon the dust within the rock...." In this epitaph, Southern finds the core of Poe's "weirdness," and his own: vengeance, the bite of savage nature.

Also in 1968 — the same year as the previously discussed *Esquire* article on the Democratic Convention in Chicago — Southern published (in *Playboy*) the short story mentioned earlier, "Plums and Prunes." The piece is written entirely in screenplay format, showing that Southern's move from cinematic prose to the very language of cinema was more or less complete at this point. It revisits the same country as "Sea-Change" (aka "A Change of Style"); in this case, "An Ideal 'Suburbia Home' in Westchester,"[5] and like the earlier story, it's basically a one-joke idea. In this case, it's an exposure of the seething lust and violence that lies beneath the bland face of white suburban mid-twentieth century culture.

Brad, returning home from work, is informed by his wife, Donna, that their teenaged daughter, Debbie, is going out for a date with Tommy. When Debbie leans over to kiss her father, "...we get (his POV) a nice CU of her well-defined young cleavage, enticingly marked at the edge of the bra by a tiny crossed ribbon, almost, it might seem, an invitation."[6] This vision launches Brad into a fantasy in which he violently murders Tommy — he snaps out of the reverie as Tommy and Debbie leave for their date:

> Brad slowly turns. CU His face is transfigured into that of an 85 YEAR OLD MAN. He moves slowly.
>
> BRAD
> (looking vaguely in Donna's direction, speaks in a voice ancient with age) Yes ... darling ... I'm coming...
>
> FADE OUT.[7]

It's a simple sketch concept, conveying the seething nature that roils in the depths beneath the calm, plastic façade of suburbia, a portrait that restates a familiar Southern theme: how age resents the vitality of youth.

But the piece is important, for it signals a "sea change" in Southern himself. As Southern aged, the familiar theme darkened, making Brad the first in a series of unflattering self-portraits of a man in defeat. And this time, it was defeat at the hands of that element Southern most trusted: nature.

18

Blue Movies

In the same December 1968 letter in which Southern jokingly tried to convince Stanley Kubrick to make a cameo in *The Magic Christian*, he then told the director that his novel-in-progress *Blue Movie*:

> ... is moving ahead at your proverbial whistling speed — though not fast enough for a certain Mr. Dumbbell Publisher, now plaguing me for having exceeded his fuddy-duddy deadline. There is no cause for alarm, however, as there have been several attractive counteroffers, so that if an extension is not forthcoming from Mr. D. we can groove with rival pub ... your experience on big *2001* has doubtless given you to understand the possibilities of delaying in completing a major work. N'est-ce pas, Stan?[1]

Southern had first conceived of *Blue Movie* during the filming of *Dr. Strangelove* in 1963, thanks to the offhand comment that Kubrick made to Southern about a big-budget pornographic film; the $35,000 advance had been given to Southern by Random House in 1965, and the novel was finally published in 1970 — by Random House, who evidently forgave the missed deadlines mentioned above.

Upon its publication, Southern was quite pleased with the finished work, calling it, in a letter to Dennis Hopper, "...the best thing I've done (or at least since *ER* ending, Den)...."[2] Peter Matthiessen, for one, was not so impressed, dismissing the novel as "puerile,"[3] while Carol Southern was also disappointed, feeling that it was "mean to women."[4]

While compiling a promotional résumé for himself shortly afterwards (probably in order to get the film adaptation going), Southern assembled a page of blurbs for *Blue Movie*, quoting from a group that Southern himself dubbed "The Great Black Humorists"[5] — a selection that included Burroughs, Krassner, Bruce Jay Friedman and Arthur Kopit.

The page also offered Southern's argument against charges, like Carol's, of chauvinism, with the following headline and blurb: "And no, it is not male-chauv, as the great Pauline Kael does attest: *Blue Movie* is the best Hollywood novel in a long time. It should be the basis for the definitive movie about the contradictions and the comedy of the picture business."[6] Friedman, echoing Southern, called it "His best novel — beyond satire and into something like grenade-throwing."[7] Burroughs found it "a great book,"[8] while Kopit enthused that it is "the most accurate book I've ever read about Hollywood, and one of the funniest I've ever read about anything."[9]

Certainly, it is Southern's most ambitious novel, more tightly structured than *Flash and Filigree*, and well beyond the loose collections of sketches that comprised *Candy* and *The Magic Christian*—which was also the structure that Southern would return to in his next and final novel, *Texas Summer*.

For once, in *Blue Movie*, Southern truly did try to develop a coherent, three-part story: the film project is conceived, filming commences, and filming falls apart. Granted, this isn't exactly ambition on the scale of *Finnegans Wake*—but it does show that screenplay structure exerted some influence and discipline on Southern's freewheeling imagination. If only that influence had been felt just a bit more, who knows in what interesting directions his work might have gone.

Leaving conjecture aside, this structure makes *Blue Movie* unique among Southern's novels: an account of a Hollywood studio's attempt to make the most expensive pornographic film ever made, it is modeled on the Marquis De Sade's novel *120 Days of Sodom*. Southern had previously said of Sade, in *Writers in Revolt*, that:

> ... in transposing the reality of his acts into the realm of the imaginary — for him, the imaginary was much more important than reality — he created and bequeathed a brutal, inspired, exasperating, often incoherent, often compelling record, a world of superhuman lusts, ambitions, urges, subjugations, abhorring abstractions and the abstract morality in which man takes refuge and in the name of which he condemns, justifies, commits with impunity and in good conscience, the most heinous crimes. Sade chose cruelty and crime, and if it is difficult or impossible to accept his solutions, it is similarly impossible to deny the validity of his attacks on hypocrisy, indifference, mediocrity, and the "flights from reality" to which man has always succumbed, to varying degrees, as if consciously denying his own existence [p. 27].[10]

Such a description could be easily applied to Southern's work as well, and demonstrates the degree to which Southern admired and was — perhaps unconsciously — influenced by Sade. Sade's novel describes how four pillars of cultural authority — The Duke, The Judge, The Bishop and The Banker — bring a veritable army of young victims to a remote castle in the Black Forest, the Chateau of Silling. There, the captives enact a series of erotic and violent fantasy tableaux for the amusement of the four libertines, a series that culminates in an orgy of depravity and death. In adapting this scenario for his Pop romp, Southern doesn't take things quite so far, though there are, to be sure, some incidents of drug overdose and necrophilia along the way.

Sade's novel had a certain hold on Southern's imagination, especially in this period. *Twice on Top, or, The Not-So-Funny Fall of a Certain Miss Charity Ball*, an unproduced screenplay that he registered with the Writer's Guild on May 15, 1973, returns to the same plot, again giving it his own Pop spin. The screenplay is a surreal sketch in which the pert, innocent Miss Charity Ball is held captive in a mansion by a general, a priest and a judge. The sketch ends — as was increasingly to become the case with Southern's tales — with the murder of youth and innocence by self-destructive age and authority, as the three men bludgeon her with phallic balloons, and the mansion is engulfed in smoke and fire.

120 Days of Sodom also served as the secret model for *The Hunters of Karinhall*, a grotesque farce about one decadent weekend at Herman Goering's country estate. At the secluded hunting lodge, Goering and his friends engage in all manner of depravity, climaxing in all-out chaos as a fireworks display goes horribly awry. *Blue Movie*, however, was the only one of these Sade-derived epics to reach the public.

The novel opens with an epigraph from T.S. Eliot, of all people — an excerpt from his critical study *The Sacred Wood*: "Poetry is not an expression of personality, it is an escape from personality; it is not an outpouring of emotion, it is a suppression of emotion — but, of course, only those who have personality and emotions can ever know what it means to want to get away from those things."[11]

What follows are the adventures of "King B." (Boris Adrian, Hollywood's top director, clearly modeled on Kubrick) and producer Sid Krassman, who acts as Sancho Panza to King B.'s Don Quixote. The director and producer are determined to make the first large-scale "artistic" porno movie — a film that will capture the truth of sex, the emotion and joy, rather than the simple mechanical acts that comprise the usual low-grade porn film.

What the epigraph from Eliot clues the reader into from the start is the impossibility of their quest; what we will see along the way is that King B. and Sid, no less than any of the other monsters that populate the Hollywood of *Blue Movie*, are devoid of true emotion. They are vacuums who themselves possess no "personality" or "emotion"; therefore, their film can never be the "poetry" that Boris so desperately wants it to be. Not possessing these qualities themselves, Boris and Sid still want their film to be "an expression" of them; not truly knowing what these things are, they desire to get to rather than "get away from those things."

Drawing on Southern's experiences over the past five years, the novel opens with a chapter that serves as an eyewitness account of Hollywood decadence. King B. and Sid are attending a party at a Malibu beach house — there, Sid is trying to convince Boris to direct his next feature under Sid's production auspices, but the producer isn't too enthused when Boris hatches his plan for an X-rated epic: "You turned down a $10 million picture — *Dante's Inferno*, and that's one hell of a property. You know that, don't you? — you turned it down and the next day you're talking about making a stag film!" (p. 28).[12]

An amusing background to this bit of dialogue demonstrates how much of his own Hollywood experience went into the writing of Southern's novel. During this very period (circa 1970), Southern was trying to sell a screenplay he had written as a vehicle for his friend Mick Jagger. Southern was pitching the screenplay, which was entitled *The Hero with a Thousand Faces*, as a modern-day retelling of Dante's *Inferno*. Nobody bit.

Sid is at first reluctant to bite at Boris's vision, as well, but soon enough, he's on board, and cast and crew set out for a castle in Liechtenstein, which agrees to provide funding and production services in return for exclusive rights to show the film for the next ten years, only within the confines of its small borders.

This plot detail was rooted in an actual fact of film production of the era: in the late sixties, it actually was cheaper for American films to be produced in Europe rather than California — this accounts for the boom times in the English and Italian film industries that led to Southern's work in those countries.

The castle in Liechtenstein is Southern's Silling, and here, the reader is treated to a series of absurd, grotesque, erotic tableaux from nature that culminates in pitched battle with a "God Squad" from the Vatican.

After this climactic battle with the forces of moral decency, the defeated Boris, Sid and Tony (the writer, modeled on Terry himself) are nursing drinks, mulling over their failure to finish the film, when Boris has an epiphany about his own project:

> "... and there I was all along thinking about Rome as being someplace where everything was on the up and up ... and where guys like Saint Peter ... Saint Paul, guys like that, come from — am I right, Tone?"
>
> "Right, Sid," said Tone, having a drink. "Not to mention the late great Nick Machiavelli."
>
> "Yeah?" said Sid, with only sullen interest. "Who is that?"
>
> "Oh..." Tony shrugged, "one of the boys. Right, B.?"
>
> Boris nodded. "Yup." And he looked over with a sad and weary smile. "Just like the rest of us ... right, Tone?"
>
> "Dig it, B." And Tone even toasted it [p. 254].[13]

Southern here makes the point that for these denizens of Hollywood (Tony — a.k.a. Terry — included), emotion and personality are simply tools to be manipulated in Machiavellian fashion. And finally, Boris gets it. As much as Southern had bemoaned the limits of prose in the early sixties, this is a novel about the limits of film; once again, nature (sex) cannot be contained by culture (film).

Despite King B.'s best intentions, film cannot show sex as anything but inhuman and mechanical, because the people who create the films are themselves inhuman and mechanical. As with *Easy Rider*, the search for Eden is doomed before the journey has even begun — because the serpent in the garden lies inside the searchers. Boris has found, like *Easy Rider*'s Captain America, that the biggest enemy is the one within: that destructive impulse seated in the human soul that Poe called "The Imp of the Perverse," and that the Catholic Church calls Original Sin. "King" B. cannot even rule over himself, and now knows the truth of the William S. Burroughs line quoted in the novel: that "the mark inside" is indeed the one "rumble nobody can cool."

In short order, Southern wrote a screenplay adaptation of *Blue Movie*: the script downplays the novel's darker undertones and emphasizes its slapstick qualities, climaxing with a Keystone Kops car chase that seems like a lost sequence from *It's a Mad Mad Mad Mad World*. Incredibly, in that strange period of artistic freedom in Hollywood, between the collapse of the Studio System Old Guard and the rise of the Blockbuster New Guard (post–*Jaws* and *Star Wars*), *Blue Movie* came very close to being made. As Southern later remembered:

> Sometime in 1970, John Calley, the extraordinary co-producer of *The Loved One* ... became president of a major studio (Warner Bros.) for a brief moment, and decided to make a film of *Blue Movie*. A number of other people had wanted to do it, but always with the idea of compromising the work by having simulated sex. Calley, however, was convinced, as was I, that the first production of a full-on erection and penetration movie using big-name stars, a talented director, and made under studio conditions, would be a blockbuster of *Gone with the Wind* proportions.
> He was living with Julie Andrews at the time, and he and Mike Nichols, who had been signed to direct, were able to persuade her (for love, art, and a lot of money) to play Angela Sterling, the heroine of the story. A $14 million budget (quite adequate for 1970) had been secured, and everything was ready. Ringo Starr had held a movie option on the book for a year, but was ready to step aside, now that there was an actual production ready to roll. He didn't want any participation; he just wanted to see the book made into a movie.
> Enter the villain of the piece, Ringo's lawyer (who shall be nameless, but whose initials are B.G.), in absolute hysteria, ranting about how he (the lawyer) was going "to look like a schmuck if the picture gets made and we don't have a piece of it." John Calley and I were prepared to do just that, but it turned out that Mike Nichols had some weird superstition against giving points to anyone not involved during the actual shooting, so the deal fell through. *Blue Movie* didn't get made, I didn't get rich, and Johnny Sixpack didn't get to see Mary Poppins *en flagrante* on the silver screen ... all because of a shyster's vanity.[14]

At this point, both Kubrick and Nichols had passed on the option of directing *Blue Movie*. Incredibly, for a time, David Lean was interested in taking on the job — but he soon decided that it was also not quite right for him. It's worth noting that *S.O.B.*, a film that Julie Andrews made a few years later with her husband, the director Blake Edwards (he also wrote the screenplay), bears more than a passing resemblance to Southern's screenplay for the movie version of *Blue Movie*.

Andrews did ultimately make her own *Blue Movie* of sorts, but without Southern. What could have been his most notorious big-screen project failed to materialize — and so, after this, did anything else.

19

Lost Weekends

Southern stayed on in Los Angeles, hoping to find more work. He enjoyed it there, finding the city "a mecca for all manner of freakishness...."[1] Throughout the seventies and eighties, Southern made a point of writing at least one screenplay a year to peddle around L.A., but none were produced until *The Telephone*, which was directed by his old friend Rip Torn in 1988.

Soon after *Easy Rider* scored a hit, Southern wrote *A Ride to the Sun*, an attempt to cash in on whatever hippy biker craze might have been generated by *Easy Rider*. A modern variation on the Icarus myth, it tells the story of a pure young soul, a hippy bike champion who resists all attempts at corruption and goes out in a blaze of glory, like "Percy Shelley in leather."

With William Claxton, he developed a television series called *On the Loose*, about a savvy cowboy who brings disgruntled city folk on camping trips and always manages to solve their problems during the trip. The proposal for the series promised original songs for each episode's soundtrack, delivered by the likes of John Lennon and the Rolling Stones, who had, according to the proposal, already promised they would provide new material. After its rejection by the networks, the authors transformed the series pitch into a feature screenplay, adding a hip photographer protagonist obviously modeled on Claxton, as well as providing a tragic rodeo clown role clearly earmarked for Slim Pickens.

There was also *God Is Love*, a treatment for a screenplay in which a woman's *Candy*-like, freely shared sexuality creates a miracle that baffles the celibate Catholic clergy. And there was *The Hero with a Thousand Faces*. This bore no relation to the Joseph Campbell book, but was conceived as a big-budget, big-screen extravaganza: "...in the tradition of *My Fair Lady* and *Around the World in Eighty Days*. The story, although wholly contemporary, is fashioned after the narrative of Dante's *Inferno* as a vehicle for Mick Jagger, about a jet-setting aristocrat who searches the world for emotional fulfillment and finds it in the wife and child he had left behind."[2]

It's impossible to read this pitch without detecting some pangs of guilt over Southern's failed marriage with Carol, and the relationship with Nile that he was working so hard to rebuild. Jagger also hired Southern to write the screenplay *Merlin*, an unproduced project in which Jagger would have played a knight in King Arthur's court.

There were also the adaptations: Southern's faithful screenplay version of the Nathanael West novel *A Cool Million* was very nearly filmed in 1972, but studio funding was cut at the last minute. In 1977, Southern wrote an excellent screenplay based on William S. Burroughs' first novel *Junky*; the screenplay is actually superior to the novel on which it is based, and is highly reminiscent of the films of Gus Van Sant (such as *Drugstore Cowboy* and *My Own Private Idaho*), made several decades later.

Like *A Cool Million*, *Junky* was one of Southern's more commercial projects, and was nearly directed by Dennis Hopper, but for one reason or another, the old friends/enemies never got this second collaboration off the ground. Inexplicably, Southern again began collaboration with Hopper in 1983, on a screenplay about the life of Jim Morrison, for a film to be produced by Althea Maye Flynt, wife of Larry Flynt, the publisher of *Hustler Magazine* (more on him below). This too went nowhere, and was their last attempt to work together.

With Larry Rivers, Southern wrote two screenplays in the seventies; the first, *Child Molester, or, It's the Little Things That Count*, is about an artist in East Hampton (where Rivers lived) who is falsely accused of molesting the neighbor's child. The second, *The Secret Life of Larry Rivers*, is a highly romanticized account of Rivers' life as a jazz musician and Pop Artist in the Greenwich Village of the fifties and sixties. The title of the first is really all one needs to know about its commercial potential; as for the second, it's not as if Larry Rivers was exactly a household name, warranting a romanticized biopic. These collaborations did not help to further the career of either party.

Southern worked constantly — but since none of the screenplays sold, he was making no money. This didn't prevent him, however, from still living the jetset life in L.A., hanging with friends like Ringo Starr, John Lennon, Keith Moon and Harry Nilsson, a talented songwriter that Southern met through Starr, and who would later become not just a favored collaborator, but also a business partner. In later years, the Texan Southern and the Brooklyn-born Swede Nilsson even came to physically resemble each other: brothers-in-arms, war veterans of long years in the trenches of the Hollywood high life.

Nilsson had first come to prominence in the late sixties when The Beatles had touted him as their favorite songwriter, and his recent cover of the Badfinger song "Without You" was an enormous worldwide smash. Starr, too, had great success in 1973 with his solo album *Ringo*—and although it's clear in retrospect that their best creative days were behind them, the Three Musketeers (Southern, Starr and Nilsson) did not waste this opportunity to celebrate, in an era of debauchery that John Lennon (who shared much of it) later remembered as "The Lost Weekend." Southern's reminiscences about this era, and the group's copious ingestion of Brandy Alexanders, led Albert Goldman, in his Lennon biography *The Lives of John Lennon*, to term it "the days of the Great Brandy Alexander Cult."[3]

Lennon called a halt to the excess and went back to New York, but for Southern, these days never seemed to end. Carol Southern recalled that Terry drank because he was actually quite shy, and he "wanted to be entertaining,"[4] and Southern himself seemed unaware of the dangers related to his alcohol intake. In an unpublished essay from the eighties called "Drugs and the Writer," he maintained that:

> I don't believe that a serious writer is in danger of becoming an alcoholic because, after a certain point, one would not be working behind it, but directly in front of it, at peril of getting wiped out blotto, thereby defeating its purpose—which is, after all, motivational, and as a hedge against the desolation of such a lonely endeavor. Good writers have so much (dare one say "beauty and excitement?") to come back to that they're not likely to go very far afield for any great length of time.... I think this may be said for other recreational drugs as well....[5]

Blinded as he may have been to his own substance abuse problems, he was not unaware of the shabby treatment he was receiving at the hands of Hollywood—this treatment spurred him out of his early seventies haze enough to create his last great short story: "Heavy Put-Away, or, A Hustle Not Wholly Devoid of a Certain Grossness, Granted." It was published in *The Paris Review* in 1975, and won the magazine's *Paris Review* Prize for Best Short Story of the Year.

The plot of the tale had been related to Southern by the producer John Calley; according to Calley, the anecdote was true. However, Southern transformed the sad, tawdry event into a chilling parable about the perils of art—and like *Blue Movie*, it is a bitter kiss-off to the industry that was no longer treating him so well. In fact, it's tempting to read it as a disguised account of how Southern feels the *Easy Rider* payment situation was handled by his collaborators.

It begins, as all of Southern's best stories of the early sixties do, with the narrator settling down to tell us the tale, speaking directly to the reader: "Recently, I was researching an article for a women's magazine, whose considerate editor had already entitled it 'Con Men: Their Games and Their Names'—aiming, with the final emphasis, for a bit of the old expose mileage, no doubt."[6]

In researching the article, the narrator finds many examples of con jobs; one particular con, however, is removed from the article by the "senior blue-coiffed lady editor," due to "certain elements ... which are simply too, how shall I say, er, ah, gross for our general readership." The con had been related to the narrator by a man named "Art ... a younger Jack Nicholson ... [at] a café restaurant on La Cienega, about two blocks below the Sunset Strip.... ('Art' is also one of those 'L.A. types,' no other way to say it....)"[7]

Art tells the narrator of a con in which his accomplice, a distinguished-looking older man, manages to convince a young woman, desperate for money due to her husband's back injury, to sleep with him, meeting at a bungalow in the Chateau Marmont. She is convinced not only to sleep with the man, but also to give him all of her clothing, her money, and her diamond wedding ring — at which point, he vanishes, leaving her with no choice but to summon her husband, in full body cast to come to the bungalow and rescue her.

After Art has finished his tale, the narrator demands to know why Art and his friend would do this to the young woman, as she had little her money and her wedding ring wasn't valuable: "He looked at me with something close to pity. 'I should have thought it obvious,' he said, a slightly pained smile on his lips."[8]

The narrator is still baffled, musing that the ring could not have been worth more than fifty dollars:

> "$100 tops," said Art, "probably less."
> "Well, that doesn't seem like much ... for all that trouble."
> He laughed. "You've got a pretty materialistic slant on things, don't you?"[9]

Ron Rosenbaum's essay on Southern discusses this tale vis à vis "The Blood of a Wig," finding that this last line reveals the two to be paired examinations of art:

> In other words, he didn't do it for the money or the sex; he did it for art. The real payoff was the pure, cold, aesthetic pleasure in creating the elaborate confabulation: art for art's sake. In fact, "Heavy Put-Away" is a slyly disguised parable about art — not Art the Con-Man, but art as a cruel con game.... In the parable, as I read it, Southern sees himself as both perpetrator and victim, both the con man and the woman in the hotel, so cruelly deceived by art. Southern, too, is a victim of art, robbed of innocence and stability but the deranging, impoverishing obsession with its cold con.[10]

This is a convincing reading; however, I can't help but apply a more personal, autobiographical interpretation to the tale — and in doing so, it seems clear that Southern is no perpetrator. He is only the victim.

The perpetrator is Hollywood itself: all the producers, all the Dennis Hoppers, anyone who is out to screw the artist (which, for Southern, means the writer). Southern (in his own view) is the one who has been screwed, who has had everything taken from him. And the two, con man and victim; Hollywood and Southern; are thrown together in this dance by Art — by greed in using art, on the side of the perpetrator, and by the desire to make art on the side of the woman, the victim — or rather, the artist, Southern.

Although its inner subject is the author being used up and spit out by art and by Hollywood, "Heavy Put-Away" is also the moment when Southern rallied himself one more time. In Calley's anecdote about the girl, he saw himself, and from that raw material he sculpted a flawless diamond-like portrait of cruelty — and his last major statement as an artist. As Rosenbaum pointed out, it "...went further than 'Blood of a Wig' in its own nasty way, in its chilling, sub-zero coldness."[11] In retrospect, these are the last words of a dying man, or at least a dying artist and creative force, bearing eyewitness testimony to the dangers of being seduced by art and fame.

Looking at the various manuscript versions of "Heavy Put-Away," it's clear that unlike most of his work in the seventies, Southern never intended this story to be peddled around to producers and studios. This was a purely literary beast that Southern wanted to bring only to *The Paris Review*, site of his first success as a literary artist — Southern was coming home, to the friends he'd left behind a decade before. The original manuscript version of "Heavy Put-Away" has a different conclusion than the published version, offering more words from Art: "He laughed. 'You've got a pretty materialistic slant on things don't you? Huh? Yes. In fact, I would say that life is passing you by because of it ... MR. *GEORGE AMES PLIMPTON*!'"[12]

This joking twist, revealing the narrator to be the *Paris Review* editor, takes some of the sting out of the preceding coldness, and was wisely discarded — but there may also be a chilling subtext to the seeming in-joke. Perhaps it's a coded message, a warning of sorts to his old friend: forget movies, stick to books — don't get screwed like I was. Art is warning Plimpton to avoid the fate of the young woman — that is to say, of Southern.

A second manuscript version ends with a wistful admission by Southern of his own failure: "And with that, he gave me his best winner-of-many-battles, Boss Charm Grin. 'Now, ain't that a real put-away?' he asked." Below this, in the typed manuscript, Southern added, in a handwritten scrawl, "And a certain Yours Truly just had to politely agree...,"[13] acknowledging his own defeat.

Yet another manuscript version ends with Art concluding the conversation by producing a snuffbox full of cocaine. With this drug, he earns the author's allegiance, perhaps even servitude — making this a rare moment in the Southern canon when drugs might seem a danger, rather than an aid, to vision.[14]

Even though this moment never made it past manuscript stage, Southern's big turn in front of the cameras makes the same point; anyone who witnessed Southern's performance in the Rolling Stones documentary *Cocksucker Blues* didn't need such a warning.

20

Grossing Out

In 1972, the Rolling Stones had invited Southern and Truman Capote to join them on tour as their official journalists-in-residence, as the Stones went out to support their album *Exile on Main Street*. Ultimately, Capote never wrote a word on the subject, while Southern only managed to cobble together one fragmentary article, "Riding the Lapping Tongue."

The article, published in *Saturday Review*, is mostly a disjointed, impressionistic screenplay that dwells far more on Capote than the Stones, but ultimately doesn't tell us much about either. The article contains an amusing collaboration between Southern and Capote on a press release about Capote "skyjacking" the Stones' private jet; but ultimately, the article is less a sustained piece of writing than it is a jumble of fragments — an unsurprising product of a tour in which "sense derangement" was the order of the day.

The attraction between the Stones and Southern is not hard to comprehend. They are almost inverse reflections of each other: the English dandies posing as Texas bluesmen and the Texas bluesman now affecting the style and pose of a mock English dandy — all of them Decadents in the tradition of Oscar Wilde, artfully manipulating masks and poses; the cowboy and the dandy fused into one being.

The *Saturday Review* article was the first in a series of collaborations between Southern and the band. He also co-authored, with photographer Annie Leibovitz, *The Rolling Stones on Tour 1978*, a memoir of the 1978 tour, on which Southern also traveled with the band. In 1992, he supplied the text for *The Early Stones*, consisting of conversations between himself and Keith Richards, as they shared reminiscences spurred on by the photographs of Michael Cooper.

The photographer Robert Frank also came along on the 1972 tour to make a record of the journey — a documentary called *Cocksucker Blues* that would then go unreleased, due to heavy litigation from the Stones. Rather than glamorizing the Age of Rock, Frank chose to shoot the ugly truth, and nobody involved was pleased with the results; but they tell us far more about both Southern and the Stones than any of Southern's writings on the subject, and amply demonstrate why Southern's *Saturday Review* reportage wound up being as incoherent and uninformative as it was.

Moreover, the scenes involving Southern go a long way towards answering the question of what happened to him in the last two decades of his life: shoveling mountains of cocaine up his nostrils, babbling incoherently, one can almost see his talent being destroyed on film. Truman Capote, who left the tour halfway through out of sheer boredom, later recalled:

> ... one night in Dallas, he [Southern] was ... taking few things ... and I was standing at the back of the stage with the chief of detectives in Dallas.... And Terry came up and started speaking to me about something, and he pulled something out of his pocket, and out rolled every conceivable kind of pill under the whole sun.
> And so the chief of detectives of Dallas just looked down at the thing and smiled and winked and I said, "Terry, don't you think you better pick up your aspirin? (laughs) ... but he's a very nice person, Terry..." [p. 261].[1]

Capote's comments come from an interview conducted by Andy Warhol, at the behest of Jann Wenner, the founder and publisher of *Rolling Stone*. Wenner had insisted that Warhol ask Capote only two questions, one of which was simply: "Terry Southern?" Capote's initial response to the question was simply a blank "Terry Southern? ... I can't imagine why that was one of Wenner's questions." The interview fails to answer that question, but it was probably rooted in Wenner's curiosity about Southern's condition — and more importantly, whether Southern was making any progress on the novel *Double-Date*, for which Wenner had already paid him a huge advance.

During the seventies, Southern was still halfheartedly dallying with *Youngblood* (originally *The Hipsters*, later to become *Texas Summer*) — mainly at the insistence of Random House, who had given him an advance. But his only other serious effort in the direction of novel-writing was *Double-Date*. The premise had developed out of an idea Southern had tossed off to Wenner one evening, about a "square" who disguises himself as his own fictional hippy brother, then simultaneously carries on affairs with two women. Wenner jumped at the concept. The advance was paid in 1971; the interview with Capote was conducted a year later, and there was still no sign of the book.

Wenner had already scored a huge success with his publication of Hunter S. Thompson's novel *Fear and Loathing in Las Vegas*, and was clearly eager to repeat that triumph by publishing a novel by the Daddy of Gonzo Journalism. It was not to be: Southern was, by this point, in no shape to focus on something as ambitious as writing a novel. In 1973 (not long after the above interview), Southern finally threw in the towel, returning the advance to Wenner.

Roughly ten pages of *Double-Date*'s manuscript survive, both handwritten and typed, veering in style from straight prose to screenplay. Southern had worked out a fairly detailed synopsis for the novel as a whole, and the plot is the stuff of pure, old-fashioned Parisian farce — from Jimmy the stockbroker disguising himself as Rod the hippy, to the crisis when he realizes that both of the women he is sleeping with have fallen in love with Rod the hippy rather than Jimmy:

> Now he's making it with Pam (as Jimmy and Rod) and with Vicky (as Rod and Jimmy). Jimmy's initial feeling about this "final conquest," and about the situation in general, is one of extreme elation; he is now, in effect, screwing four different girls at the same time. It is a grand ego trip for him, and his highly buoyant spirits reflect his sense of triumph. Gradually, however, he becomes vaguely disturbed by the realization that both girls have betrayed him.[2]

The put-on goes wrong, ending in madness and death, with the man unable to decide which of his masks is the true face:

> ... Behind the wheel we intercut quick five frame freezes of his face and CU and the face of "Rod" peering out the window above — back and forth, back and forth like a shutter action, faster and faster — signaling the nadir of schizo-dominance. Both have nightmarish grins frozen on their faces. As the ever-faster intercut attains speed beyond visual recognition (one-frame cuts), and the motor sound of Jimmy's car reaching a screaming crescendo of burning rubber, there is a tremendous explosion as the car plummets over the precipice of the hairpin turn, in a sensational soaring crash.[3]

Like the man veering between two masks, Southern himself is veering between styles, unable to settle on prose or screenplay. This uncertainty with form betrays a deeper uncertainty with the project — and perhaps with the author himself. The unfinished novel explored the nightmare side of playing with masks, with personae: the absolute loss of any essential self or vision.

This situation was epitomized for Southern by the final scene of the old British horror film *Dead of Night*, in which Michael Redgrave as the ventriloquist has been completely taken over by his dummy Sylvester: he speaks in the dummy's voice, while shadows falling on his face create the illusion of a carved mouth (the scene was later borrowed by Hitchcock for the final moments of *Psycho*, in which Norman Bates is completely submerged in Mother).

The *Dead of Night* sequence had a peculiar hold on Southern over the years, as he returned to it repeatedly over the decades — it crops up in "Love Is a Many-Splendored," as well as a nineties column for *The Nation*, written shortly before his death.

This is the dark side of the put-on: the hipster who never recovers from sampling the blood of a wig. *Double-Date* demonstrates a sea change in the art of making it hot for them; the seventies tales are increasingly dark meditations on the theme. Southern was growing fearful that he was losing his vision, and his self.

The reasons are many for this growing fear; both Peter Matthiessen and Carol Southern feel that reality overtook his outrageous vision, and what had been shocking in the fifties and early sixties was passé and routine by the time the seventies rolled around.

In an unpublished, taped conversation from 1982, Southern and Albert Goldman ruminated on the reasons why Lenny Bruce had fallen in cultural stature so quickly, from troublemaker and trailblazer to obscure, forgotten footnote. Goldman's reasoning is as valid for Southern's reputation as it is for Bruce's, seeing that the problem with "...being a great influence ... [is that] after awhile you sort of atomize yourself into the culture.... You're everywhere, so therefore you're nowhere.... It's like the culture consumes you."[4]

To this, Southern could only glumly agree, knowing that what had made Bruce—and himself—unique, was now universal, and that as a result, they were both now passé.

Things seemed to be looking up, however, as the seventies turned the corner into the eighties. The editor on *The Loved One*, Hal Ashby, had gone on to a successful career in directing, and just had a big hit with Peter Sellers on *Being There*. Fresh off their successful collaboration on that film, the duo approached Southern to write their next venture, which was to be a satire about the global weapons trade, in the tradition of *Dr. Strangelove*.

Sellers had conceived of the idea after spending a weekend in the company of an Arab arms dealer, observing his lavish lifestyle up close. Southern and Sellers immediately went to work on research for the screenplay, as Southern recalled in his conversation with Goldman: "We went to a couple of the arms bazaars that they had in England, and they were fantastic. They're right in the middle of ... these sleepy, fabulous old Elizabethan towns.... The people come, and they have their nation set up their concession booths [to sell weapons]...."[5]

The resulting screenplay, *Grossing Out*, was an episodic montage of vignettes exploring governmental and personal deceit—it's *Syriana* played as farce. For narrative unity's sake, the plot focuses on one heavily armed British battle cruiser, which would have been captained by Sellers' character; Southern had learned in his research that "the English maintain this ship which is like a floating showcase of weapons, and they go all around the world and they invite these people ... [to] these arms bazaars...."⁶ It was a perfect setup for a series of comic sequences, with Sellers as the mad weapons merchant piloting his own floating arsenal.

This was Southern's most promising screen project in more than a decade, and came close to being filmed — unfortunately, right before production began, Sellers suffered a fatal heart attack. Ashby, who had just staged his own comeback with *Being There*, after years of personal and reputation damage due to his own substance abuse, died soon after. *Grossing Out* was finished.

However, right on the heels of this disaster, Southern finally secured what Carol Southern called "the only job he ever held"⁷: a staff writer on *Saturday Night Live*.

21

Saturday Nights of Terror, Days of Weird

By 1981, after several early years of glory, *Saturday Night Live* had fallen on hard times; the show's original cast had left, and the replacements weren't quite measuring up, to put it kindly. The original producer, Lorne Michaels, had also departed, and his replacement, Dick Ebersol, didn't seem to know what to do to fix the flailing show. After a season of creative chaos, Ebersol brought back one of the most talented of the original writers, Michael O'Donoghue, to act as Show Runner.

One of O'Donoghue's first acts in his new capacity was to hire Southern, who had been a hero at least since O'Donoghue's days at Brentano's back in the mid-sixties, when he was peddling *Candy* to unsuspecting matrons.

In the seventies, when O'Donoghue was an editor at *National Lampoon*, he had elicited three articles from Southern: "Strange Sex We Have Known," a collaboration with William S. Burroughs; "Reflections for Independence Day on Our Golden Heritage, or, Puritan Porn," a short one-act play satirizing school history pageants; and "Hard-Corpse Pornography, or, Gook Rimming in America," a disturbing account of grotesque sexual acts by American soldiers in Vietnam.

All three articles detailed deviant sexual practices; in keeping with that spirit, Southern began contributing sketches to *SNL* with titles like "Hooker Brides," "KY Madness in High Places," and "Sex with Brookie," in which two men discuss the best means of getting in bed with the then-pubescent Brooke Shields. How Southern or O'Donoghue could ever have thought this material was going to be suitable for network television, even during late night, is anyone's guess.

Southern had also, since *Dr. Strangelove*, acquired a reputation as a political satirist, though this was largely unwarranted: shrewd political commentary was never his greatest strength as a writer — as he told a radio interviewer in 1964, "I'm not interested in social reform." Politics was just part and parcel of the whole cultural apparatus he was out to dismantle — even *Strangelove* isn't satire proper but, rather, broad farce employing politicians and soldiers as its buffoons.

Still, Southern tried gamely to go along with his reputation, offering sketches like "Go Ahead, Mister Khomeini ... Make My Day!," in which then–President Reagan bases all of his policy decisions on scenes from favorite old movies. These efforts met with no greater success than the others. Tony Rosato, who was a cast member at the time, recalled (to Doug Hill and Jeff Weingrad, in their history *Saturday Night*) a day when Southern trudged into his office and slouched dejectedly into a chair, reporting that his latest sketch had been rejected by the producer. When Rosato asked why, Southern replied that "Dick told me we did politics last week."[1]

It's up for discussion just how much of his *SNL* material Southern actually wrote. In *Mr. Mike*, his biography of O'Donoghue, Dennis Perrin asserts that:

> The reasons given for Southern's low output on *SNL* that year depended on who did the talking. Southern himself said little about the experience, but [Nelson] Lyon (a fellow writer) remembered encountering the writer in a bar before the show premiered. Southern nervously sipped from a glass of scotch and confessed to Lyon his fear of doing the show. Southern asked if Lyon would add his name to Lyon's scripts and keep him on staff. Lyon agreed. After all, this was a comic genius at low ebb; slack had to be given ... [p. 380].[2]

Southern was proud of arranging for an appearance by Miles Davis on the show, but aside from that achievement — and the copious amounts of cocaine drifting around the studio ("toot by the truckful,"[3] as he phrased it) — the experience of writing for *SNL* was not pleasant for him.

Ebersol's high hopes in bringing back one of the original architects of the show didn't pan out: lightning did not strike twice for O'Donoghue, and *Saturday Night Live* was still awful. At the end of the 1981–1982 season, O'Donoghue was fired; Southern, too, was not asked to return.

In 1984, in one of the more bizarre and amusing incidents in Southern's later life, he was hired by Larry Flynt, publisher of *Hustler Magazine*, to be head speech writer in Flynt's presidential campaign. Southern lived for a time at Flynt's mansion in Los Angeles: unfortunately, no speech drafts survive, leading one to speculate on how much planning went into this bid for the presidency. This is also the period when Flynt's wife, Althea Maye, was trying to get her Jim Morrison biopic off the ground, with Southern as writer (though he doesn't seem to ever have actually written a word of the script, either).

The campaign was short and unsurprisingly unsuccessful, but did lead

Southern to write a series of erotic reminiscences about his Texas youth for the magazine. Only one ("Virgin Love; or, Fab First Fuck") was published, in the July 1985 issue — it is significant in being his first and only published piece of openly autobiographical writing (the memoir *Making It Hot for Them*, begun nearly a decade later, would remain unfinished at his death).

Despite his professional setbacks in these decades, Southern found solace by retreating to Blackberry River Farm. Nile Southern later wrote a touching memoir of life there with his father:

> I enjoyed what I imagine to have been a classic Texas boyhood, in the northwest corner of Connecticut. Our farm dated from 1757, and our twenty-nine acres were nestled in a rural valley. We had an apple orchard and pond, giant field, barns — all surrounded by the amazing wild nature of the Berkshires. Terry was always enhancing the visuals, planting flowers, mosses and ground cover. He was a gentleman farmer. We raised organic beef, sheep, chickens and guinea fowl. We'd take buckets of steaming gruel out to the pigs by snowmobile on subzero nights.[4]

Here, Southern found and reveled in the twilight world that his best prose evokes, pinpointed by Algren in "The Donkeyman by Twilight." Father and son made short films together, in which Southern's Poe-like imagination was given freest rein, unfettered by studio demands, still alive and well in his Hawthorne woods.

Nile recalls one of their collaborations, a short called "Night of Terror, Day of Weird," in which Nile played Larry Rivers, painting a portrait of Southern:

> Terry wears a half-beauty/half-beast mask, and as I finished painting his portrait, beauty side facing me, I say "Kindly turn this way, Madame," and the weirdo slowly, painfully swings the hideous profile into full, leering close-up.
> "Not a pretty sight, is it ... *Mister Portrait Painter!*" he exclaims in falsetto, parting the long white hair to reveal the full horror of her hamburger meat face — at which point I begin blasting with a miniature pistol in slow-mo ECU.[5]

The flip side of beauty is always horror, for Southern — one is incomplete without the other, the two always joining to create a whole. Left to his own devices, Southern could paint that picture clearly. And yet, outside of those woods, the vision was stunted, despite his best efforts to gain control of his work.

In 1985, Southern and his old friend Harry Nilsson formed a film production company together called Hawkeye Productions; for the first time since *The End of the Road*, Southern seemed to be taking control of his work, rather than relying on the whims and needs of others. In its brief career, Hawkeye did prove successful in returning Southern's work to the big screen for the first time in nearly two decades — the only problem was that the resulting film seemed hardly worth the wait.

Hawkeye's first project was a Southern/Nilsson collaboration called *Obits*, which stemmed from a story idea by Nilsson that Southern developed more fully into a screenplay. Harkening back to "The Blood of a Wig's" evocation of seedy low-end journalism, the unproduced script reads like a cross between *Miss Lonelyhearts* and *The Texas Chainsaw Massacre*. A burned out journalist from Manhattan heads to Texas to investigate the wealthiest family in America, who turn out to be a bizarre incestuous clan inhabiting a crumbling Victorian mansion in the middle of nowhere — a Texas version of the House of Usher.

Southern took Nilsson's original idea of a star reporter going after weird tales, and transformed it into an exercise in Texas Gothic. Along with the three brief erotic memoirs he wrote for *Hustler* in the eighties, as well as *Texas Summer* and the unproduced nineties screenplay *Whut?*, *Obits* indicates that in his final years, Southern's imagination was returning more and more to Texas. Brooding in the twilight of his northern Hawthorne woods, Southern's reveries alternated between the dreamy nostalgia of the *Hustler* essays and the horror of *Obits*— Texas was still the landscape of his blues, a region of dreams and nightmares.

It was not *Obits* that was filmed, however — that honor went to their second collaboration, *The Telephone*. Like *Obits*, it is an exercise in Gothic Horror, though on a far more restrained, psychological level — the subject is, in Southern's words, "...an out-of-work actor who gets so into hallucinations that he would make up phone calls for himself."[6] Neither *Obits* nor *The Telephone* screams "box-office smash" in terms of subject matter; both are odd fruits for the collaboration between a noted humor writer and a tunesmith known for pleasing pop confections.

It's even more bizarre that this unsettling character study called *The Telephone* was conceived as a vehicle for Robin Williams, with whom Nilsson had collaborated on the film *Popeye*. Then again, though light on humor, the script demands an actor adept at multiple voices and fast improvisation.

Williams passed on the script, and the part eventually went to Whoopie Goldberg; Rip Torn agreed to direct. According to Southern, Goldberg insisted on improvising new material, which led to clashes between her and Torn, and, ultimately, a battle over who got final cut, star or director.

Southern preferred Torn's version to Goldberg's, but whatever the behind-the-scenes story might be, the finished film that was ultimately released adheres quite closely to Southern and Nilsson's script, after they had revised it to suit Goldberg rather than Williams. As a nightmarish vision of a person lost in role-playing, in masks and put-ons, artifice and illusion, *The Telephone* is a work conceived in the same spirit as *Double-Date*— and in some ways, *The Year of the Weasel*. This is a portrait of someone lost in the fun house, cut adrift from any coherent sense of self, her life nothing but an endless stream of bizarre reflections and masks. It is another indication of Southern's darkening vision in his later years, as he called his entire artistic project into question.

As mentioned above, Southern had made comparisons, in his Journal from the Fifties, between the writer and the actor. It was the manipulation of many styles that he admired in the writing of Henry Green, as well as in the acting of Peter Sellers (not to mention Brando and Olivier, the two actors mentioned in the Fifties Journal). He told Albert Goldman, in their taped conversation, that what he admired most in Sellers and Lenny Bruce was their ability to play many characters. Recalling all this, it is impossible not to see *The Telephone* as a form of dark autobiography.

The screenplay is again structured a bit like a Roald Dahl story, recalling "Sea-Change" in that aspect. The dark ending twist sheds new light on all that came before: this was not light-hearted comedy, but chilling madness. The entire action of the film takes place in one San Francisco apartment, where a young woman sits alone with her pet owl (recall John Phillips' memoir of Southern's early New York days, when he'd sit in his darkened apartment with his own pet owl). She spends the evening performing a series of comic monologues and impersonations as she speaks to various friends and relatives on the telephone, though we learn during the climax that the phone has been cut off for three months — when the telephone man informs her of this fact, she beats him to death with the telephone.

The put-on is now deadly, a source of unease and horror. Cut off from Hollywood and from his muse, alone in the woods, Southern conjured characters that court madness and death. His 1973 short story "Fixing Up Ert" had echoed "The Tell-Tale Heart" (see below), but still in the service of raucous gross-out belly laughs. *The Telephone*, on the other hand, moves into the nightmare country of such fevered Poe narratives as "The Black Cat" and "The Cask of Amontillado." Any laughter afforded by this screenplay leaves a very bitter aftertaste.

The problem with *The Telephone* as a film rather than a screenplay is that there is very little laughter indeed, although Goldberg gamely goes for it. Though a talented performer, her strength doesn't lie in mimicry and impersonation; the screenplay is obviously tailored for the skills of someone like Williams or Peter Sellers, someone who can fly effortlessly from characterization to characterization. Watching Goldberg struggle with accents and dialects is painful; every routine falls flat. The ending is effectively creepy — but coming after ninety minutes of mind-numbingly dull "comedy," it's too little, too late. The film's fast disappearing act in theaters was unsurprising.

The Telephone was Hawkeye's first and last hurrah, though financial problems associated with the company plagued the partners for the rest of their days (Nilsson died in early 1994, a year before Southern). Their business manager, according to Southern, failed to file the company's income tax and then "absconded with all of the funds that Harry and I had put aside for tax,"[7] leaving Southern and Nilsson in a great deal of trouble with the IRS, even after she was reportedly jailed for the theft. On this sour note, Southern's film career came to its definitive end.

22

Limbo

The Terry Southern Archives contain a large body of unproduced screenplays and story fragments from these last decades; most of them are disjointed, bizarre vignettes, frequently set in Texas, nearly all careening from prose to screenplay, seemingly at random. There was no focus, no discipline, and the published work provides corroborating evidence of a failing vision.

Nearly all of the screenplays could be summarized in script coverage with basically identical plot summaries: protagonists come to strange location and become enmeshed in even stranger sexual practices. There was *The Brightest and the Best*, inspired by Dr. William Shockley's controversial seventies theories on using test tube babies to create a master race, and detailing the misadventures of patients chosen to breed that race; *Sex Therapy Script* (the only title that survives on the manuscripts), about the doomed attempts by a laboratory to map sexuality (again, culture tries to control nature and pays the price); and *George and Linda*, the dark tale of a couple whose car breaks down, not unlike David and Vivian in "Janus" — but unlike David and Vivian, George and Linda take refuge in the isolated farmhouse of an elderly couple who watch them having sex, and then grotesquely mimic George and Linda's lovemaking (age feeds on youth).

The discerning reader will detect a pattern here — a pattern that has nothing to do with moviegoer tastes or movie industry demands. The screenplays show an uncommercial preoccupation with aberrant sexuality; in the prose, Southern seemed increasingly preoccupied with the prospect of put-ons and masks, to the exclusion of all other topics. He had already composed his greatest tribute to the art of the put-on in *The Magic Christian*— but where Grand's hoaxes were clever and, as Southern insisted, were "never meant to harm anyone," the same could not be said of later subjects.

In the low-rent skin magazine *Oui*, he published a short story in 1976, the previously mentioned "Fixing Up Ert." One has to admire the protean skills of a writer who could follow up the 1975 *Paris Review* Award for Best Short Story of the Year with what is basically a dirty joke in a porn book. But "Ert," while undeniably funny, is also childish in its raunch, as the narrator pits his monstrous coworker "Ertegun Barff" against a blueblood Duchess. Southern's version of "The Telltale Heart" is far more light-hearted than Poe's, and nature's triumph over culture in this case is Southern at his most scatological.

"Tito Bandini; or, Doggy Dope Run" was published in a 1978 issue of *High Times*: a portrait of a dope dealer who smuggles drugs into America in the bars of animal cages, the article seeks to make of Bandini another Guy Grand. Southern is lost in admiration of the drug smuggler's con, seemingly oblivious to the fact that Bandini is no more than a thug.

"The Straight Dope on the Private Dick," also written in the late seventies (but not published until after Southern's death), begins with a series of put-ons aimed at confounding private detectives, but builds to a climax that describes what Southern sees as the ultimate put-on: the one perpetrated by the U.S. government in its persecution of Lenny Bruce, who Southern also considered a master of the put-on. The whole art of the con turns on itself, as the laughter grows sour.

By the early nineties, the joke was over; all laughter had faded. Even Southern must have realized he was now simply writing for an audience of one, and that he had drifted, to borrow the title of a late story fragment, into "Limbo." The story survives only in scattered typed and handwritten pieces, and revisits the same terrain as *Obits*.

In the remote farmhouse of a bizarre redneck family, "Ma" complains to her son about her husband, who has now secreted himself in a closet in order to observe a couple making love in the next room:

> John sighed. "You hate him, don't you, Ma?"
> "It isn't him I hate, son," she said gently. "It's what he's become."
> "How do you mean, Ma?"
> "I don't know, son. He's just ... well, he's just lost it."
> "Lost it? Lost what, Ma?"
> "His vision. He's become some kind of creepy voyeur."[1]

Southern heeds the female voice — the voice of nature — in this exercise in self-laceration. It was from this limbo state that he rallied himself, beginning in 1991, to compose a series of short op-ed pieces for his old stomping grounds at *The Nation*. The essays are critiques of such issues of the day as the first Iraq War and Mother Theresa's anti-contraception stance. In the essay "Looking for Dr. Strangelove; or, How I Learned to Stop Worrying and Groove Behind Instant Gratification," he again employs the *Dead of*

Night image of Michael Redgrave and his dummy Sylvester — this time, America is the ventriloquist, now controlled by its supposed puppet Israel. None of the essays is particularly inspired — again, political analysis wasn't his strength — but they seem to have finally given Southern's writing a modicum of focus again.

Conceding that his career in film was over, Southern tried to get a regular job as a columnist for *The Nation* or *Esquire*: he seems to have acquired, near the end, a certain zeal for the role of pundit. It was not the first time that he had dallied with the notion of being a columnist; as early as 1970, a minor skin magazine called *Screw* had offered him the post for sixty dollars a column, telling him that "believe it or not, that will make you our highest paid columnist."[2] Southern rejected the offer, but did briefly serve as *Oui*'s television critic around the time of "Fixing Up Ert." Actually, both of the critical columns he submitted were actually humor pieces: one about a *Waltons* sex cult, the other about imagined (and depraved) new offerings for the fall season.

Unfortunately, no such columnist gig was forthcoming in the nineties, aside from three mock exposes in *Hamptons Magazine*, all under the title "New Age Ethics." He had to settle for publishing more op-ed pieces wherever he could. His last piece of "political satire" appeared in a small local paper in Connecticut called *The Millerton News and the Lakeville Journal*, on May 12, 1994. "Good Golly, Colonel Ollie! Is Virginia Ready for You?" was a mock dialogue between Newt Gingrich, Bob Dole and Oliver North, spurred on by North's bid for the senate in Virginia. In 1964, it might have gotten attention, reading like a lost scene from *Dr. Strangelove*. In 1994, it just seemed charming, like a familiar song from a forgotten singer.

So too did the previously discussed "Repentance," when it appeared in Jean Stein's *Grand Street* in 1992. In the context of Southern's career, the tale was fascinating. For those unfamiliar with his work, Southern's last published short story was no doubt dismissed as merely puzzling. He published a few more short pieces in *Grand Street*: a memoir of Maurice Girodias called "Flashing on Gid," a mock interview with an outrageously gay Donald Trump under the title "Gay Man's Nook, Gay Man's Cranny." Nothing made much of an impact.

His very last column, written for Nile Southern's website *Alt-X* in 1995, did show a spark of life, as he once again conjured the mood of the *Confidential* exposes that Carol recalled him loving back in the fifties, and that had inspired his *Realist* articles back in the sixties. Under the old *Olympia Journal* heading "Terry Southern's Spy's Corner," he conjured a new alter ego, in the spirit of Hunter S. Thompson's Raoul Duke: "Cody McAllister," a

Texas Ranger taking up the crusade to wage war on "Rash Lamebrain."[3] In Rush Limbaugh's wildly popular conservative program, Southern had found a new target for demolition.

This character harkens back to the epigraph for *The Magic Christian*: "Little man whip a big man every time if the little man is in the right and keeps a-comin,'" which Southern had credited as the "Motto of the Texas Rangers." The Ranger Cody McCallister was no Guy Grand, but at least Southern went down fighting, his old zest for combat in the face of "smug complacency" seemingly renewed. Still, with the emerging internet offering a vast platform for every conceivable viewpoint and agenda, Southern's voice was easily lost in the shuffle.

Serving as mouthpiece for a Texas redneck always granted Southern's later writings a vitality they might otherwise have lacked: the screenplay and novel fragment *Whut?* concerns the adventures of Buck and Roy, two good ol' boys (actually, morons) who strike it rich in the oil business and head out to Hollywood to conquer the movie business as producers. Southern had first conceived of Buck and Roy in several letters to the artist Neil Welliver, whose work Southern had first analyzed in his unpublished essay "The Centaur in the Stable," back in the fifties (see above). *Whut?* contains some of the funniest writing of Southern's final years, but he never completed either the novel or screenplay version. Again, we are only left with tantalizing hints of unrealized projects.

There seems little point in discussing all of the output from these last years in great detail: all drive home, in various ways, the points already made — of a writer who has lost touch, lost focus, lost youth, and is painfully aware of all of this. It was noticeable to others, as well. Gore Vidal, in his memoir *Palimpsest*, recalls seeing Southern at a party in the early nineties, noting that Southern "...is now large and unlike the lean, sharp youth I first knew."[4]

Southern's 1992 screenplay *Festival*, done at the behest of *Magic Christian* director Joseph McGrath, is a kaleidoscopic farce about the Cannes Film Festival — and serves as a prime example of just how much, and why, Southern had drifted into irrelevance and obscurity.

McGrath conceived of the project and story, mesmerized by the precession of the simulacra in Cannes, as people on film filming people on film, images capturing images in an endless cycle. It's a good basic concept, and perhaps he wanted something along the lines of a Robert Altman movie; what he got was another *Casino Royale*. Southern does nothing with the endless looping of filmic images that McGrath spoke of in interviews — the action is basic slapstick. Thirty years after Marvin Barrett's article, Southern was still strip-mining his old fifties gags; even the "New Art Museum in Hamburg" piece from *The Olympia Journal* gets recycled here.

It's astonishing how redolent of the fifties and early sixties the *Festival* screenplay is: what is most forcefully conveyed by the cast of lascivious Russians and Playboy bunnies is just how stuck in that period old-timers like Southern and McGrath had become, forever dwelling in the era of their greatest success (if interviews are any indication, McGrath seemed pleased with the screenplay, however ambitious his original concept was).

This brings us to the final question: even if his current work was subpar, why did the early work never get rediscovered? Why did Southern's career never receive the renaissance granted to like-minded contemporaries like William S. Burroughs? We have answered the question of what happened to Southern himself—but what of his reputation, a matter over which he had little or no control?

As mentioned previously, Burroughs' reputation in the later years was carefully managed by his assistant James Grauerholz, who was largely responsible for turning the old Beat into a brand name. Southern had no such assistant, but that isn't the whole of the reason for his reputation's inability to make a comeback.

The answer, I think, can be found in the fact that his vision is so evocative of that *Mad Men* Era of Hugh Hefner and Madison Avenue that oozes out of every scene in *Festival*: a vanished world, one that Southern had been dedicated to blowing up when he burst on the scene. Once it was gone, however, so was he.

Too Much Playboy, Not Enough Punk: this can serve as an apt enough solution for the riddle of why Southern's vanished street cred has never been rediscovered. During his renaissance, Burroughs did readings in punk clubs, courting new generations. Southern, on the other hand, stayed at Blackberry River farm, only deigning to drop some disparaging remarks about punk music in *Virgin* (see below); rock (and its various mutations) was never his thing. Despite his fondness for The Beatles, the Rolling Stones and Nilsson as people, he was a Jazz man through and through, to the end, and he wasn't going to budge for anyone.

Likewise, his attitude towards sexuality, once daring, seemed positively antique after the sexual revolution, as if it came from the same time capsule as Hugh Hefner's—it's wonderful that he was against Puritan restraint, but by the time Southern reached old age, who in America wasn't? Not very many—more's the pity for Southern's notoriety.

The post-sixties generations, who aided Grauerholz in keeping the Burroughs flame burning on into the present, loved the explicit violence, the brutal sexuality, and most of all, the Hieronymous Bosch–like fantasy landscapes that remove Burroughs's work from any one specific time period; the science-fiction aspect of his work allows Burroughs to belong to the ages.

These same readers found little to relate to, on the other hand, in the very Fifties landscape of Southern's imagination — as Southern himself found little to relate to, once that cocktail-set universe was gone. Without the dragon, the knight was lost, as he ruefully realized. After all, the epigraph to *Making It Hot for Them* was a quote from Beavis and Butthead: "Plus ca change, plus ca suck."[5]

Texas Summer was a pleasant curtain call when it was finally published in 1992, but hardly the sort of work that would re-establish his reputation or connect him to the young firebrands of the new generations. It contained some wonderful new material, especially Chapter 11's visit to the Big Red Onion Carnival; but no one could pretend it was anything more than a nostalgia trip, collecting mostly old material in a somewhat new package. The book is, in a word, complacent — a worrying product from an author whose avowed earlier mission was to smash complacency.

But that was done. All he could do, at this point, was look back, at a time and a career that was slipping farther and farther away into the past.

Conclusion to Part Two: The Priest of Pagan Nature Laid to Rest

It is, perhaps, not surprising that Southern brought so little creative fire to his writing at the end; taking his health into account, it's admirable that he did any writing at all. In 1991, he was diagnosed with stomach cancer and had half of his stomach removed; in 1992, he suffered a minor stroke — for the rest of his life, Southern couldn't walk without the aid of a cane. In 1993, he returned to Texas for the first time in decades, on a reading tour with Tess Gallagher; a reporter who interviewed Southern in Dallas noted that the stomach operation had no visible effect on his consumption of spareribs and whiskey.

During these last years, Southern taught a few screenwriting classes in the graduate writing program at Yale, and then got a steady (although low-paying) position as a writing instructor for the graduate film writing program at Columbia. His colleague Robert Fitzpatrick recalled him as "a generous mentor to young writers."[1]

Gail Gerber, who was living with Southern at Blackberry River Farm, would drive him down from Connecticut to the 125th Street campus, dropping him off at the base of a steep set of stairs that led from the parking lot to the building in which he taught.

One day in late October of 1995, she dropped him off and went in search of a parking spot; happening to glance in the rearview mirror, Gerber saw Southern stagger and fall. He was rushed to the nearby Saint Luke's Hospital. A doctor there asked Nile if his father had ever worked in a coal mine; a lifetime of heavy smoking had caused so much damage that he appeared to be suffering from Black Lung Disease.

On Sunday, October 28, at the age of seventy-one, Terry Southern died of respiratory failure — just a few days shy of Halloween, missing his last chance to put on the masks once more. The night nurse who found him told Nile that Southern "...looked radiant, his long silver hair" spread out on the pillow beneath him, "the angelic trickster laid to rest."[2]

In early 1996, a few months after his death, Richard Branson's Virgin Press issued *Virgin*, mainly a scrapbook collection of photographs charting the history of the record label. The text (such as it is) consists of Southern's witty comments on the photographs assembled, making it similar to earlier "scrapbooks" he had collaborated on, like *The Journal of the Loved One* with William Claxton, *The Rolling Stones on Tour '78* with Annie Leibovitz, and *The Early Stones* with Michael Cooper and Keith Richards.

Southern himself dismissed such books, as well as his 1991 *Spin* cover story on Texas band ZZ Top, and his limited edition biography of Southern Rock band The Black Crowes, written in 1992. He described these forays into rock journalism as "deadly, tedious, enervating work,"[3] taken purely for the paycheck.

It was not exactly a triumphant swan song, but *Virgin* was his final published book; the Texas bluesman had played his last riff. The final bedtime story had been told.

Carol Southern described what happened to his life and enormous talent as "a tragedy,"[4] and so it was, ending not with a bang but an unfocused whimper. But right up until the end, through all the haze and chaos, we still catch those fast glimpses he offered of another world, an American twilight zone of freedom and darkness where lies explode, plastic melts and nature looms triumphantly, enervating — and enabling — our culture.

The cultural clothes might have changed, and that might have caused the tales to be discarded like yesterday's news, never picked up again. That's regrettable, because the core is eternal.

The priest of pagan nature took his own road out of Axotle, and he hit that fence too soon. It's a shame he never tried to go over, to search for that knowledge on the other side that would have made his vision expand further; something that would have taken him beyond an existential delight in watching his insufficient culture crumble in the face of an abundant nature.

Existentialism can be the gateway to higher knowledge, after the old constructs of knowing have been blown up. It can also be just a closed fence at the end of the road — and for Southern, it seems that ultimately, it was. It's too bad he never tried to figure out what lies further up that road ... to follow it, like Arthur Gordon Pym, all the way to the end, whatever that end might be. Then again, he went farther than many go, and that may be far enough for us.

Because in doing so, he left behind these existential lessons from nature, these wisdom fables of monsters and innocents ... these tales of the American Grotesque.

That's of lasting value. That's what endures.

Source Notes

Introduction to Part One

1. Perry Meisel, *The Cowboy and the Dandy* (New York: Oxford University Press, 1999): 132.
2. Terry Southern, "Grooving in Chi," *Esquire*, November 1968: 86.
3. *Ibid.* 86.
4. Nelson Algren, "The Donkeyman by Twilight," *The Nation*, 18 May 1964: 508.
5. Dust Jacket Copy, *Flash and Filigree* (New York: Coward-McCann, 1958).
6. Terry Southern, "The Loved One: Terry Southern's Last Interview," *Paper*, December 1995: 83.
7. *Ibid.* 83.
8. Kenneth Silverman, *Edgar A. Poe: Mournful and Never-Ending Remembrance* (New York: Harper Perennials): 133.
9. Carol Southern, personal interview, 9 October 1997.
10. Lee Hill quoting Kurt Vonnegut, "Southern Discomfort," *Scenario*, Spring 1999: 166.
11. Terry Southern quoting Henry Green, ms. personal journal, The Terry Southern Archives (henceforth, all material contained in the Southern Archives will be designated TSA).
12. Terry Southern quoting Samuel Beckett, ms. personal journal, TSA.
13. Nelson Algren, "The Donkeyman by Twilight," *The Nation*, 18 May 1964: 508.
14. Greil Marcus, *Invisible Republic: Bob Dylan's Basement Tapes* (New York: Henry Holt, 1997): 87.
15. Camille Paglia, *Sexual Personae* (New Haven: Yale University Press, 1990): 137.
16. Peter Matthiessen, personal interview, 27 July 2000.
17. Nile Southern, personal interview, 20 August 1999.
18. Albert Goldman, *Freakshow* (New York: Atheneum, 1971): 333.
19. Terry Southern, "A Creative Capacity to Astonish," *Life*, 21 August 1964: 40.
20. Terry Southern, "Interview with Terry Southern by Maggie Paley," ms. interview, TSA.
21. Greil Marcus, *Invisible Republic: Bob Dylan's Basement Tapes* (New York: Henry Holt, 1997): 87.
22. William S. Burroughs, "Introduction to *Flash and Filigree*," ms. essay, TSA.
23. Terry Southern, "The Refreshing Ambiguity of the Deja Vu," ms. story, TSA.
24. Ray Bradbury, *Something Wicked This Way Comes* (New York: Avon Books, 1996): 25.
25. Camille Paglia, *The Birds* (London: British Film Institute Press, 1998): 99.

Chapter 1

1. Carol Southern, personal interview, 9 October 1997.
2. Terry Southern, *Texas Summer* (New York: Arcade, 1991): 102.
3. Terry Southern, "You were born in Alvarado ..." ms. interview, TSA: 1.
4. Terry Southern, "The Loved One: Terry Southern's Last Interview," *Paper*, December 1995: 83.
5. Terry Southern, "Trib to *Pym*," ms. essay, TSA.
6. Terry Southern, "An Impolite Interview with Terry Southern," *Best of the Realist*, ed. Paul Krassner (Philadelphia: Running Press, 1982): 134.
7. Terry Southern, "Ten Minutes with Terry Southern," *The Catalog of Cool*, ed. Gene Sculatti (New York: Warner Books, 1982): 83.
8. *Ibid.* 84.
9. William Styron, "Transcontinental with Tex," *The Paris Review*, Vol. 38, No. 138, Spring 1996: 224.

10. Carol Southern, personal interview, 9 October 1997.
11. Terry Southern, interview, "Buried Beneath the Haze," *Dallas Observer*, 2 April 1992: 16.
12. Terry Southern, interview, "No Limits," *Newsweek*, 22 June 1964: 86.
13. *Ibid.*
14. Terry Southern, "You were born in Alvarado...," ms. interview, TSA: 5.
15. Carol Southern, personal interview, 9 October 1997.
16. Helen Southern, letter to Terry and Pud Southern, undated, "It was so nice to talk with you...," TSA.
17. Terry Southern I, letter to Terry Southern II, 3 March 1956, TSA.
18. Joseph H. Davis, M.D., letter to Mrs. L.J. Barrett, 29 January 1957, TSA.
19. Carol Southern, personal interview, 9 October 1997.
20. Nile Southern, interview, "Buried Beneath the Haze," *Dallas Observer*, 2 April 1992: 16.

Chapter 2

1. Terry Southern, "You were born in Alvarado...," ms. interview, TSA: 5.
2. *Ibid.* 2.
3. Terry Southern, "The Face of the Arena," *Red-Dirt Marijuana and Other Tastes* (New York: Citadel, 1990): 207.
4. *Ibid.* 207.
5. *Ibid.* 211.
6. *Ibid.* 212.
7. Terry Southern, interview, "Buried Beneath the Haze," *Dallas Observer*, 2 April 1992: 16.
8. Terry Southern, "You were born in Alvarado...," ms. interview, TSA: 3.
9. Terry Southern, "The Automatic Gate," *Red-Dirt Marijuana and Other Tastes* (New York: Citadel, 1990): 200.
10. *Ibid.* 200.
11. *Ibid.* 201.
12. Terry Southern, "The Butcher," *Red-Dirt Marijuana and Other Tastes* (New York: Citadel, 1990): 190.
13. *Ibid.* 192–193.

Chapter 3

1. Terry Southern, "The Sun and the Still-Born Stars," *Red-Dirt Marijuana and Other Tastes* (New York: Citadel, 1990): 35.
2. *Ibid.* 37.
3. *Ibid.* 39.
4. *Ibid.* 42.
5. *Ibid.* 43.
6. *Ibid.* 41.
7. Peter Matthiessen, personal interview, 27 July 2000.
8. Terry Southern, *Flash and Filigree* (New York: Grove, 1996): 29–31.
9. Terry Southern, "The Accident," ms. story, TSA.
10. George Plimpton, "Introduction to the Citadel Underground Edition," *Red-Dirt Marijuana and Other Tastes* (New York: Citadel, 1990): ix.
11. Peter Matthiessen, personal interview, 27 July 2000.
12. William Styron, "Transcontinental with Tex," *The Paris Review* Vol. 38, No. 138, Spring 1996: 217.
13. John Phillips, "Long ago in 1951..., " ms. essay, TSA: 5–6.
14. *Ibid.* 8.
15. *Ibid.* 9.
16. George Plimpton, "Introduction to the Citadel Underground Edition," *Red-Dirt Marijuana and Other Tastes* (New York: Citadel, 1990): x.
17. *Ibid.* x.
18. Terry Southern, "His Second Most Interesting Case," ms. story, TSA: 1.
19. *Ibid.* 6.
20. Terry Southern, "Now dig this...," ms. interview, TSA: 2–3.
21. Carol Southern, letter to Nile Southern, 17 November 1995, TSA.
22. John Phillips, "Long ago in 1951...," ms. essay, TSA: 9.
23. *Ibid.* 9.
24. Terry Southern, "You were born in Alvarado...," ms. interview, TSA: 37.
25. Terry Southern, *The Hipsters*, ms. novel, TSA: 2.
26. *Ibid.* 42.
27. Terry Southern, "You Gotta Leave Your Mark," *Red-Dirt Marijuana and Other Tastes* (New York: Citadel, 1990): 89–90.
28. *Ibid.* 105–106.
29. Terry Southern, "Children at Play," ms. screenplay, TSA: 2.
30. Terry Southern, "The Pusher," ms. story, TSA.
31. Terry Southern, "Song of the Old Hemp-Smoking Woman by the Fireside," *Two Songs and a Game*, ms. poem, TSA.
32. Terry Southern, "Funny Little Children's Song," *Two Songs and a Game*, ms. poem, TSA.

33. Terry Southern, "Play a Game of Diplomats," *Two Songs and a Game*, ms. poem, TSA.
34. Mckay Jenkins quoting Gay Talese, "Introduction," *The Peter Matthiessen Reader* (New York: Vintage Books, 2000): xx.
35. Terry Southern, "The Bird Is Gone," ms. essay, TSA.
36. Terry Southern, "The Night the Bird Blew for Doctor Warner," *Red-Dirt Marijuana and Other Tastes* (New York: Citadel, 1990): 45–46.
37. *Ibid*. 55.
38. Terry Southern, "Paul's Problem," ms. story, TSA: 1.
39. *Ibid*. 5–6.
40. *Ibid*. 18.
41. Terry Southern, "A Run of Dimes," ms. story, TSA: 1–2.
42. *Ibid*. 2.
43. *Ibid*. 7–10.
44. Terry Southern, *The Magic Christian* (New York: Grove, 1996): 10.

Chapter 4

1. Carol Southern, personal interview, 9 October 1997.
2. *Ibid*.
3. Terry Southern, "A South Summer Idyll," *Red-Dirt Marijuana and Other Tastes* (New York: Citadel, 1990): 57.
4. *Ibid*. 60.
5. *Ibid*. 62.
6. *Ibid*. 67.
7. Carol Southern, personal interview, 9 October 1997.
8. Terry Southern, "You were born in Alvarado…," ms. interview, TSA: 4.
9. Terry Southern, *The Year of the Weasel*, ms. play, TSA: cast page.
10. *Ibid*. 1–1–2.
11. *Ibid*. 1–1–2.
12. *Ibid*. 1–1–18.
13. Terry Southern, *The Donkey and the Darling*, ms. story, TSA: 1.
14. *Ibid*. 2–3.
15. *Ibid*. 34.
16. *Ibid*. 35.
17. *Ibid*. 36.
18. Terry Southern, "C'est Toi Alors: A Scenario for Existing Props and French Cat," ms. play, TSA: 1.
19. *Ibid*. 4.
20. *Ibid*. 4.
21. Terry Southern, "Janus," ms. story, TSA.
22. *Ibid*.
23. Terry Southern, "Brandy for Heroes," ms. story, TSA: 11–12.
24. *Ibid*. 10.
25. *Ibid*. 15–16.
26. Terry Southern, "(TS INTERVIEW CONT'D.) Jean Stein said…," ms. interview, TSA.
27. Terry Southern, "Color-Blind," ms. story, TSA: 3.
28. *Ibid*. 6–7.
29. *Ibid*. 7.
30. Terry Southern, "The Strangest Breed," ms. story, TSA: 5.
31. *Ibid*. 5.
32. Terry Southern, *Making It Hot for Them*, ms. memoir, TSA: 45–46.
33. Carol Southern, personal interview, 9 October 1997.
34. Terry Southern, letter to Mason Hoffenberg, 19 May 1957, TSA.
35. Carol Southern, personal interview, 9 October 1997.
36. Terry Southern, letter to Mason Hoffenberg, 19 May 1957, TSA.
37. Terry Southern, *Candy* (New York: Grove, 1996): 133.
38. *Ibid*. 136.
39. *Ibid*. 149.
40. George Plimpton, "Introduction to the Citadel Underground Edition," *Red-Dirt Marijuana and Other Tastes* (New York: Citadel, 1990): xii.
41. *Ibid*. xii.
42. Camille Paglia, *Sexual Personae* (New Haven: Yale University Press, 1990): 5.
43. *Ibid*. 5.
44. Terry Southern, "Just what sort of operation…," ms. interview, TSA: 4.
45. Carol Southern, personal interview, 9 October 1997.
46. John De St. Jorre quoting Maurice Girodias in *Venus Bound* (New York: Random House, 1994): 137.

Chapter 5

1. Terry Southern, *The Accident*, ms. screenplay, TSA.
2. Harold Bloom, *The American Religion: The Emergence of the Post-Christian Nation* (New York: Simon & Schuster, 1992): 3.
3. Terry Southern, *A Fairly Stubborn Case*, ms. screenplay, TSA: 4.
4. Terry Southern, *Flash and Filigree*, ms. novel, TSA.

5. Terry Southern, *Flash and Filigree* (New York: Grove, 1996): 202–203.
6. Terry Southern, "An Impolite Interview with Terry Southern," *Best of the Realist*, ed. Paul Krassner (Philadelphia: Running Press, 1982): 135.
7. Terry Southern, *Flash and Filigree* (New York: Grove, 1996): 203–204.
8. Terry Southern, *Nut-Case: First Scene and Screenplay Synopsis*, ms. screenplay, TSA: 16.
9. Malcolm Bradbury, *The Modern American Novel* (New York: Oxford University Press, 1983): 177.
10. Terry Southern, *Flash and Filigree* (New York: Grove, 1996): 11–12.
11. *Ibid*. 167–168.
12. Terry Southern, *Candy* (London: Grove, 1996): 147.
13. Terry Southern, "A Creative Capacity to Astonish," *Life*, 21 August 1964: 40.
14. Terry Southern, "You were born in Alvarado…," ms. interview, TSA: 3.
15. V.S. Pritchett, "Green on Doting," *The New Yorker*, 17 May 1952: 137.
16. George Plimpton, "Introduction to the Citadel Underground Edition," *Red-Dirt Marijuana and Other Tastes* (New York: Citadel, 1990): xii.
17. John Updike, "Introduction," *Surviving: The Uncollected Writings of Henry Green*. ed. Matthew Yorke (London: Chatto & Windus, 1992): xvi.
18. Henry Green, letter to Terry Southern, "Dear Southern, It is amazingly good…," TSA.
19. Carol Southern, personal interview, 9 October 1997.
20. George Plimpton, letter to Terry Southern, 11 February 1948 [sic], TSA.
21. Carol Southern, personal interview, 9 October 1997.

Chapter 6

1. Terry Southern, letter to Mason Hoffenberg, "Thanks for your letter of November 7th," TSA.
2. Carol Southern, personal interview, 9 October 1997.
3. Terry Southern, *The Magic Christian* (New York: Grove, 1996): 10.
4. *Ibid*. 6–7.
5. Terry Southern, *The Magic Christian*, ms. novel, TSA: 113–117.
6. *Ibid*. 119.
7. *Ibid*. 120.
8. *Ibid*. 127–128.
9. Terry Southern, *The Magic Christian* (New York: Grove, 1996): 148.
10. Henry Allen quoting Hunter S. Thompson, "To Him, Hip Was a Funny Bone," *Washington Post*, 3 October 1995: B1.
11. Terry Southern, "The Perils of Publishing," *Best of the Realist*, ed. Paul Krassner (Philadelphia: Running Press, 1982): 137.
12. Terry Southern, "The Spy's Corner: New Art Museum in Hamburg Blown Up," ms. story, TSA: 1.
13. *Ibid*. 3.
14. Carol Southern, personal interview, 9 October 1997.
15. Terry Southern, "Put-Down," *Red-Dirt Marijuana and Other Tastes* (New York: Citadel, 1990): 69.
16. *Ibid*. 74.
17. Carol Southern, personal interview, 9 October 1997.
18. *Ibid*.

Chapter 7

1. Terry Southern, "Interview with Terry Southern by Maggie Paley," ms. interview, TSA.
2. Carol Southern, personal interview, 9 October 1997.
3. Terry Southern, "(TS INTERVIEW CONT'D.), Jean Stein said…," ms. interview, TSA.
4. Terry Southern, "The Case of William Faulkner and the Cross-Bearing Liberals," ms. essay, TSA: 1.
5. *Ibid*. 3.
6. Terry Southern, "Tom Swift in the Brothel," ms. essay, TSA: 4–5.
7. Terry Southern, interview, "Were you interested in movies…?" ms. interview, TSA: 1–2.
8. Terry Southern, "Red-Dirt Marijuana," *Red-Dirt Marijuana and Other Tastes* (New York: Citadel, 1990): 4.
9. *Ibid*. 12.
10. *Ibid*. 13.
11. Terry Southern, *Texas Summer* (New York: Arcade, 1991): 174.
12. Terry Southern, "Razor Fight," *Red-Dirt Marijuana and Other Tastes* (New York: Citadel, 1990): 17–22.
13. *Ibid*. 29.
14. *Ibid*. 32.
15. Terry Southern, "Pellet of Nihilism," *The Nation*, 21 May 1960: 440.

16. Terry Southern, "Toward a New Ethics," ms. essay, TSA.
17. Terry Southern, "New Trends and Old Hats, *The Nation*, 19 November 1960: 380.
18. *Ibid.* 383.
19. Terry Southern, "Christ Seen Darkly," *The Nation*, 25 February 1961: 170.
20. *Ibid.* 171.
21. *Ibid.* 170.
22. Terry Southern, "Miller: Only the Beginning," *The Nation*, 18 November 1961.
23. Terry Southern, "The Theatre," *Queen*, 30 January 1963: 11.
24. Terry Southern, "When Film Gets Good…," *The Nation*, 17 November 1962: 330.
25. Terry Southern, "You were born in Alvarado…," ms. interview, TSA: 38–39.
26. Peter Matthiessen, personal interview, 27 July 2000.
27. Terry Southern, "Love Is a Many Splendored," *Red-Dirt Marijuana and Other Tastes* (New York: Citadel, 1990): 140.
28. *Ibid.* 142.
29. *Ibid.* 144.
30. Terry Southern, "Apartment to Exchange," *Red-Dirt Marijuana and Other Tastes* (New York: Citadel, 1990): 136.
31. *Ibid.* 137.
32. Terry Southern, "The Moon-Shot Scandal," *Red-Dirt Marijuana and Other Tastes* (New York Citadel, 1990): 214.
33. *Ibid.* 215.
34. *Ibid.* 217–218.
35. Terry Southern, "Red Giant on Our Doorstep!" *Red-Dirt Marijuana and Other Tastes* (New York: Citadel, 1990): 217–218.
36. Terry Southern, "Scandale at the Dumpling Shop," *Red-Dirt Marijuana and Other Tastes* (New York: Citadel, 1990): 219.
37. *Ibid.* 220.
38. Terry Southern, "Terry Southern Interviews a Faggot Male Nurse," *Red-Dirt Marijuana and Other Tastes* (New York: Citadel, 1990): 225–226.

Chapter 8

1. Tom Wolfe, "Preface," *The New Journalism*, eds. Tom Wolfe and E.W. Johnson (New York: Harper & Row, 1973).
2. Terry Southern, "An Impolite Interview with Terry Southern," *Best of the Realist*, ed. Paul Krassner (Philadelphia: Running Press, 1982): 137.
3. Albert Goldman, *Ladies and Gentlemen: Lenny Bruce!!!* (New York: Penguin Books, 1971): 228–229.

4. Terry Southern, "The Road Out of Axotle," *Red-Dirt Marijuana and Other Tastes* (New York: Citadel, 1990): 107.
5. *Ibid.* 108.
6. *Ibid.* 111.
7. *Ibid.* 124.
8. *Ibid.* 124–125.
9. *Ibid.* 127.
10. Tom Wolfe, introduction to Terry Southern, *The New Journalism*, eds. Tom Wolfe and E.W. Johnson (New York: Harper & Row, 1973): 161.
11. Terry Southern, "Twirling at Ole Miss," *Red-Dirt Marijuana and Other Tastes* (New York: Citadel, 1990): 145.
12. *Ibid.* 145.
13. *Ibid.* 145.
14. *Ibid.* 146.
15. *Ibid.* 152–153.
16. *Ibid.* 157.
17. Terry Southern, "You're Too Hip, Baby," *Red-Dirt Marijuana and Other Tastes* (New York: Citadel, 1990): 75.
18. *Ibid.* 79.
19. *Ibid.* 86.
20. *Ibid.* 87.
21. Terry Southern, "Recruiting for the Big Parade," *Red-Dirt Marijuana and Other Tastes* (New York: Citadel, 1990): 159.
22. Terry Southern, "I *Am* Mike Hammer!" *Red-Dirt Marijuana and Other Tastes* (New York: Citadel, 1990): 179–180.
23. *Ibid.* 176.
24. *Ibid.* 177.
25. Terry Southern, "A Change of Style," *Red-Dirt Marijuana and Other Tastes* (New York: Citadel, 1990): 203.
26. *Ibid.* 206.
27. Terry Southern, "After the Bomb, Dad Came Up with Ice," *The New York Times Book Review*, 2 June 1963.

Chapter 9

1. Terry Southern, letter to Carol Southern, "Sunday Night," TSA.
2. *Ibid.*
3. Albert Goldman, *Ladies and Gentlemen: Lenny Bruce!!!* (New York: Penguin, 1971): 589.
4. *Ibid.* 588.
5. Terry Southern, *Making It Hot for Them*, ms. memoir, TSA: 47.
6. Terry Southern, "The Burroughs Express," ms. essay, TSA.
7. Terry Southern, "Rolling Over Our Nerve-Endings," *Book Week*, 8 November 1964.

8. Victor Bockris, *With William Burroughs: A Report from the Bunker* (New York: St. Martin's, 1996): 256.
9. *Ibid.* 95.
10. *Ibid.* 64.
11. Terry Southern, "Toward a New Ethic," ms. essay, TSA.
12. Terry Southern, *Beyond the Beat*, ms. anthology, TSA.
13. Terry Southern, "Introduction: Toward the Ethics of a Golden Age," *Writers in Revolt*, eds. Terry Southern, Richard Seaver, and Alexander Trocchi (New York: Berkeley Medallion Books, 1965): 13–14.
14. *Ibid.* 16.
15. *Ibid.* 17.
16. Terry Southern, "The Blood of a Wig," *Red-Dirt Marijuana and Other Tastes* (New York: Citadel, 1990): 232.
17. *Ibid.* 242.
18. *Ibid.* 246.
19. Ron Rosenbaum, "The Edgy Enthusiast," *The New York Observer*, 19 December 1995: 32.

Conclusion to Part One

1. Terry Southern, personal journal, TSA.
2. Albert Goldman, *Freakshow* (New York: Atheneum, 1971): 333.
3. Terry Southern, "A Creative Capacity to Astonish," *Life*, August 1964: 40.

Introduction to Part Two: The Movie Years

1. Mark Singer, "Whose Movie Is It, Anyway?" *The New Yorker*, 22 June 1998: 110.
2. Terry Southern, interview, "...now dig this..." (an interview with Terry Southern," ms. interview), TSA.
3. Robert McKee, *Story* (New York: Regan Books, 1997), 46.
4. Stephen King, *On Writing* (New York: Pocket Books, 2002).
5. Terry Southern, letter to Allen Ginsberg, "Dear Allen...," ms. letter, TSA.

Chapter 10

1. Terry Southern and Stanley Kubrick, "An Interview with Stanley Kubrick," ms. interview, TSA.
2. *Ibid.*
3. *Ibid.*
4. Terry Southern, *Making It Hot for Them*, ms. memoir, TSA.
5. *Ibid.*
6. *Ibid.*
7. Terry Southern, "Screenwriting: An Interview with Terry Southern," ms. interview, TSA.
8. Terry Southern, interview, "Were you interested in movies...?" ms. interview.
9. Terry Southern, *Making It Hot for Them*, ms. memoir, TSA.
10. Terry Southern, "True Darl," ms. letter, TSA.
11. *Ibid.*
12. Terry Southern, "Memories of *Dr. Strangelove*," ms. essay, TSA.
13. *Ibid.*
14. John Baxter, *Stanley Kubrick: A Biography* (New York: HarperCollins, 1997), 194.
15. Terry Southern, interview, "Were you interested in movies...?" ms. interview, TSA.
16. Carol Southern, personal interview, 9 October 1997.
17. John Baxter, *Stanley Kubrick: A Biography* (New York: HarperCollins, 1997), 179–180.
18. *Ibid.*
19. *Ibid.*
20. Nile Southern, "Dad Strangelove," *Scenario*, Spring 1999: 185.
21. John Baxter, *Stanley Kubrick: A Biography* (New York: HarperCollins, 1997), 181.
22. Terry Southern, *Making It Hot for Them*, ms. autobiography, TSA.
23. *Ibid.*
24. Stanley Kubrick, letter to Terry Southern, "Dear Terry, Thank you very much...," ms. letter, TSA.

Chapter 11

1. Terry Southern, interview, "...now dig this...," ms. interview, TSA.
2. *Ibid.*
3. Dennis Perrin quoting Alfred Chester, *Mr. Mike: The Life and Work of Michael O'Donoghue* (New York: Avon Books, 1998), 113.
4. *Ibid.* 116.
5. Conrad Knickerbocker, "Black Humor," *New York Times*, May 1964.
6. Robert Scholes, *The Fabulators* (New York: Oxford University Press, 1967).
7. Conrad Knickerbocker, "Humor with a Mortal Sting," *New York Times*, 27 September 1964.
8. Terry Southern, "A Creative Capacity to Astonish," *Life*, August 1964: 40.

9. Steven Weisenburger, *Fables of Subversion: Satire and the American Novel, 1930–1980* (Athens and London: University of Georgia Press, 1995).
10. Albert Goldman, "Boy-Man Schlemiel" in *Freakshow* (New York: Atheneum, 1971).
11. Albert Goldman, "Pop Is Mom" in *Freakshow* (New York: Atheneum, 1971).
12. *Ibid.*
13. *Ibid.*
14. *Ibid.*
15. *Ibid.*

Chapter 12

1. Terry Southern and Stanley Kubrick, interview, "An Interview with Stanley Kubrick," ms. interview, TSA.
2. William Styron, "Transcontinental with Tex," *The Paris Review*, Vol. 38, No. 138, Spring 1996: 215–226.
3. *Ibid.*
4. *Ibid.*
5. *Ibid.*
6. *Ibid.*
7. Carol Southern, personal interview, 9 October 1997.
8. Tony Richardson, *The Long-Distance Runner: An Autobiography* (New York: William Morrow, 1993), 195.
9. *Ibid.* 201.
10. Terry Southern, *The Journal of The Loved One*, ms. essay, TSA.
11. Terry Southern, "A Creative Capacity to Astonish," *Life*, August 1964: 40.
12. Conrad Knickerbocker, "Humor with a Mortal Sting," *New York Times*, 27 September 1964.
13. Terry Southern, interview, "No Limits," *Newsweek*, 22 June 1964.
14. *Ibid.*
15. Terry Southern, "A Creative Capacity to Astonish," *Life*, August 1964.
16. Terry Southern, interview, "No Limits," *Newsweek*, 22 June 1964.
17. Nelson Algren, "The Donkeyman by Twilight," *The Nation*, 18 May 1964: 508.
18. *Ibid.*
19. *Ibid.*
20. Marvin Barrett, "At the Movies: The Southern Way of Death," *The Reporter*, 18 November 1965: 40–42.
21. *Ibid.*
22. Tony Richardson, *The Long-Distance Runner: An Autobiography* (New York: William Morrow, 1993).
23. Terry Southern, interview, "Were you interested in movies...?" ms. interview, TSA.
24. Terry Southern, interview, "You were born in Alvarado, Texas...," ms. interview, TSA.

Chapter 13

1. Terry Southern, interview by Lee Hill for *Patrick McGilligan's Backstory* 3, ms. interview, TSA.
2. Terry Southern, interview, "Were you interested in movies...?" ms. interview, TSA.
3. Terry Southern, interview with Lee Hill for *Patrick McGilligan's Backstory* 3, ms. interview, TSA.
4. Terry Southern, "Dennis Hopper Profile," *Vogue*.
5. Terry Southern, interview with Lee Hill for *Patrick McGilligan's Backstory* 3, ms. interview, TSA.
6. *Ibid.*
7. *Ibid.*
8. *Ibid.*
9. *Ibid.*
10. Carol Southern, personal interview, 9 October 1997.
11. Terry Southern, interview, "You were born in Alvarado, Texas...," ms. interview, TSA.
12. *Ibid.*

Chapter 14

1. Terry Southern, interview with Lee Hill for *Patrick McGilligan's Backstory* 3, ms. interview, TSA.
2. *Ibid.*
3. Terry Southern, interview, "Screenwriting: An Interview with Terry Southern," ms. interview, TSA.
4. Terry Southern, Interview with Lee Hill for *Patrick McGilligan's Backstory* 3, ms. interview, TSA.
5. "Court Ruling Doubles the 'Easy' Score." 11 May 1999. CNN.com.
6. Terry Southern, profile of Rip Torn, *Saturday Review of the Arts*.
7. Terry Southern, interview with Mike Golden, "...now dig this...," ms. interview, TSA.
8. Terry Southern, "Brothel Sequence/*Easy Rider*," ms. screenplay, TSA.
9. Terry Southern quoted by Lee Hill, BFI Modern Classics: *Easy Rider*. London: British Film Institute, 1996.

10. Terry Southern, letter to Dennis Hopper, "Dear Den, I'm sorry to bug you...," ms. letter, TSA.

Chapter 15

1. Terry Southern, interview with Lee Hill for *Patrick McGilligan's Backstory 3*, ms. interview, TSA.
2. *Ibid.*
3. Terry Southern, interview, "Screenwriting: An Interview with Terry Southern," ms. interview, TSA.

Chapter 16

1. Terry Southern, interview, "Were you interested in movies...?" ms. interview, TSA.
2. Terry Southern, letter to Stanley Kubrick, "Dear Stanley, I was delighted beyond all expressing...," ms. Letter, TSA.
3. Terry Southern, interview with Lee Hill for *Patrick McGilligan's Backstory 3*, ms. interview, TSA.
4. Ringo Starr, liner notes, *Goodnight Vienna* (Los Angeles: Capitol Records, 1974).
5. George Plimpton, "Terry Southern: Introduction," *The Paris Review*, Vol. 38, No. 138, Spring 1996: 197.

Chapter 17

1. Nile Southern, "Dad Strangelove." *Scenario*, Spring 1999: 7, 185.
2. Terry Southern, interview, "Your magazine articles in the early 60s...," ms. interview, TSA.
3. Terry Southern, "Trib to *Pym*," ms. essay, TSA.
4. *Ibid.*
5. Terry Southern, "Plums and Prunes," ms. short story, TSA.
6. *Ibid.*
7. *Ibid.*

Chapter 18

1. Terry Southern, letter to Stanley Kubrick, "Dear Stanley, I was delighted beyond all expressing...," ms. letter, TSA.
2. Terry Southern, letter to Dennis Hopper, "Dear Den, I'm sorry to bug you...," ms. letter, TSA.
3. Peter Matthiessen, personal interview, 27 July 2000.

4. Carol Southern, personal interview, 9 October 1997.
5. Terry Southern, "What the Great Black Humorists are Saying..." ms. page, TSA.
6. *Ibid.*
7. *Ibid.*
8. *Ibid.*
9. *Ibid.*
10. Terry Southern, "Introduction to Sade," *Writers in Revolt*, Eds. Terry Southern, Richard Seaver, and Alexander Trocchi (New York: Berkeley Medallion Books, 1965).
11. Terry Southern quoting T.S. Eliot, *Blue Movie* (New York: Grove, 1996).
12. *Ibid.*
13. *Ibid.*
14. Terry Southern, interview, "You were born in Alvarado, Texas," ms. interview, TSA.

Chapter 19

1. Terry Southern, interview, "Why does there seem to be a homosexual aura...," ms. interview, TSA.
2. Terry Southern, *The Hero with a 1000 Faces*, ms. screenplay, TSA.
3. Albert Goldman, *The Lives of John Lennon* (New York: William Morrow, 1988), 490.
4. Carol Southern, personal interview, 9 October 1997.
5. Terry Southern, "Drugs and the Writer," ms. essay, TSA.
6. Terry Southern, "Heavy Put-Away," Fourth version ms. short story, TSA.
7. *Ibid.*
8. *Ibid.*
9. *Ibid.*
10. Ron Rosenbaum, "The Edgy Enthusiast," *The New York Observer*, 19 December 1995: 32.
11. *Ibid.* 32.
12. Terry Southern, "Heavy Put-Away," First version, ms. short story, TSA.
13. Terry Southern, "Heavy Put-Away," Second version, ms. short story, TSA.
14. Terry Southern, "Heavy Put-Away," Third version, ms. short story, TSA.

Chapter 20

1. Truman Capote, interview with Andy Warhol, *Truman Capote: Conversations*. Ed. M. Thomas Inge (Jackson and London: University of Mississippi Press, 1987).

2. Terry Southern, *Double-Date*, ms. novel, TSA.
3. *Ibid.*
4. Terry Southern, "Came in for a quiet drink…," Interview with Albert Goldman, Tape Transcript (Transcribed by Author), 10 December 1982, TSA.
5. *Ibid.*
6. *Ibid.*
7. Carol Southern, personal interview, 9 October 1997.

Chapter 21

1. Tony Rosato quoting Terry Southern to Doug Hill and Jeff Weingrad, *Saturday Night: A Backstage History of Saturday Night Live* (New York: Vintage Books, 1986), 450–453.
2. Dennis Perrin, *Mr. Mike: The Life and Work of Michael O'Donoghue* (New York: Avon Books, 1998).
3. Doug Hill and Jeff Weingrad quoting Terry Southern, *Saturday Night: A Backstage History of Saturday Night Live* (New York: Vintage Books, 1986), 450–453.
4. Nile Southern, "Dad Strangelove." *Scenario*, Spring 1999: 7, 185.
5. *Ibid.*
6. Terry Southern, interview with Lee Hill for *Patrick McGilligan's Backstory* 3, ms. interview, TSA.
7. *Ibid.*

Chapter 22

1. Terry Southern, "Limbo," ms. short story, TSA.
2. *Screw* Magazine, letter to Terry Southern, "Dear Terry, Good to from you…" ms. Letter, TSA.
3. Terry Southern, "Terry Southern's Spy Corner," ms. essay, TSA.
4. Gore Vidal, *Palimpsest: A Memoir* (New York: Penguin Books, 1995), 213.
5. Terry Southern, *Making It Hot for Them*, ms. memoir, TSA.

Conclusion to Part Two

1. William S. Burroughs quoting Robert Fitzpatrick, "WSB: A Sketch of Terry Southern (1924–1995)," WSB.com.
2. Nile Southern, "Envoi." *The Paris Review*, Vol. 38, No. 138, Spring 1996: 240–241.
3. Terry Southern, interview, "Buried Beneath the Haze," *Dallas Observer*, 2 April 1992: 16.
4. Carol Southern, personal interview, 9 October 1997.

Bibliography

Note: All materials designated "TSA" are contained in the Terry Southern Archives, now housed in the Berg Collection, New York Public Library.

Algren, Nelson. "The Donkeyman by Twilight." *The Nation*, 18 May 1964: 509–512.

Allen, Henry. "To Him, Hip Was a Funny Bone." *Washington Post*, 3 October 1995: B1, B5.

Barrett, Marvin. "At the Movies: The Southern Way of Death." *The Reporter*, 18 November 1965.

Baxter, John. *Stanley Kubrick: A Biography*. New York: Carroll & Graf, 1997.

Bloom, Harold. *The American Religion: The Emergence of the Post-Christian Nation*. New York: Simon & Schuster, 1992.

Bockris, Victor. *With William Burroughs: A Report from the Bunker*. New York: St. Martin's, 1996.

Bradbury, Malcolm. *The Modern American Novel*. New York: Oxford University Press, 1983.

Bradbury, Ray. *Something Wicked This Way Comes*. New York: Avon Books, 1996.

Breton, Andre, ed. *Anthology of Black Humor*. Translation by Mark Polizzotti. San Francisco: City Lights Books, 1997.

Davis, Joseph H., M.D. Letter to Mrs. L.J. Barrett. 29 January 1957. TSA.

De St. Jorre, John. *Venus Bound: The Erotic Voyage of the Olympia Press and Its Writers*. New York: Random House, 1994.

Fiedler, Leslie. *Freaks: Myths & Images of the Secret Self*. New York: Simon & Schuster, 1978.

_____. *Love and Death in the American Novel*. New York: Delta Books, 1966.

Goldman, Albert. *Freakshow*. New York: Atheneum, 1971.

_____. *Ladies and Gentlemen: Lenny Bruce!!!* New York: Penguin Books, 1971.

Goodstone, Tony, ed. *The Pulps*. New York: Chelsea House, 1970.

Green, Henry. Letter to Terry Southern. "Dear Southern. It is amazingly good...," 9–13, George Street, Manchester Square, London. W.1. TSA.

_____. *Loving, Living, and Party-Going*. New York: Penguin Books, 1993.

_____. *Surviving: The Uncollected Writings of Henry Green*. Edited by Matthew Yorke. London: Chatto & Windus, 1992.

Hawthorne, Nathaniel. *Tales & Sketches*. New York: Library of America, 1982.

Hill, Lee. *Easy Rider. BFI Modern Classics*. London: British Film Institute, 1996.

_____. "Southern Discomfort." *Scenario*, Spring 1999: 164–171, 192.

Hollowell, John. *Fact & Fiction: The New Journalism and the Nonfiction Novel*. Chapel Hill: University of North Carolina Press, 1977.

Hopper, Dennis, Peter Fonda and Terry Southern, Screenwriters. *Easy Rider*. Dir. Dennis Hopper. With Dennis Hopper, Peter Fonda. Columbia Pictures, 1968.

Jenkins, Mckay. "Introduction." *The Peter Matthiessen Reader*. Edited by Mckay Jenkins. New York: Vintage Books, 2000: xx.

Johnson, Michael L. *The New Journalism: The Underground Press, The Artists of Nonfiction and Changes in Established Media*. Lawrence: University Press of Kansas, 1971.

Knickerbocker, Conrad. "Humor with a Mortal Sting." *New York Times*, 27 September 1964.

Krassner, Paul. *Confessions of a Raving Unconfined Nut: Misadventures in the*

Counterculture. New York: Simon & Schuster, 1993.
Kubrick, Stanley. "An Interview [by Terry Southern] with Stanley Kubrick," Ms. interview. TSA.
_____. Letter to Terry Southern. 1 August 1963, TSA.
Kubrick, Stanley, Peter George and Terry Southern, Screenwriters. *Dr. Strangelove*. Dir. Stanley Kubrick. With Peter Sellers. Columbia Pictures, 1964.
Marcus, Greil. *Invisible Republic: Bob Dylan's Basement Tapes*. New York: Henry Holt, 1997.
_____. *Lipstick Traces: A Secret History of the 20th Century*. Cambridge: Harvard University Press, 1990.
Matthiessen, Peter. Personal interview. 27 July 2000.
McKee, Robert. *Story: Substance, Structure, Style, and the Principles of Screenwriting*. New York: Regan Books Harper Collins, 1997.
Meisel, Perry. *The Cowboy & the Dandy*. New York: Oxford University Press, 1998.
Morgan, Ted. *Literary Outlaw: The Life & Times of William S. Burroughs*. New York: Avon Books, 1988.
Paglia, Camille. *The Birds*. BFI Modern Classics. London: British Film Institute Press, 1998.
_____. *Sexual Personae: Art and Decadence from Nefertiti to Emily Dickinson*. New York: Vintage Books, 1991.
Perrin, Dennis. *Mr. Mike: The Life and Work of Michael O'Donoghue*. New York: Avon Books, 1998.
Phillips, John. "Long ago in 1951..." Ms. essay. TSA.
Plimpton, George. "Introduction to the Citadel Underground Edition." *Red-Dirt Marijuana and Other Tastes*. New York: Citadel Press, 1990.
_____. Letter to Terry Southern. 11 February 1948 [sic]. TSA.
_____. "Terry Southern: Introduction." *The Paris Review* Vol. 38, No. 138, Spring 1996: 197.
Poe, Edgar Allan. *Poetry and Tales*. New York: Library of America, 1984.
Pritchett, V.S. "Green On Doting." *The New Yorker*, 17 May 1952: 137–138.
Richardson, Tony. *The Long-Distance Runner: An Autobiography*. New York: William Morrow, 1993.
Rosenbaum, Ron. "The Edgy Enthusiast." *The New York Observer*, 18 December 1995: 32.
Scholes, Robert. *The Fabulators*. New York: Oxford University Press, 1967.
Silverman, Kenneth. *Edgar A. Poe: Mournful and Never-ending Remembrance*. New York: Harper Perennial, 1992.
Singer, Mark. "Whose Movie Is It, Anyway?" *The New Yorker*, 22 June 1998: 110.
Southern, Carol. Letter to Nile Southern, 17 November 1995. TSA.
_____. Personal interview. 9 October 1997.
Southern, Helen. Letter to Terry and Pud Southern. "Dearest Terry and Pud, It was so nice to talk with you..." TSA.
Southern, Nile. "Dad Strangelove." *Scenario*, Spring 1999: 7, 185.
_____. "Envoi." *The Paris Review*, Vol. 38, No. 138, Spring 1996: 240–241
_____. Personal interview. 20 August 1999.
Southern, Terry, Sr. Letter to Terry Southern, Jr. 3 March 1956. TSA.
Southern, Terry, Jr. *The Accident*. Ms. screenplay. TSA.
_____. "After the Bomb, Dad Came Up with Ice." *The New York Times Book Review*, 2 June 1963: 7.
_____, screenwriter. *Barbarella*. Dir. Roger Vadim. With Jane Fonda. Paramount Pictures, 1967.
_____. *Beyond the Beat*. Ms. anthology. TSA.
_____. *Beyond the Shadows*. Ms. screenplay. TSA.
_____. *The Big Touch*. Ms. screenplay. TSA.
_____. "The Bird Is Gone." Ms. essay. TSA.
_____. *Blue Movie*. New York: Grove Press, 1996.
_____. *Blue Movie*. Ms. screenplay. TSA.
_____. "Brandy for Heroes." Ms. story. TSA.
_____. *The Brightest and the Best*. Ms. screenplay. TSA.
_____. "Brothel Sequence/*Easy Rider*." Ms. screenplay. TSA.
_____. "The Burroughs Express." Ms. essay. TSA.
_____. *Candy*. New York: Grove Press, 1996.
_____. *Candy*. Ms. essay. TSA.
_____. *Candy Kisses*. Ms. screenplay. TSA.

———. "The Case of William Faulkner and the Cross-Bearing Liberals." Ms. essay. TSA.
———. "C'est Toi Alors: A Scenario for Existing Props and French Cat." Ms. play. TSA.
———. *Children at Play*. Ms. screenplay. TSA.
———. "Christ Seen Darkly." *The Nation*. 25 February 1961: 170–171.
———. "Color-Blind." Ms. story. TSA.
———. "Dark Laughter in the Towers." *The Nation*, 23 April 1960: 348–350.
———. *The Donkey and the Darling*. Ms. story. TSA.
———. *Double-Date*. Ms. novel. TSA.
———. "Drugs and the Writer." Ms. essay. TSA.
———. *The Early Stones*. New York: Hyperion Books, 1992.
———, screenwriter. *The End of the Road*. Dir. Aram Avakian. With Stacy Keach, James Earl Jones. Columbia Pictures, 1969.
———. *A Fairly Stubborn Case*. Ms. screenplay. TSA.
———. *Festival*. Ms. screenplay. TSA.
———. "Fixing Up Ert." Ms. story. TSA.
———. *Flash & Filigree*. New York: Grove Press, 1996.
———. *Flash and Filigree*. Ms. novel. TSA.
———. "Funny Little Children's Song," *Two Songs and a Game*. Ms. poem. TSA.
———. *George and Linda*. Ms. screenplay. TSA.
———. *God Is Love*. Ms. screenplay treatment. TSA.
———. "Grooving in Chi." *Esquire*, November 1968: 83–86.
———. *Grossing Out*. Ms. screenplay. TSA.
———. "Heavy Put-Away; or, A Hustle Not Wholly Devoid of a Certain Grossness, Granted." Ms. story. Three versions. TSA.
———. *The Hero with a 1000 Faces*. TSA.
———. *The Hipsters*. Ms. novel. TSA.
———. *The Hunters of Karinhall*. Ms. screenplay. TSA.
———. "An Impolite Interview with Terry Southern." *Best of the Realist*. With Paul Krassner. Philadelphia: Running Press, 1982.
———. Interview. "Buried Beneath the Haze: Digging into Terry Southern's Buried Texas Roots." With Robert Wilonsky. *Dallas Observer*, 2 April 1993: 13–19.
———. Interview. "Came in for a quiet drink..." Tape Transcript (transcribed by Author). With Albert Goldman. 10 December 1982. Cassette tape given to Author; transcript now in TSA.
———. Interview. "A Creative Capacity to Astonish." With Jane Howard. *Life*, 21 August 1964: 39–41.
———. "(TS Interview Cont'd.) Jean Stein said..." Ms. interview. TSA.
———. Interview. "Just what sort of operation..." Ms. interview. TSA.
———. Interview. "The Loved One: Terry Southern's Last Interview." With Carlo McCormack. *Paper*, December 1995: 83.
———. Interview. "No Limits." *Newsweek*, 22 June 1964: 86–87.
———. Interview. "...Now Dig This..." June 1990. With Michael Golden. Ms. interview. TSA.
———. Interview. For *Patrick McGilligan's Backstory* 3, with Lee Hill. Ms. interview. TSA.
———. Interview. "Screenwriting: An Interview with Terry Southern." Ms. interview. TSA.
———. Interview. "Ten Minutes with Terry Southern." With Richard Blaikhen. *The Catalog of Cool*. Ed. Gene Sculatti. New York: Warner Books, 1982.
———. Interview. "Were you interested in movies...?" Ms. interview. TSA.
———. "Interview with Terry Southern by Maggie Paley." Ms. interview. TSA.
———. Interview. "You were born in Alvarado..." Ms. interview. TSA.
———. "Introduction: Sade." *Writers in Revolt*. Eds. Terry Southern, Richard Seaver, and Alexander Trocchi. New York: Berkeley Medallion Books, 1965.
———. "Introduction: Toward the Ethics of a Golden Age." *Writers in Revolt*. Eds. Terry Southern, Richard Seaver, and Alexander Trocchi. (New York: Berkeley Medallion Books, 1965.
———. "Janus." Ms. story. TSA.
———, with William Claxton, photographer. *The Journal of The Loved One*. New York: Random House, 1965.

———. Letter to Allen Ginsberg. "Dear Allen." TSA.
———. Letter to Carol Southern. "Sunday Night." TSA.
———. Letter to Dennis Hopper. 5 December 1970, TSA.
———. Letter to Mason Hoffenberg. 19 May 1957, TSA.
———. Letter to Mason Hoffenberg. "Thanks for your letter of November 7th." TSA.
———. Letter to Stanley Kubrick. TSA.
———. "Limbo." Ms. story, TSA.
———. "The Loved House of the Dennis Hoppers." *Vogue*, 146. August 1, 1965: 138–143, 153, 162, 164.
———. *The Magic Christian*. New York: Grove Press, 1996.
———. *The Magic Christian*. Ms. novel. TSA.
———. *The Magic Christian*. Ms. screenplay. TSA.
———. *Making It Hot for Them*. Ms. memoir. TSA.
———. *Making It Hot for Them*. Ms. screenplay. TSA.
———. "Memories of *Dr. Strangelove*." Ms. essay. TSA.
———. *Merlin*. Ms. screenplay. TSA.
———. "Miller: Only the Beginning." *The Nation*, 18 November 1961: 399–401.
———. "New Trends and Old Hats." *The Nation*, 1960: 380–383.
———. *Night-Light*. Ms. screenplay. TSA.
———. *Nut Case: First Scene and Screenplay Synopsis*. Ms. screenplay. TSA.
———, and Harry Nilsson, screenwriters. *Obits*. Ms. screenplay. TSA.
———. "Paul's Problem." Ms. story. TSA.
———. "Pellet of Nihilism." *The Nation*, 21 May 1960: 440.
———. "The Perils of Publishing." *The Best of the Realist*. Ed. Paul Krassner. Philadelphia Running Press, 1982.
———. Personal Journal. Ms. journal. TSA.
———. "Play a Game of Diplomats." *Two Songs and a Game*. Ms. poem. TSA.
———. "The Pusher." Ms. story. TSA.
———. *Red-Dirt Marijuana and Other Tastes*. New York: Citadel, 1990.
———. *A Ride to the Sun*. Ms. screenplay. TSA.
———. "Riding the Lapping Tongue." Ms. essay. TSA.
———. "Rolling Over Our Nerve-Endings. *Book Week*, 8 November 1964: 5, 31.
———. "A Run of Dimes." Ms. story. TSA.
———. "Song of the Old Hemp-Smoking Woman by the Fireside." *Two Songs and a Game*. Ms. poem. TSA.
———. "The Spy's Corner: New Art Museum in Hamburg Blown Up." Ms. story. TSA.
———. "The Strangest Breed." Ms. story. TSA.
———. "Spy Corner." Networked Interzones. Edited by Mark America (sponsored by Degenerative Prose), 1995, Alt-X.com. http://www.alt.com/interzones/ts/gulf.html.
———. *Texas Summer*. New York: Arcade Publishing, 1991.
———. "The Theatre." *Queen*, 30 January 1963: 9–12.
———. "Tom Swift in the Brothel." Ms. essay. TSA.
———. "Towards A New Ethic." Ms. essay. TSA.
———. *Twice On Top; or, The Not So Funny Fall of a Certain Miss Charity Ball*. Ms. screenplay. TSA.
———. "Untitled Narcotics Sequence." Ms. screenplay. TSA.
———. *Virgin: A History of Virgin Records*. New York: Publishing Company Limited, 1995.
———. "When Film Gets Good…" *The Nation*, 17 November 1962: 330–332.
———. *Whut?* Ms. screenplay. TSA.
———. "Why Not Hire the REAL Rip TORN?," *Saturday Review of the Arts*, 1. April 1973: 36–40.
———. *The Year of the Weasel*. Ms. play. TSA.
———, and Christopher Isherwood, screenwriters. *The Loved One*. Dir. Tony Richardson. With Robert Morse, Jonathan Winters. MGM, 1965.
———, and Stanley Kubrick, screenwriters. *Dr. Strangelove*. Dir. Stanley Kubrick. With Peter Sellers. Columbia Pictures, 1964.
———, and Ring Lardner, Jr., screenwriters. *The Cincinnati Kid*. Dir. Norman Jewison. With Steve McQueen. MGM, 1966.
———, with Annie Leibovitz, photographer.

The Rolling Stones on Tour '78. New York: Dragon's Dream/Phin Publishing, 1978.

_____, and Harry Nilsson, screenwriters. *The Telephone.* Ms. screenplay, TSA.

_____, and Harry Nilsson, screenwriters. *The Telephone.* Dir. Rip Torn. With Whoopie Goldberg. New World Pictures, 1988.

Styron, William. "Transcontinental with Tex." *The Paris Review,* Vol. 38, No. 138, Spring 1996: 215–226.

Updike, John. "Introduction." *Surviving: The Uncollected Writings of Henry Green.* ed. Matthew Yorke. London: Chatto & Windus, 1992.

Vidal, Gore. *Palimpsest: A Memoir.* New York: Penguin Books, 1995.

Weisenburger, Steven. *Fables of Subversion: Satire and the American Novel, 1930–1980.* Athens & London: University of Georgia Press, 1995.

Wolfe, Tom. "Preface." *The New Journalism.* Eds. Tom Wolfe and E.W. Johnson. New York: Harper & Row, 1973.

Index

The Accident (screenplay) 65–66, 68, 84
"The Accident" (short story) 31–34
"The Adventures of the Vomiting Priest" 78–79
"After the Bomb, Dad Came Up with Ice" 84
Algren, Nelson 12, 141, 145–146
Allen, Woody 93
Alt-X 196
Alvarado (Texas) 19
American Grotesque (definition) 16, 18
The Anatomy of Criticism 65
Andrews, Julie 175–176
"Apartment to Exchange" 93
Ashby, Hal 186–187
Attenborough, Richard 164
"The Automatic Gate" 28–29
Avakian, Aram 27, 160–162

Barbarella 153–154, 167
Barbarella 2 154
Barrett, Marvin 126, 146–148, 197
Barth, John 88
Baudelaire, Charles 64, 111, 169
Baxter, John 132–133
The Beatles 11–12, 145, 150, 198
Beavis and Butthead 199
Beckett, Samuel 14, 27
Beyond the Beat (Writers in Revolt) 110–111
Beyond the Shadows 84, 144
The Big Sleep 69
The Big Touch 84–85
"The Bird Is Gone" 37, 42–43
"The Black Cat" 53–54, 192
Black Humor 118, 136–139
"The Blood of a Wig" 97, 112–114, 168, 181
Bloom, Harold 66
Blue Movie (novel) 13, 65, 97, 134, 150, 165, 171–176, 179
Blue Movie (screenplay) 175–176
Bockris, Victor 109
Bradbury, Malcolm 69
Bradbury, Ray 18, 131
Brando, Marlon 152, 192
"Brandy for Heroes" 55–57

The Brightest and the Best 194
Bruce, Lenny 94, 108–110, 137, 186, 192
Buchwald, Art 34
Burgess, Anthony 134
Burnett, David 34
Burroughs, William S. 9, 10, 11, 17, 27, 38, 103, 105, 108–110, 137, 171, 172, 175, 178, 198–199
Burton, Richard 152
"The Butcher" 26, 29

Calley, John 126, 175, 179, 181
Candy (film) 151–152
Candy (novel) 11, 15, 16, 34, 60–64, 65, 67, 69, 73, 74, 78, 99, 106, 132, 136–139, 153, 172, 177
Candy (Southern screenplay) 151
"Candy Christian" (short story) 17, 60, 66
"Candy Kisses" 35
Capote, Truman 27, 183–184
Carroll, Lewis 71, 118, 145
Carver, Raymond 69
"The Case of William Faulkner and the Cross-Bearing Liberals" 83
Casino Royale 150–151, 153
"C'est Toi, Alors!" 15, 50, 51, 53–54
Chandler, Raymond 69, 70
"A Change of Style" ("Sea Change") 105, 170, 192
Chapman, Graham 164
Chessman, Caryl 87–88
Un Chien Andalou 18
"Child Molester; Or, It's the Little Things That Count" 178
"Children at Play" 35–36, 40, 51
"Christ Seen Darkly" 87–88
The Cincinnati Kid (film) 85, 117, 149–150, 154
The Cincinnati Kid (novel) 149
Claxton, William 143, 167
Cleese, John 164
A Clockwork Orange (film) 134
A Clockwork Orange (novel) 134
A Clockwork Orange (Southern screenplay) 134, 151

219

Cocksucker Blues 182, 183–184
Cocteau, Jean 27, 60
Coleridge, Samuel Taylor 16
The Collector (film) 150
The Collector (novel) 150
"Color-Blind" 57–58
The Confidence-Man 76
A Cool Million 178
Cooper, Alice 18
Cooper, Michael 134, 151, 183
Corso, Gregory 27, 108
The Cowboy and the Dandy 9
The Crying of Lot 49 69

Dallas (Texas) 20–25
Davis, Miles 26, 118, 189
Dead of Night 185, 195–196
Decadence (definition) 15
DeLaurentiis, Dino 153–154
Didion, Joan 150
Dr. Strangelove 78, 106, 116, 117, 126, 128–135, 137, 139, 140, 154, 162
The Donkey and the Darling 36, 52–53, 107, 154
"The Donkeyman By Twilight" 12, 145–146, 190
Don't Make Waves 153
Double-Date 184–186

The Early Stones 183
East Canaan (Connecticut) 11–12
Easy Rider 12, 16, 17, 60, 85, 98, 100, 117, 124, 154, 155–159, 160, 161–162, 164, 166, 175, 177, 179
Easy Rider (Southern screenplay) 157–158
Ebersol, Dick 188–189
"The Edgy Enthusiast" 113, 180
The Electric Kool-Aid Acid Test 157
Eliot, T.S. 173
The Emperor Jones 84
The End of the Road (film) 85, 117, 159, 160–162, 165, 166, 190
The End of the Road (novel) 160–161, 162
Esquire 9, 10, 94, 100, 101, 102, 103, 104, 105, 106, 111, 128, 135, 169, 196
The Evergreen Review 80, 81, 85, 112
Eyes Wide Shut 135

The Fabulators 137
"The Face of the Arena" 26, 56
A Fairly Stubborn Case 65–66
Family Guy 78
Faulkner, William 55–57, 82–83
Festival 164, 197–198
"Fiasco Reverie" 104
"Fixing Up Ert" 192, 194–195, 196
Flash and Filigree 6, 12, 13, 31, 50, 65–73, 74, 78, 172
"Flashing on Gid" 60, 196
Flynt, Althea Maye 178, 188

Flynt, Larry 178, 188
Fonda, Jane 153–154, 167
Fonda, Peter 12, 154, 155–159, 162
Frank, Robert 183
Fraser, Robert 151
Freud, Sigmund 69, 91, 92–93
Frye, Northrop 65
"Funny Little Children's Song" 41

Gadiot, Pud 35, 36
"Gay Man's Nook, Gay Man's Cranny" 196
Genet, Jean 9, 10, 105
George and Linda 194
Gerber, Gail 142, 167, 200
Ginsberg, Allen 9, 10, 11, 27, 42, 105
Girodias, Maurice 60–64, 196
God Is Love 77
Goering, Herman 173
Goldberg, Whoopie 191–192
Golden, Mike 78
Goldman, Albert 15, 98, 118, 108, 138–139, 186, 192
"Good Golly, Colonel Ollie! Is Virginia Ready for You?" 196
Goodnight Vienna 165
Grand Street 82, 196
Green, Henry 11, 14, 47, 68, 71–73, 84, 192
Grgurevich, Boris 103
"Grooving in Chi" 9–10, 12, 105, 169
Grossing Out 133, 186–187
The Grotesque (definition) 16

Hamptons magazine 196
Harper's Bazaar 36, 43, 48, 81
Harvard Lampoon 91
Hawkeye Productions 190–193
Hawthorne, Nathaniel 12, 14, 16, 97, 101
"Heavy Put-Away; Or, a Hustle Not Wholly Devoid of a Certain Grossness, Granted" 126, 133, 179–182
Heller, Joseph 137
Hemingway, Ernest 26, 55–57
Henry, Buck 152
The Hero with a Thousand Faces 174, 177
High Times magazine 195
Hill, Lee 151, 166
The Hipsters 37–39, 42, 48, 51, 80, 84, 87, 102, 144
"His Second Most Interesting Case" 34–35, 40
Hoffenberg, Mason 27, 37, 48, 59, 60–64, 108–109
Hopper, Dennis 12, 150, 155–159, 160, 162, 178, 180
Howl 42, 97
Humes, Harold "Doc" 27–28
The Hunters of Karinhall 173
Hustler magazine 178, 188–189

"I AM Mike Hammer!" 104–105
The Iliad 6, 66

Jagger, Mick 134, 151, 174, 177–178
James, Henry 80
"Janus" 54–55, 57, 194
Jessup, Richard 149
Jewison, Norman 149–150
Jones, James Earl 160
The Journal of the Loved One 143–144
Junky (novel) 178
Junky (screenplay) 178

Kafka, Franz 13, 28, 44, 56, 91, 92–93
Keats, John 114
Kelly, Grace 76
Kerouac, Jack 73
Kesey, Ken 157
Kotcheff, Ted 84
Krassner, Paul 78–79, 91
Kubrick, Stanley 112, 116, 128–135, 163–164, 171, 176

Lardner, Ring, Jr. 149
Lean, David 176
Lennon, John 179
Lester, Richard 164
Levine, David 145
Life Magazine 15, 83, 107, 140, 144–145
"Limbo" 195–196
"Looking for Hemingway" 41–42
Lord, Sterling 81
"Love Is a Many-Splendored" 5–6, 91–92
Lovecraft, H.P. 6, 13, 30
"The Loved House of the Dennis Hoppers" 150
The Loved One (film) 117, 126, 140–143, 154
The Loved One (novel) 140, 142, 147, 161
Lyon, Nelson 189

MacKendrick, Alexander 153
Mad Magazine 91
The Magic Christian (film) 159, 163–165, 171
The Magic Christian (novel) 13, 46, 49, 65, 66, 69, 73, 74–78, 84, 108, 129, 172, 197
The Magic Christian (Southern screenplay) 151–153, 165
Mailer, Norman 11, 42
Making It Hot for Them 130, 190, 199
Marcus, Greil 14–15
Mathiessen, Peter 6, 15, 27, 33, 49, 73, 88–89, 91, 108, 120
McCallister, Cody 196–197
McCartney, Paul 165
McGrath, Joseph 164, 197–198
Meisel, Perry 9, 13
Melville, Herman 76
"Memories of Dr. Strangelove" 131
Merlin 178
Miller, Henry 27, 88, 111, 146, 168
Miller, Jonathan 128–129
"Miller: Only the Beginning" 88, 97
"The Moon-Shot Scandal" 93–94

Naked Lunch 108–109
The Narrative of Arthur Gordon Pym. of Nantucket. 12, 13, 16, 17, 20, 27, 168–169, 201
The Nation 43, 84, 87, 88, 90, 97, 196
National Lampoon 78, 91, 137
"New Art Museum in Hamburg Blown Up" 79, 94
The New Journalism 96
"New Trends and Old Hats" 88–89
The New Yorker 71, 124
Newsweek Magazine 143–144
Nichols, Mike 175–176
Nietzsche, Friedrich 6
"Night Light" 36
"The Night the Bird Blew for Doctor Warner" 43
"Nights of Terror, Days of Weird" 190
Nilsson, Harry 178–179, 190–193, 198
Northwestern University 25
Nut-Case 68–69

Obits 191, 195
O'Conner, Flannery 18, 30
O'Donoghue, Michael 136, 188–189
O'Hara, Frank 38
Olympia Journal 79, 94, 196, 198
Olympia Press 59
On the Road 97
One Hundred and Twenty Days of Sodom 13, 172–173
O'Neill, Eugene 84
Oui magazine 194, 196

Paglia, Camille 15, 18, 118
"The Panthers" ("You Gotta Leave Your Mark") 39–40, 41, 48
Paris Review 6, 27, 31, 32–33, 48, 72–73, 133, 179, 181
Parker, Charlie 26, 42–43
"Paul's Problem" 44–45
"Pellet of Nihilism" 87–88
Philips, John 33–35, 36, 76, 192
Pickens, Slim 133
"Play a Game of Diplomats" 41
Playboy 169, 198
Plimpton, George 6, 27, 72–73, 82, 165, 181
"Plums and Prunes" 169–170
Poe, Edgar Allan 6, 12, 13, 14, 16, 17, 20, 53–54, 70, 168–169, 175
Pop Art 79, 118, 138
Presley, Elvis 142, 167
"The Pusher" 40
"Put-Down" 37, 39, 80, 102
Pynchon, Thomas 69, 137

"Razor-Fight" 39, 86–87, 149
The Realist 78–79, 90–91, 94–95, 134
"Recruiting for the Big Parade" 94, 103–104, 168
"Red-Dirt Marijuana" 39, 49, 85–86, 149

Red-Dirt Marijuana and Other Tastes 26, 37, 112, 167–168
"Red Giant on Our Doorstep!" 94, 104
"The Refreshing Ambiguity of the Deja Vu" ("Repentance") 17, 196
The Reivers 83
"Repentance" ("The Refreshing Ambiguity of the Deja Vu") 17, 196
Richards, Keith 139, 151, 183
Richardson, Tony 11, 140–143
A Ride to the Sun 177
"Riding the Lapping Tongue" 183
Rivers, Larry 52, 178, 190
"The Road Out of Axotle" 97–100, 157
Rolling Stone Magazine 184
The Rolling Stones 183, 150–151, 182, 183–184, 198
The Rolling Stones on Tour 1978 183
Rosato, Tony 189
Rosenbaum, Ron 113, 180–181
"A Run of Dimes" 45–46

Sade, Marquis De 7, 13, 15, 110–111, 172–173
Sartre, Jean-Paul 26
Saturday Night Live 78, 91, 137, 187, 188–189
"Scandale at the Dumpling Shop" 94–95
Scholes, Robert 137
Screw Magazine 196
"Sea Change" ("A Change of Style") 105, 170, 192
Seaver, Richard 27
The Secret Life of Larry Rivers 178
Sellers, Peter 133, 150–151, 163–165, 186–187, 192
Sergeant Pepper's Lonely Hearts Club Band 11–12, 151
"Sex Therapy Script" 194
Shockley, Dr. William 194
Short Cuts 69
Silverman, Kenneth A. 13
The Simpsons 78
Singer, Mark 124
"Song of the Old Hemp-Smoking Woman by the Fireside" 40–41
"A South Summer Idyll" 22, 39, 48–49
Southern, Carol (Kauffman) 19, 20, 23, 24, 33, 35, 36–37, 47, 48, 49, 54–55, 62, 80, 81, 82, 107, 131, 140, 142, 153, 166, 167, 177–178, 179, 186, 187, 201
Southern, Helen 19, 20, 23, 24
Southern, Nile 15, 60, 107, 131, 140, 167, 177–178, 190, 196, 200–201
Southern, Terry, Sr. 19, 20, 22, 23, 24
Southern Methodist University 25
"The Southern Way of Death" 126, 146–148

Spin Magazine 201
Starr, Ringo 163, 165, 178–179
Stein, Jean 73, 82, 196
"The Straight Dope on the Private Dick" 195
"The Strangest Breed" 58–59
Styron, William 27, 33, 88, 141–142
"The Sun and the Still-Born Stars" 26, 30–31, 34, 36, 48, 59, 78, 82

Talese, Gay 41–42
The Telephone 177, 191–193
"Terry Southern's Spy's Corner" 94, 196
Texas Summer 22, 37, 48, 74, 80, 199
"Theatre Review" 89–90
Thompson, Hunter S. 78, 97,116, 168, 184, 196
Time Magazine 136, 137
"Tito Bandini; or, Doggy Dope Run" 133, 195
Torn, Rip 150, 157, 177, 191–192
Traumnovelle 135
"Trib to *Pym*" 168–169
Trocchi, Alex 27, 36, 59
The Twice on Top; Or Not-So-Funny Fall of a Certain Miss Charity Ball 173
Twilight of the Idols 6
"Twirling at Ole Miss" 100–101, 102, 103, 168

"Untitled Narcotics Sequence" 50
Updike, John 72, 88–89

Venus Bound: A History of the Olympia Press 60
Vidal, Gore 197
Virgin: An Illustrated History 198, 201
"Virgin Love; or, Fab First Fuck" 190
Vogue 150
Vonnegut, Kurt 14, 83–84, 105, 137

Warhol, Andy 79, 184
Waugh, Evelyn 11, 140, 142, 147, 161
Weird Tales 13, 78
Wenner, Jann 184–185
West, Nathanael 44, 70, 178
"When Film Gets Good..." 84, 90, 104, 115
Whut? 197
Williams, Robin 191–192
Wolfe, Tom 96–97, 157, 168
Woolf, Virginia 71
Writers in Revolt (Beyond the Beat) 110–111, 172

The Year of the Weasel 50–52, 68, 75
"You Gotta Leave Your Mark" ("The Panthers") 39–40
"You're Too Hip, Baby" 39, 97, 102–103

Zombie, Rob 18

www.ingramcontent.com/pod-product-compliance
Ingram Content Group UK Ltd.
Pitfield, Milton Keynes, MK11 3LW, UK
UKHW041950140426
5217IPUK00014B/728